ORAZALY SABDEN

ABAI,
FUTURE OF KAZAKHSTAN
AND WORLD CIVILIZATION

**EURASIAN
CREATIVE
GUILD**
LONDON

Academy

Cambridge International Press
Imprint of Hertfordshire Press Ltd © 2018
e-mail: publisher@hertfordshirepress.com
www.hertfordshirepress.com

On behalf of Eurasian Creative Guild, London

ABAI, FUTURE OF KAZAKHSTAN
AND WORLD CIVILIZATION
by ORAZALY SABDEN ©

English editor: Gareth Stamp
Academics: A. Kaydar, T. Kakishev, C. Kirabayev,
A. Koshanov, M. Myrzahmetov.
Public figures: A. Osman, T. Tokhtarov, K. Gabzhalilov

The book is intended for a wide audience of readers, especially youth and for those who are not indifferent to the future of human civilization. The author hopes that his book will make a fair share of contribution in Kazakhstan's entering the list of developed democratic states of the world in perspective.

*British Library Catalogue in Publication Data
A catalogue record for this book is available from the British Library
Library of Congress in Publication Data
A catalogue record for this book has been requested*

ISBN: 978-1-910886-78-6

Instead of wasting life fill it with an idea.
Show us the right way for the welfare of future descendants.
                                                    Shakarim

FROM THE AUTHOR

An outstanding thinker of our nation Abai who raised the Kazakh poetry to an unprecedented level lived only 59 years – the same as Nostradamus [1-4].

The words of edification of Abai for two centuries already serve for the intellectual development of humanity and especially today they are actual and vitally important. However, the world changes and nowadays we have already the XXI century and the process of globalization is light years away. Ensuing from big changes in the world the society doesn't have time to scrutinize and understand it thoroughly though we can observe them via the Internet and many other sources.

In this connection we believe that those novelties which happen in science and education, technology and mental prosperity prove once again that it is necessary to change cardinally our world view, to search the new approaches for their realization. They will give us a new impulse for the civilizations development [5]. Thus, we can divine our further steps for the future creation over and over again returning to *The words of edification* of Abai and all our conscience. This is because Abai thanks to his deep and keen understanding could always give a sharp estimation of any person, his actions and especially his ethical principles.

What did the great poet speak about? How did he say it? What did he predict? To solve an idea of his thoughts and to give an answer on them that is what was bequeathed to us his descendants. For this reason, relying on the Abai's creations and analyzing his thoughts I began to search the answers on the following

What Abai would say and how would he react if he would be alive looking over his nation's heartfelt cry, irreversible cataclysms which happen pretty often, severity and cruelty of reality of the modern existence? I am interested if Abai is still respected today as an eminent personality by the representatives of authority as he was before, if they react on the poet's severe criticism which penetrates to the bones?

In words **Abai is an ideal for all Kazakhs.** He is not only an outstanding personality of his time but a wise teacher who still gives the advices how to solve the challenges of the epoch. By his creation the poet-philosopher famed by Kazakhs all over the world. **Abai became the symbol of the thought and word freedom.** As Akhmet Baitursynov said: Every self-respecting Kazakh should know Abai's works and quote them by heart! It seems that the representatives of authority forgot about it at all. Even deputies, Government members and representatives of administrative structures don't use the wise advice and thoughts of Abai in their everyday work. This brings up the question: why? Indeed, the Kazakh people as poor as rich love the great Abai, appreciate him as a phenomenon; respect the fidelity and precision of his sayings. But when the action comes to point they forget about it and the others do conversely. To find the answer on this question is very hard.

I had to touch this strategically important problem for the sake of national interest and future of my nation. The purpose is to identify the possible ways of solution the questions targeted on the development of nation, state, science and life values. Whereby of course we need to consider the differences in the views of life between the modern man and Abai who paid more attention to the vices of his contemporaries which slowed down their spiritual and moral development what led to a material welfare of the whole nation.

The modern Kazakh nation came to its independence from the Soviet Union when words didn't correspond to actions with the baggage of more than 70 years of indifference and reticence of the true history, derogation of national culture and language. Even today within 25 years of sovereignty along with weighty achievements we continue to speak more than to do.

For example, in amount of developed programs Kazakhstan can even pretend to enter the Guinness Book of Records. And to their real introduction, though the costs on it are big, Kazakhstan in the tail of the big list of countries. Our ideas are light-weight, the doings are unfruitful. Still we cannot get rid of vainglory and conceitedness; we often conceal and hide the vices.

In former times people said: «The caravan will line up on the way». But when will we change? What should we do for it? These questions troubled me for a long time, I spent a lot of forces and I thought oceans of dreamless nights before I came to a definite conclusion because I was distressed a lot for our country's future.

I live a considerable amount of years in this world. I visited a lot of countries to present day. I became a master of sport of the USSR in free-style wrestling, joined the ranks of the famous scientists of the Republic and four times ran for a seat on the Parliament of RK. Nowadays I participate in many international congress-conferences, have more than 650 scientific works, among them 72 monographic books and course books. On the scientific field I exchanged views with many scientists of the world including the Nobel laureates: Joseph Stiglitz, yisrael Robert John Aumann, S. Timasheff. In total I visited more than 60 countries of the world and that's why I mustn't grumble. I have enough observaions and forethought. The Abai's creation became a push to rethinking of all seen and bygone, especially when I reread *The words of edification* and the Shakarim's works again in order to fill in time during the long flights to Europe and USA [1, 6]. I wrote my thoughts to notebook and then even titled «15 words of Oshan» under the name which I (the youngest among my 13 sisters) bore some time ago in childhood and which was given to me by my maternal grandmother Kenzhegul.

The phenomenon of Abai is that he who was situated far away from the big civilization (in boorish aul) advanced the genius ideas of spirituality. The evidence of this could serve his learning about *appropriate man*, moral philosophy, poetry, *The words of edification* and the other humanistic and intellectual values. Over and over again rereading *the words of edification* of Abai which inspired me and seeing the happening around of mess and chaos which saddened my sense it became subhuman for me to sit idle. And I came to a conclusion that anyhow I will write a book and will try to answer the following pressing questions: How do we see our future? What to change today and how to do it tomorrow? What will be the fate of next generation if we'll continue to live this way? Will the consequences of the world encounters influence us? The point is not in voluminous book but in the truth discovering, telling about the problems of society and the ways of their solution.

I tried to use my time fruitfully when I was aimed at removing away the science, especially after the fact when in 2012 (at bidding from above) I was released from the position of director of the academic Institute of Economics of the Ministry of Education and Science of RK... Just then I worked pretty well under the several **International Megaprojects'** working in respect to the new conditions of life and world development.

This is the method of the entire universal measurement and the world currency regulation (by means of kW to currency) on the model of «Power»; «The creation of new mentally-technological cluster for turning Turkestan into the capital of the nation's spiritual renovation under the name of the Turkistan's region»»; «The new global model of the world order»; «The humanization of society and safety are the basis of the new world order»; «The construction of the human survival strategy in the XXI century»; «The system of the world processes regulation and management model» [5,7]. These projects were supported and auditioned on the international congresses and conferences and received the positive feedbacks from the authorized scientists including the Nobel laureate [5].

In these hard times which sharply needs the cardinal decisions maybe modern generation will become the first in the history which rouse to challenge on the way of a new century in the development of our society. Because we are the generation of humanity which stands at the turn of the mentally-moral evolution disappearance.

I was inspired to the creative understanding and generalization of my speculations into one whole and then to writing of this book by the wise *The words of edification* of the great Abai, the writings of Mukhtar Auezov who discovered a panoramic portrait of Abai, the works and writings of the eminent state and public man of the international level Turar Ryskulov who supported Mukhtar Auezov in his time [1-3,8]. I was always worried by the warnings and aspirations of my nation and that's why I devote this book to the questions of forming the renewed thinking of present and I hope future generation.

Suffering all the difficulties of his time Abai didn't abjure his native soil and didn't call people for uprising. Conversely thanks to the force of his mind and poetic power he found the other way for mental uplift of his nation. It could be called a mental revolution of Abai. The author also alludes on this way... The meaning of thinking of the scientist is that **without the right point of view on the problems of society, on the national development, on the scientific and educational role and on the establishment of social relations it is very dubious for us to become the country of high culture and civilization.** Following Abai's conceptual ideas and directives we can advice to every citizen of the Republic thinking about the real future of his country, consequently according to the time requirements, to pass through the heart and write down all seen and heard and then search the mechanisms of their realization.

Of course Abai didn't indicate and present the ready answers to those problems which bother us today. However we, learning the poet's genius thoughts and analyzing the depth and accuracy of his sayings, should work out our own concept of the moral and spiritual values' of the establishment of our civilization in the XXI century in accordance with the present changes happening in the country and world. In this book I'd like to pay a special attention of our young generation in that it should follow Abai's wise words respecting and honouring his world view and world outlook, even though he lived in other times with the other social patterns, but still useful during the decision of any everyday or social problem [5].

The value of 'The words of edification of Abai' is that learning and rethinking them we can find the answers on actual questions. Abai teaches us to be honest and make any doing honestly. People should always tend to know more. They are obliged to educate themselves to be brave and straight in the back, to love their nation.

Only in such a manner we can get rid of self-assurance and bumptiousness. Only knowledge would open our eyes. If people will get knowledge they can defend their nation and soil legally correctly and will get the possibility to enter the relations with other civil countries. It makes it necessary to look at oneself and one's doings critically. Abai teaches: **«There are three things which make people helpless and despicable. They are unenlightenment, indolence and insidiousness»**.

Truly speaking up to now during the decision making for any question I consult with the departed great thinkers imaginatively as if they were alive and ask the questions: "How would you do in this or those situations? What right decision should I make?" And I noticed that all the decisions which I made after the imaginative dialogue with them were closer to the truth. Though the glum thoughts visited me either: Would I support this idea? Anyway I decided by the example of the great thinker Abai to write my vision and give the answers on those questions which bother my contemporaries and I hope that this book '15 words of thinking' will pay shot in forming a new thinking of the society for the sake of a new generations revival of the Kazakh nation – proud and respecting the language and culture of its forefathers and the heritage of the great thinkers, poets and writers who left us an order that every Kazakh should remember his "roots".

There are a lot of books about Abai's creation and heritage. No doubt, it is a scientists', specialists' fate. This book has the other mission and new methods of presentation. Every word in the "15 words of thinking" consists of two parts. The first: **What did you achieve? What is the situation for today?** The second: **To give the answers and the mechanisms of decisions.** And thanks to that to show my nation the ways of high civilization level achievement. And advice the base values of the nation the efficient usage of which will lead the society forward:

- **the global natural wealth;**
- **the spirituality, national genetic pool;**
- **the new knowledge, science, health, sport and youth**
- **the aul's destiny;**
- **the economy and technology;**
- **the harmony of man and nature;**
- **the man's life journey in the XXI century;**
- **the democratic and effective state management.**

with due account for all these and other raised vital questions.

Truly speaking no matter how good was the former Soviet-socialistic epoch or the present capitalistic market system I don't like either, because the humanity rates the best. They created and create for humanity more and more negative events, hurdles which the people are forced to overcome. By the day the authorities more and more estrange from the nation. That's why I constantly search for 'true and fair' because there are no other ways.

For this purpose we, especially young people, let's for the be-ginning free the tied hands and thoughts and achieve the realization of ideal of the mental reformer, great thinker and democrat Abai. Because Abai is our teacher, not alien. That's why the realization of his legacies is our cherished cause, our sacred duty.

Abai Kunanbaev
Nostradamus

The blue fog – the age of after years,
With hope the glance goes ahead
The days fly away hurrying up the years,
No picture, no imagination,
The eyes get tired...
Abai

THE WORD FIRST

In what direction the world goes?

Within recent memory the world changed so much that it is impossible to divine what waits us in future. The most important question is how to go out of crisis, what to do in order to free humanity from the global concussions? These are global climate warming, the lack of water and food, social-economic and political dislocations, migration and the other negative changes and processes, catastrophes.

Never before has humanity forced such problems which dont find their solution. That's why up to now USA, EU, UN, G 8 and other international organizations are unable to find the right decision of these questions, including the crisis in Ukraine and Syria.

It is impossible to un riddle such puzzles of contradictions only by means of sanctions or military involvement and bombing. The problems' solution is on another level. The world suffers a deep transformation, a mental corruption of the society's layers. The situation in the countries of the Near East and Africa and the other regions of the world complicates matters.

The reason of it is in the objective economic rules of the societies development of non-compliance, the rules of wildlife in violation and of the cyclic development management rules. Besides the United Nations Organization (UN) doesn't enforce its regulations (international human rights and others).

The big authorities including the states of G 8 day by day loose the credit of the international community. Nowadays more than a half of the Gross Domestic Product (GDP) is owned by these states and the international transnational companies own more than 50 percent of their capital. At the same time USA, Russia, China and Northern Korea arm themselves on a massive scale. So USA has more than 50 percent of armament. If consider this it seems that we stand on the cusp of the third world war. Nowadays the whole world is in danger and we can say that its further development is under question.

After that it begs the questions: Where do we go? Where are we led? And we don't know where we go? And the leaders themselves don't know where to lead us (I mean USA and G 8). In the age of globalization, it is impossible to solve such problems all alone. Even one of super countries – USA is at a loss, the evidence of that is a terrorist attack in New York on September 11, 2001. In order to avoid such events, we need to unite the forces, to use the common ideas and integrate the development.

In our opinion the world can follow two ways. The first was mentioned above. Because the developed countries are intended only on wealth accumulation, at the same time leaving the questions of the soil resources usage, power production, economy development without any changes in former frames tying them only to business. The others are involved in a fight with it. The result is the world crisis.

The second way is to conduct duly the transformation of society, spiritual renewal and to be ready for new basic changes in everything. This is a pending task.

Because of such situations I made the following conclusion: it's time for radical changes in people's minds and through them to way finding in order to change the world psychology, to revive the mental and moral worth, to call the humanity for a high responsibility and in every family for a right to child-rearing.

As a scientist in this sphere I wrote straight to UNO, G8, G20 (September 2014), gave lectures on different international congresses. I offered to be found the international legal organization – The Global Parliament. Surely, many problems are solved separately by each country. And the Global Parliament should issue the laws for solution of the most global international questions. Among them are the world crises, climate warming, unleashing of war prevention, food supply security, fighting hunger, political world reorganization, space exploration, etc. One of the forthcoming tasks is new radical reforms implementa t i o n referring to the United Nations Organization transferring their general Headquarters to Asia or on the other continent, as to the row of international organizations and their transformation. These structures should solve the most important global problems. The points of views of these problems are presented in a separate book [5].

About a quarter of century passed from the day of getting independence. The Kazakh nation should find where it belongs in the world civilization and by an indefatigable labour to join the ranks of developed countries using the heritage of the great Steppe's prominent figures, including Abai's study.

The second opportunity to use all our wealth
efficiently for the welfare of people.
Otherwise we'll be immersed by the others.

THE WORD SECOND

Whom we were? Who are we now? Where are we going? What awaits us?

In order to find the answers to these questions we need to remember our history, because if we don't know the history it is impossible to divine the future. We cannot overlook the logic of histories course the meaning of which is that our land had a paramount importance in the development of the whole world. For example, we know about the existence of Sacks on the territory of ancient Eurasia, in Kazakhstan – the ancient states of Huns, Chanls, Uysuns; Turkic khanates and other medieval states and khanates. Either we know about the Kazakh civilization existence of that time on the wide areas from the Caspian Sea to China. To be specific the history of our nation began much earlier than the khan's Shaibani Abul-Khaira government and then it continued under the aegis of the Kazakh khanate during such Khans' as Kerey, Zhanibek, Kassym, and others ministry. The Kazakh Khans and national Batyrs, spilling their blood during severe fights for their congeners rights to own the native soils and courageously defending them during the often aliens' invasions, made a tremendous contribution in the border strengthening and the following destiny of their nation. In the period of khans' government the Kazakh soils with Turkistan as a capital had an important strategic role in geopolicy of that time.

So, during 550 years of the khans' government the heavy political, moral and spiritual, social and economic processes happened.

And today, the history of independent Kazakhstan, having enough authority in the world and going to join the ranks of the most developed countries, consists of difficult stages. 25 years have past from the day of independence gaining by the Republic of Kazakhstan.

I am proud that when I was a deputy in parliament I took a direct participation in the first law adoption – the Constitution of the country, and especially when the own national currency – Tenge was accepted, for the first time in history of the Kazakh nation. In such moments the tears well up in my eyes because of the pride that the centuries long dream of my forefathers came into being. But even now in the epoch of global reformations and world crisis when Kazakhstan got an appreciable prest and we are in the list of many succeeding countries we should understand the necessity of perspective measures and taking of the right decisions in order not to lose all our achievements in this unstable world. We need to do a lot.

If we consider the history of other nations – each of them has its own way of development. Under the rethinking of our history, the history of Asia and European development in whole, the history of China, only one though appears that **the fate supported two opportunities** for eastern nations: the first couldn't be used by our forefathers and the other shouldn't be missed in order not to disappear as a nation in foreign history, not to be swallowed. If we won't rebuild ourselves other than being a primary producing country, we'll serve to other more industrially developed countries and we'll be dependant from them buying this product in finished form by more expensive price. The life puts this question squarely [7].

The first missed opportunity relates to the period of 1000-1500 years ago when the eastern nations were very developed. The evidence of this are the works of Al-Farabi, Ibn Sin, Ul-ugbek and other globally well-known persons in the sphere of mathematics, medicine, philosophy which are required even now [20]. The Europe of that time developed very slowly because it was wallowed in internecine wars, etc.

The last 500 years the nations of Europe adopted a lot of discoveries from the nations of East especially Turkic creating the steam machine, steam navigation, building the plants and factories and putting in great efforts to develop the manufacturing industry. The evidence of this was the London Olympics of 2012, the opening of which was viewed by the whole world within several hours by TV, where their historical development was shown. Two great world imperials – China and Eastern countries fell much further behind.

The well-known European scientists – Albert Einstein, Isaac Newton, Thomas Alva Edison, Michael Faraday and then Hegel, Ricardo and Marx made an inappreciable contribution in the development of their society. Nowadays Europe ' teaches' us. The advanced top-universities are also located on the territories of Europe and USA. However, our young countrymen who study abroad shouldn't forget that one of the world knowledge's' ancestors were our eastern forefathers. The empirical sources of science, the questions of life and peace, the wise ancient philosophy originated in India and China, the Eastern countries. Even the Islamic civilization contributed the science and culture birth. However, the West is the "capitalistic" and "rationalistic" engine of these life spheres. In our time we couldn't continue our rich and deep beginning. Only China for the recent 20-30 years made a great leap forward in economics purchasing a worldwide recognition. Today China plays second fiddle after USA in economic potential.

There are the prognoses that the XXI century will be for China the century of domination on the world market.

The second opportunity is a heritage conquered by the point of a spear and the force of square shoulders of our forefathers left us for its accruement. **The Kazakh nation's nobleness and blood purity was supported by a prohibition on marriages between relatives closer than on 7 generations. We believe this fact raises the national immunity and will give an intellectual and highly educated generation.** That's why the national genetic pool and natural wealth are of priority for our nation. However, being one of the richest countries in the world we live poor. Why? First of all, it is necessary to use this illimitable wealth not allowing bargaining them away for the welfare of our nation.

The set goal is to achieve the level of developed countries. In other ancient words we can say as "the camel's burden is on our back". Besides nowadays the important role plays the strengthening of our national, qualitative, competitive, highly-moral human capital.

Well known that the ancient Turkistan took a special place on the great Silk Route as a spiritual center looking through the world atlas you can see such big ancient cities of Central Asia as Turkistan, Samarkand, Bukhara and Taraz.

If we analyze the whole human history, it becomes clear that even without reference to ancient times in the VI-VIII centuries these areas were occupied by Turkic-Speaking nations or more precisely by **Turkic Khanate** [10]. In that Turkic Khanate, Turkistan as a spiritual capital had a historical value. After that as time passed the Turkic-Speaking nations disunited. For example, a small part went to Anadols. There as a result of rapid development the Ottoman Empire was established and became a new civilized state. Nowadays Turkey with its 80 million population entered the group of 20 developed countries. The rest of the Turkic-Speaking countries created their own states and are also in the process of development.

I think that if Turkey will continue to develop so rapid forming new science, education, technologies and paying a special attention to human capital thus it will have a rich future. I won't be surprised if by 2030 Turkey using its geographic opportunities and mental patriotic power of its nation will precede many European countries and even will become the leader of all the Muslim states.

In this unstable world of globalization, we need as never before the integrative ideas, projects which unite around themselves the whole nations and ethnic groups.

Maybe it will be an integrative idea of peoples and nations' union in the epoch of global and irreversible changes. After these processes the new opportunities will appear for our nations' spiritual wealth revival. We need to make a leap forward in integration not tarnish our honour, keeping safety and not degrading. The human world view should correspond the requirements of the XXI century and the level of new civilized society. This is the demand of modern civilization.

And as to our nation – **we need new ideas and projects which will promote the whole nation.** They could be withdrawn from the world civilization development and also from the Abai's learning and heritage of great historical persons who are listed in the second part of the book.

Our country is one of richest in the world
regarding the mineral deposits reserves.
It begs the question: Why do we live poor?

THE WORD THIRD

What wealth do we have? Do we have a potential? How do we use that potential? What measures should be taken in future?

The khans Kerey and Zhanibek – the Kazakh Khanate founders were the first among the dozens of famous khans of the Kazakh Steppes (1465). It was written in detail in the Muhammad Haydar Dulati's book called Tarihi-i-Rashidi and also in many other sources [11, 12].

Our nation owning such illimitable wealth should be a w a r e what happens with those soils which our forefathers saved for their descendants defending them from aliens by the point of a spear and the force of mighty hands.

Of course, within the period of independence Kazakhstan transformed, improved the economy, brought prosperity to its people, earned a great reputation and prestige in the world – this is the fact and nobody can neglect it. But it helps to remember that Kazakhstan is one of richest countries in the world. Its interiors contain 99 from 110 elements of Mendeleev's law, but we use only about 60 of them. Kazakhstan is ahead of all countries regarding the natural deposits under calculation for every person, specifically for the world resources of **wolframium** – 50%, **uranium** – 25%, **chrome ores** – 23%, **Lead** – 19%, **Zinc** – 13%, **cuprum and baryta** – 10%, **manganese, fluoride,** etc. Either Kazakhstan takes the world leading place according the very rear natural expensive nonferrous metals which contain **rhenium, osmium, beryllium, titanium, tantalum, thallium, aurum, argentum,** etc. Besides, **oil and gas,** carbon of different types, hydrocarbonic minerals, we can say, are in plenty in the interior of our soils [13]. Having such wealth, to the envy of many neighbour countries and the whole world either, why we still, saying the understandable for every Kazakh Abai's words – Неге шеңгел шайнап жүрміз? i.e. literally – Why do we chew a bare spine?.

The native people are Kazakhs. They often come from faraway auls where unemployment is everywhere and in order to survive anyhow they obtain credits by any means possible and get to previously dug debt pit. Why we cannot live as Arabs? Why the state doesn't open an infant capital under the baby's birth like Arabs do (for example, in Arab Emirates – 100 thousand of US dollars), taking care of his future? Maybe we are the worst? May be our knowledge are not on required level? Comparing and analyzing we came to a conclusion that we are better, and our knowledge is deeper! Than what does bar us? These questions have bothered me a long time and, I hope, that it is not only me.

The area of soils with oil deposits in Kazakhstan occupies 1 million 700 thousand square kilometers (62%), the resources of natural gas – 3 trillion cubic meters. Till nowadays only 50% of territories are investigated. The state didn't conduct any other big investigations and till nowadays uses the discoveries' benefits of our scientist and academician Kanysh Satpaev and his teammates (academicians Grigory Sherba, Aryktay Kayupov, Aitmukhamed Abdulin, German Zhilinskiy and others) and continues all 24 years of independence to export and sell the initial products abroad. Because of our tender mindedness many foreign countries became rich and we already have our

own oligarchs. People have a little. The quantity of geological explorations sharply decreased. Unfortunately, scientists who discovered the deposits and their families didn't receive a Tenge for their incentive.

It mustn't concealed that such rich mountain ranges as Dzhungar, Altay, Kalba and regions of Karatau, Mugodzhar, Torgay,

Mangystau wait for more precise geological exploratory investigations [14, 15, 16].

Abai emphasized: In our time a saying appeared – The core is not in problem, but in person. The meaning of it that you can achieve a purpose not by a right action, but by your cunning and tricks. That's why Abai believed that it's useless to speak about vices; we should apprehend what will be tomorrow and what should be done in this situation. The answers on such questions should be scientifically proven and we should search and use the required levers.

The matter in hand requires a serious approach on the level of government and Parliament. What would Abai say if he saw a shameful squandering of the Kazakh people's national wealth? I imagine a reproach and a mental pain in his eyes: My descendants, why you don't use rich soil resources rationally having such opportunities and deep knowledge in all science spheres learning in the best foreign universities of USA and Europe?

Abai wrote in his Edifications: We can impede the thieves, but how to pacify the rich men who breed the mischiefmakers? [1].

What should we do in further?

First of all, to make a thorough investigation beginning from surface till the deep layers of earth on all the territories of Kazakhstan, then analyzing the results to make a full account on presence of rare earth and other elements which were not discovered before. For example, Russian scientists discovered a new field on the territory of Kostanay region where the big reserves of gas hydrogen are located. Considering that the future depends on hydrogen energy when the automobiles will be fuelled by it thus already in the near future we'll meet the need to investigate this extreme wealth.

Secondly, to adopt a law on Parliament level which will contain a separate paragraph that the mineral deposits on our territory belong to Kazakhstan or pursuant to the law to government. By the example of Arabic countries to bring in practice of the leading highly qualified specialists' from abroad recruitment: top managers, engineers, etc. while our growing generation of young specialists is taught in the best world universities. Then to change them gradually by our own specialists. To give an opportunity under the government's support to those citizens who got rich earlier by honest employment to develop themselves further from a new angle and to take charge of bigger enterprises in order to raise labour productivity. If nowadays we'll continue to increase oil extraction to 100 million barrels and more thus what will we leave to next generations?

It is necessary to take into account the experience of other countries. For example the Norwegian Parliament adopted a special law which regulates the oil subject. One of super countries which consume oil and energy – USA – keeps its natural resources especially oil deposits for future.

Today the potential of a growing generation is especially high. It is far away from a colonial conscience, mastered a modern technology, can speak several world languages. That's why a progressive youth can become a legal owner of our forefathers' heritage and we, in our turn, should cooperate fully in all the beginnings. Besides knowledge, professionalism and labour of young people should be analyzed in a flexible manner and grow according to means of social mobility. Such approach can stimulate the production increase and a desire to make a carrier on its specialty.

Thirdly it is necessary to revise the old international contracts accepted knowingly or innocently, which contravene the national interests. Because only 22% of refined oil belongs us and the rest 78% belong to the international companies. The share of China companies in an entire volume of oil extraction on the territory of Kazakhstan accounts 24%. The amount of oil resources which belong to Chinese companies on deposits in maintenance accounts about 480 million tons or 14%. So, many developing countries (Saudi Arabia, Venezuela and Malaysia) revised a range of signed before international contracts and founded their own national companies. Such serious steps requires firmness and courage from Parliament and government. As an academician Dmitry lvov says in Russia the rent accounts 75%. And our country can also raise the rent to such figures. If we refined oil here and sold the ready product abroad it could increase the economy of Kazakhstan and thus the prosperity of people would be improved. We cannot develop if we won't produce and refine ourselves. This is an indisputable truth!

Passing all heard and seen,
Through justice and mind,
It is necessary to get message to others,
In order to prevent the meeting of the match.
Abai

THE WORD FOURTH

What and on what level are our intellectual values? How can we revive them?

It is well known that in a huge area between the Caspian Sea and China a highest civilization existed. Found in V-VI centuries the ancient Turkistan became one of the centers of the Asian continent. This is a historical fact. That's why it promoted the establishment of relations between nations, the Islamic religion advancement and a wide development of culture.

The sacred soil of the Big Turkistan hides in itself a deep history of Muslim nations, because Turkistan in XVI – XVIII centuries was the capital of the Kazakh Khanate, there the mausoleum of Hoja Ahmet yassawi is located which was build on the order of the lame Timur and till nowadays it didn't lose its spiritual values. In addition to that still on people's lips the outstanding works of different spheres of science of such remarkable and great historical persons, state and public people as **the Queen Tomyris, the King Attila, YerTonga, Tonykok, Arystan bab, Al-Farabi, Yusuf Balasaguni, Manas, Nizami Ganjavi, Hoja Ahmet Yassawi, Makhmut Kashgari, Genghis Khan, Baybars Sultan, Emir Timur, Ulugbek, Alisher Navoi, Muhammad Haydar Dulati, Korkyt, Abylay Khan, Maktumkuli, Abai Kunanbayev, Ataturk, Bektash Veli, Chokan Valikhanov, Gabdolla Tukay, Turar Ryskulov, Dinmukhamed Kunaev, Mukhtar Auezov, Berdy**

Karbabayev, Rassul Gamzatov, Chingiz Aitmatov and others. [7, 17, 18, 19, 20, 21].

In the second part of this book the short data about the great Historical Persons are presented (pages 123-174). We can be proud of our history because the great forefathers left a big heritage to us the future generation. Taking this in account it is necessary to build pantheons and landmarks in our mental capital – Turkistan. In order to revive these intellectual values it is necessary to conduct different events of interest and conferences, Only with these measures we can propagandize and acquaint the other countries with our intellectual values. Our intellectual values beginning from Anaharsis to Abai and the follwing periods should be uppermost beyond measure.

In his world outlook Abai explained a wide philosophy meaning of *intellectual values and reality (existence)* tied to conscience and inward of man as humanism, fear of god, kindness, honesty, respectfulness, etc. and tried to cultivate these qualities to his people through customs and traditions, beliefs and others. Deeply learning the poet's world outlook **Mukhtar Auezov** came to a conclusion: ***Abai put humanity, moral philosophy before all else.*** The evidence of it is the Abai's thoughts in his fourth *Words of edifications.* **Socrates** believed that ***in the philosophy thought development a special place is taken by a Man.*** The questions of existence and ethics understood by Abai regarding the human conscience and inner thoughts coincide very much with Socrates' saying. Simply speaking the both thinkers said about the same fact – humanism (humanity).

Crises opened our eyes. We have intellectual and moral values in centuries-long history which nowadays lose their meaning gradually. We should revive them. Today all over the world the necessity of humanism and justice ideas appears because the intellectual values and humanity norms are the result of civilizations development. Social catastrophes, natural cataclysms and dictatorial regimes thrill the whole world.

In The *words of edification* of Abai quarrels and discords, slanderous suits disuniting people are shown as concrete examples. Thus, the poet reveals such shortfalls and negative features indignantly and anxiously called people for unity, agreement and mutual understanding masterly using for it the examples of spiritual values and human existence, widely spread customs and traditions in the country.

We often forget to live in accordance with the law of nature and in the epoch of the world historical development – about the humanization of society. **Because the laws are realized in practice only when they correspond the panhuman norms.** The society in its development first of all should care for environmental protection, because nature and human life are dependable upon each other. Unfortunately, there is not enough attention paid to nature and human capital; especially the spiritual values are forgotten. For this reason the laws of harmonic society development are broken; the invisible market levers had their effect. It connected to the fact that even developed countries are still in the grip of world crisis.

In common, the idea of Kazakh, Turkish society humanization was born in XI-XIII centuries already on the basis of the learning "жауанмартлик и хал" or The Philosophy of Moral. Besides in XIX century the Abai's learning about *an appropriate man* appeared. These learning were originated from a heroic dastan told by lips of the great Turan's Khan – yer Tonga about himself as an edification of "аки" (free-hearted). Absorbing all positive from these learning the idea of Abai about an appropriate man continued the traditions of our forefathers. The reason of this learning appearance was an intention of Kazakhs to discover the secrets of the invisible side of world and to cognize it. An immense force was paid to cognition in unity of visible and invisible sides of universe.

The society is the world of majorities and separate groups which are divided by contradictions. A man can cognize such "disease" of universe by calling to his inner world. If a man cannot cognize itself, he won't cognize a surrounding media. Because of the big love to his nation Abai criticized its shortfalls in social life and tried to free his people from them. He under-stood well as nobody else that the one who doesn't see his guilt will never strive for civilization. This thought corresponds to any science and nation. That's why khakim Abai criticized sharply and fought against negatively reaction morals and customs calling for unity.

Meanwhile Europeans striving for secrets disclosure of "vis-ible world side" chased only for wealth accumulation and chose a materialistic and atheistic route. They believe that it is mean-ingless to cognize the "invisible world sides" and severed connection with the spiritual world. It led them to moral degradation and inanition.

Today they cannot avoid this disaster. The only way of survival is to learn and cognize the "invisible world side". But this target is hardly reachable for them. Because Europeans have formed a materialistic world view which dominates over them for more than five centuries . It is very hard to ruin it. Secondly the scientific achievements they turned on a way of unbelief (sacrilege). Chose an icy intelligence. But Abai's *appropriate man* rests on clear mind and puts the science achievements on a way of nobleness (fear of god). Learning khakim Abai's study about *an appropriate man* we can humanize the society's life and will newly relate to civilization.

In Abai's *Words* his philosophical thoughts about natural phenomena, human manners, and ways of his own knowing of historical course of his epoch, people's interests and ideals have been put.

Abai noted: "People are born with a cry and then die. Not knowing where is a life delight, conflict to each other, addict to boasting – so passing time in vain, to no purpose, doing negative actions. And when life is in its wane they cannot buy a day for all their wealth (cattle). Equivocation, mendicancy is a cat's business. First of all, pray to God, hope on yourself and work. To work the soil will answer in spades".

There are social problems that influence directly a world society development. These problems were accrued for years in different regions of the world and naturally don't pass without consequences. Day by day the quantity of such negative facts as mental segregation, bribery, etc. increases because of inequity and indifference of local authorities to the needs of simple people. Many countries in the absence of state ideology became backward and developed countries went on a way of excessive consumption. And Kazakhstan didn't stay on sidelines of these imperfections [5].

How will we revive our mental values?

Every state needs a new national idea directed on intellectually mental activity of people. We need to arouse passion and adopt the best practices of "raising the voices" of intelligentsia humbled recently. This measure should be based on principles of national union, development of language, culture and tradition. The national idea is not only a mental axiological phenomenon but an act of nature which arouses national interests and further which enables their realization. However in new epoch there is no nation which can exist apart from other nations and opposing its interests to the interests of others what certainly leads to negative events and wars.

The depth of Abai's *Words of edification* content could be traced by the subject raised in them essential public and humanitarian problems tied to human's conscience and inner self . The poet-philosopher proficiently used the traditions and customs, morals, rhetoric of Kazakh nation in order to get youth on board of art, belief and nobleness.

That's why an understanding of national ideas, interests and mutual confidence is the only way of their realization.

That's why the Turkic-Speaking nations considering Turk-istan their spiritual capital and second Mecca gathering there as in a sacred place and honour it [10]. We still cannot freely use a spiritual and economic potential of Turkistan. To consider this region as a tourist object is absolutely not enough. The base of Turkish world, its nurse with such deep history could be and is necessary to use in order to raise a spirituality, economy and regional technology on a new higher step. Proceeding from such considerations I advance **a national idea to turn Turkistan to a spiritual capital [7]. The name of this megaproject will sound as follows: about "creation of spiritually technological cluster "Turkistan region – the way of humanization of Kazakh society".**

The main purpose of the project is to turn Turkistan to spiritual complex (megacity), to make a step in supporting an inter-national safety. For the first time in history here on an example of one region it is necessary to solve two big problems which include from one side a spiritually cultural and historical development of humanity and from the other – a formation of new sixth technological mode. The realization of these measures could be shown to an entire world as an etalon of Kazakhstani revival (renaissance), innovational development. For this purpose it is necessary to make the following:

1)   The Parliament should adopt a law – "New Turkistan is a spiritual capital";

2)   To legislate the status of Turkistan region as a "Free economic zone";

3)   To exempt the Turkistan region from taxes for five years;

4)   To open an International Spiritual Academy, to organizea center of religiology;

5)   To institute a scientific centre of society humanization. To open an Academy of Social Sciences (China has). To institute a Cultural University;

6)   To open a museum "The Treasures of History" from ancient times till nowadays (in London there is a geographical museum).

7)   To build a new city according to old, ancient architecture. Under the construction of new Turkistan it is necessary to use the eastern examples of town-building, etc.

There is a hope that during the construction of new Turkistan Turks, Uzbeks, Azerbaijani, Turkmen, Kirghiz, Tatars and others will lend effective help as to motherland of their forefathers, because all of them are of Turkistan steppes descents. And the entire Muslim world represented by Arabs, Egyptians, Iranians and others will also lend a helping hand as Muslims. And they would also build new objects on our example in their countries.

Visiting Turkistan our Muslim brothers would remember the past history of their countries.

The project consists of **6 clusters: spiritual, technological, new aul, tourism, logistic and infrastructural.**

Uniting here in one process the spiritual, cultural and techno-logical practices we will provide an effective usage of the most valuable people's capital. Speaking about people's capital, we can suppose that in the Big Turkistan and around it an interest of not less than 400 million people to this project can appear. Undoubtedly such know-how will be distributed around the world very quickly. Compare: the number of nations affiliated with EU (European Union) – about 500 million people. We can imagine a high scale of this project. Considering that a number of Muslim populations in 2009 exceeded 1.3 billion people and to 2020 will achieve 1.8 billion people (25 percent of the world population) we can easily believe in Turkistan's project verisimilitude [22]. The difference of this project from technocratic project of **Silicon Valley** in USA is in intension to stick a spiritually cultural, historical development and revival of aul, tourism, logistics and infrastructure according to requirements of new time, with the fourth innovational technological practice, to force them to work in the interest of humanity.

A cognitive top of Abai's *Words of edification* in what he con-siders a main dignity and wealth of people – perfection of their conscience and inward. Because a man using his opportunities acquires science and knowledge directing them on practice of humanization and jus-tice in society. *Abai considered that the science is not only valu-able and successful, but eventually it will lead to a wide philosoph-ical notion "spiritual values and existence". As Abai said – they are* *the core of human existence. He believed that spirituality, science and knowledge are the main wealth of humanity. "Agriculture and sowing, obtained knowledge is the main. Without work everything is fault" said th*e

poet. The main wealth of human Abai considered his spiritual values as a result of cognition of his inner self. In short, *The words of edification* of the poet aim at feeling of humanism revival and its perfection and through them the social relations change.

From the point of view of a spiritual cluster it is necessary to build a new capital city in Turkistan. The architecture of this city should account in project and during its construction the most advanced architectonic examples of Ancient East and Turkic civilization and either in a national spirit of Kazakhs to use ornaments, mosaic and colors. If Astana in XXI century be-came the capital of a new modern country[23] thus the revived Turkistan will become a new spiritual capital which saved its ancient culturally historical view. Besides it is necessary to open in the city an International Academy of Religion, an Academy of Culture, a museum The Park of Nuclear Security Baikonur – Semey, an Archeological Museum, etc. There is a necessity to institute an Academy of Humanization of Society and a meaning of Moral Codes of XXI century.

Taking into account uniqueness of entity and community of Turkic Muslim world, its spirituality, culture and religion, Turkistan should symbolize a Second Mecca, that's why there should be a center of patriotic education. For this purpose it is necessary to legalize officially the status of Turkistan as a spiritual capital. In future from a strategic point of view it is necessary for us to strive for intellectual leadership. Of course, it requires an acceptation of a large number of measures, conduction of big scientific, cultural, and ideological works. Why not to institute in Turkistan a university and an investigational center which would teach the rich scientific and cultural heritage of Eastern nations?! It's not a secret that nowadays science develops in spirit of Euro-centrism. **That's why it is necessary to** turn the way of science development in the East.

We face a target by means of spirituality revival to turn Turkistan to a historical center. I think that from a geopolitic point of view the world centre will move towards the Pacific Ocean. In this context the role of Turkistan revival project is great. The New Turkistan ,on an international level, will tie West and East, thus will raise the so-cially economic opportunities of the great Silk Road. Thanks to its centuries-long history and culture will change a spiritual conscience of humanity. Consequently the collaboration between nations will be consolidated, the system of stable development of region and the Eurasian area in whole will be formed.

In Kentau city it is necessary to build new plants of sixth technological mode. Taking into account such modern processes us-ing human and production potential of the city it is necessary to upgrade excavating and transformer plants, Achpolymetal JSC and other production powers. A specialists' training regime is necessary according to new technologies. We need to open the park of nuclear security, etc.

A necessity of construction of transport logistical cluster, a small centre of innovation business, technopolis, technical col-lege and other infrastructures of the great Silk Road also ap-pears in Kentau. Speaking modernly, we need to form a new technological cluster. In such a manner, first of all, we will create a spiritual centre in Turkistan; secondly, we will form a new sixth technological mode in Kentau. And in the interest of country we will have a new spiritu-ally technological cluster.

Consider logistics for example. On the great Silk Road by a motorway from Western China – Western Europe through Ka-zakhstan travel vehicular and railway transportation of all states of Central Asia. By the project only from the logistical cluster will there be realization of about 30% of profit will come from Turk-istan region.

It is necessary to create and develop a tourist cluster along the great Silk Road. It will give the big opportunities for monocities development program realization.

The Aul cluster creation is an imperative of our time. It will answer a question: What the Aul of XXI century should be? Through new dawn and development of aul we develop the entire country. Such Aul dawn is reached by means of new workplaces creation, thanks to Aul cluster, what will result a constant living of population on one place. Hence the demographic condition improvement. I believe that this project is conformable to centuries-long dream of our forefathers and it promotes a natural growth of population. That's why the demographic question should be in priority. **Without a population growth it is hardly believed that we will become a prosperous and strong state.**

This megaproject is issued by a separate book on three lan-guages: Kazakh, Russian and English. It was discussed in international conferences, approved unanimously and in type of offers and recommendations were sent to corresponding state authorities. A financially economic calculation was developed. A total sum is more than 8 billion US dollars. The project shows the costs of monetary means of separate clusters [7].

Turkistan is the center of Turkic speaking nations. All of us are of Big Turkistan descents. It is our common home. There is a surety that this project will be actual and realized in future. The process of society development itself will lead to this re-sult. Not creating spiritual elite it is hardly believed that we will enter the list of developed countries, and the basis of it is a spiritual development of Turkistan. There is still no alternative to this progressive idea.

The main aim is to create **an Academy of society humanization, basing on spiritual values, and forming in Kazakhstan spiritual elite, to make a step towards a new civilization.**

The winning philosophy thoughts in Abai's Words of edification remember about values of human soul. Though a human has a lot of interesting in life, the core is world cognition. That's why Abai considers a principle of humanism comparing with greedy wealth accumulation to the damage of morals, typical to human – the most human performance. In Abai's Words of edification the core of human existence is a cognition of spiritual values, because the core of existence connected to mental activity and his inner self is mind, intellectual thinking and justice, their increase is applied to present-day conditions of Kazakh nation, his peaceful life and strong entity.

Today the idea, which unites nation and nations and considers interests and needs of separate family is a crying need.

Such idea could be **the National Idea of Turkistan Re-vival.** Please, don't lose such opportunity!

The science is wealth and heritage,
Try only to pay it attention.
Abai

A man without science is like an animal,
By any means acquire it.
And science needs man,
If he's not clever, science is like an orphan.
Shakarim

THE WORD FIFTH

On what level are science and education? How can we give a push for their development?

If we remember our historical persons, we are doubtless gently born and educated nations. This list includes such great figures as **Al-Farabi, Al-Horezmi, Al-Biruni, Makhmut Kashgari, Mohammed Babur, Ussuf Balassaguni, Hoja Ah-met Yassawi, Mukhamed Haidar Dulati, Hafiz, Baki Turke-stani, Kydyrgali Zhalairi, Chokan Valikhanov, Abai Kunanbaev, Shakarim Kudaiberdiuly, Ybyrai Altynsarin, Alikhan Bokeikhanuly, Akhmet Baitursynov, Magzhan Zhumabaev, Mustafa Shokai, Sanzhar Asfendiyarov, Saken Seifullin, Nazir Torekulov, Turar Ryskulov, Mukhametzhan Tynysh-bayev, Mirzhakyp Dulatuly, Gabdolla Tuqay, Dinmukha-med Kunaev, Mukhtar Auezov, Berdy Kerbabaev, Zhussip-bek Aimauytov, Chingiz Aitmatov, Gerold Belger,** etc.

We can be proud that the first in the world of the technology of paper production was developed by Salim (in China – Cai lun). He was a native of Kashgariya. The scientists speak about his Turkish origin. In his time the quality and volume of Samarkand paper's production were widely known. Either today generation knows the names of Shora Kotani, Babur, Ulugbek, Zhalairi and a list of other scientists who participated in this affair. Besides, the first university and madras were found in Central Asia where the subjects of different spheres of science and art were taught. The list of their graduates is completed by many famous doers. The evidence of it is the works of famous Venetian traveller Marco Polo.

Abai teaches that science and knowledge help to learn and determine the roots and meaning of any phenomenon for what ambition and interest are necessary.

Cognition, science and knowledge are intended on humanism and kindness and are human in and of themselves. In such a manner a link between cognition and humanism is love. The cognition and science itself are induced by this love. The cognition and humanism based on love are humanness and they form it. Allah is the truth itself and love to him is humanness – said Abai. If we'll understand that life itself is a fight between right and wrong, humanism and insidiousness thus we consider the fight of love with these negative phenomena as humanism and humanness.

After the USSR formation there were contradictions in society notwithstanding development of education and science. Because of Stalin's hard regime some of advanced Alash Orda members were repressed – a lot of outstanding individuals of Kazakh intelligentsia, elite of nation. If in 1897 8.1% of Kazakh population were literate, in 1920 this rate reached 12%. In the following years of Soviet authority Kazakhstan became a country of full literacy. Later after getting independence (in 2012) the level of literacy of population reached 99%. It was a great progress. From Soviet Union along with sovereignty we acquired a big culture and scientifically technical potential. The Kazakh Academy of Sciences at that time took third place on a Union scale in order of importance. 29 scientists of our Republic were granted the titles of laureates of Lenin's, Stalin's and State Prizes for discoveries in the spheres of science and techniques, literature and art [3, 14, 16, 24, 25, 26]. For the years of Soviet power the names of Kanysh Satpaev, Mukhtar Auezov, Murat Aitkhozhin, Salyk Zimanov, Dmitry Sokolskiy, Alkey Margulan, Alexander Baraev, T.N.Sherba, Ufa Akhmetsafin, O.Sultangazin, Umirbek Dzholdasbekov, etc. became well known around the world.

When for the first time in history Jury Gagarin flew to the cosmos, USA admitted the high level of Soviet science and began to adopt our experience.

Where are those world achievements and experiences? Why did we fall behind in science? Where is a sectored science? Why our Kazakhs began to chase after honours and career? Nowadays a lot of public officials have the status of Doctor or Candidate of Sciences. And who are these scientists actually? They are ministers, deputies, akims and other public officials ravenous for fame and honours but who doesn't give anything and don't pursue science. Naturally that's why we see a declension of science. The main problem of modern science is an absence or lack of importantance for scientists' activity moral imperatives. This particular circumstance – a change of human development character itself, has today menacing forms and proportions. It is the moral imperatives break down that underlie in contradictions between science, society and state.

We lost the generation of talented scientists. The advanced young people who graduated Moscow, Leningrad and Novosi-birsk Universities after our country's independence reaching for survival went away to business, bank and other systems where they were able to get rich. Among them are B. Mergenov, N.Subhanberdin, O.Zhandossov, M.Essenbaev, Z.Kakimzhanov, M.Ablyazov, N.Kapparov and the representatives of other nations too. Some of them are still abroad. By this fact the Kazakhstani science lost because the government didn't take care and didn't provide conditions for science pursuit. Considering that in order to prepare a young scientist we need 30 years, thus we made a big and irretrievable mistake. Even nowadays we don't attract youth to science. For example, instead of working in scientific institutes for 44 thousand Tenge, the young special-ists prefer to go to banks on positions of managers or simple clerks and earn solid money. Because the wages there are much higher. There is guilt of the older generation which doesn't give way to youth and doesn't pay enough attention for scientific brain-power training. The mission of science is not determined.

Then again let's address to Abai. In his Words of edification he noted: for science and knowledge pursue a human nature has mind, energy and heart; in order to achieve the target they should be used at most. This is a philosophic creed of the great poet.

He considered the basic condition of common prosperity – humanness and personal enlightenment. Because perfecting his acquirements a man perfects his humanism. An individual becomes a real man.

Khakim Abai in Words spoke a lot about intellectual values having in mind humanism, respectfulness, belief (fear of god). In a piece of poetry What people need? He set them on the following values:

What people need?
Love, feeling, aggravation? To act, to run,
Wisely, advisedly speak.

In second line of this rhyme we see feeling (heart), in third – energy, in last – sense (mind). Combining them in one entire human nature Abai called them spiritual values which inspire people by conscience and inner self. That's just a philosophic conception of Abai in this question.

Nowadays prestige of scientists is not as high as it was under Kanysh Satpaev. A special concern of nation and scientific society is caused by closing of the National Academy of Sciences of the Republic of Kazakhstan. Meanwhile today in all CIS countries of former USSR the national academies of sciences remain in force financed by governments. Is this excusable?! Surely the guilty will be found and eventually they will face the music. It is bound to happen. The recovery of the National Academy of Sciences as a state organization is fateful for state which wants to enter the number of 30 developed countries of the world. The Republican civic organization The Council of Scientists of Kazakhstan offered this in its time to state authorities.

Abai in Words raised an issue about the general education demand. He advised: Who wants to pursue science and knowledge, need to know for what. And here he explained: an addiction to science and knowledge. This is a wealth; you cannot to learn just in case. If learn hard and with love the acquired knowledge will become food for existence for the whole life.

Whereby the science will extend mercy to you. Secondly, pursue science for the sake of truth and justice achievement but not for competing to somebody – making a mash on somebody. Then Abai said that the science loves truth, thus be honest to science

In Words he continues: Eventually a man can differ from another man by his mind, erudition and knowledge, disposition (character). Take it or leave it. And all rest is folly.

Though from the day of independence getting by our Republic 24 years passed, the science and education are slowly progressing in their development and we still cannot praise ourselves for great successes. Of course it began from economic fall, termination or complete halt of production enterprises which resulted a science crisis. We can understand it. However within many years the economy (beginning from 2000) grew multi-fold (annually the GDP growth reached 9-10%), but the science and education didn't get a priority and the funds for their development were not budgeted. Nowadays the material and technical resources are weak, everything is outmoded and initially we – scientists lead a wretched existence. The example of this could serve the following figures: in 1991 for the needs of science 0.68% of funds were budgeted from the total volume of GPD, today in 2015 – 0.16% in total. Instead of growth the science financing decreased on 4.5 times. Is that what influences the science development? In this case against our will we can remember the following Abai's word:

The science will result sorrow
The knowledge of course aggravation
When sorrow and aggravation press
Then I'm in hell – I have a brocard.

In the project of industrially innovative development in 2015 it is planned to budget for science 2.5% from GPD. The senior ranks of authorities even talked large officially and stated to increase this figure to 3%, but nothing changed and everything stayed in words. Notwithstanding a good growth of economy, the problem is still not solved. In Kazakhstan per head of the population for science 11 US dollars are budgeted, in USA – 1000$, in Japan $816, in Russia – $100. And as to the number of scientists, for these years it decreased from 41 thousand to 13 thousand, only recently it grew to 18 thousand, a slight increase.

If it comes to a showdown the devoted funds for the needs of science amount to the budget of a moderate university in USA. Afterwards what innovation are we speaking about? One may ask how is it? Because of insufficient budgeting for the needs of science equivalent to world competitiveness (as abroad). We are lagging behind other countries.

The volume of science financing in our country is on 20-25 times fewer in comparison with developed countries. They have 3-4% from a total volume of GDP. Being in such deficiency of funds for science how can we learn and support the scientists of world level? Besides doctor of sciences has the same salary as any company security, maybe even smaller. What do we have after that? There is only one decision – to find another work in business structures, etc. There is a popular saying and even songs: 'Be an akim, but closer to people'. In our time is all about financial standing and money. And what do the scientists have? They have mind, scientific potential, but holed pockets. But what consideration do the akims have is well-known. But there is no doubt that they live in easy circumstances, in clover. Even with all things considered it is necessary to do justice to those public officials who by their mind and doings honestly serve the people.

In spite of all the above listed dislocations our scientists on an international level in the sphere of mathematics and other exact sciences do the significant investigations and make discoveries. The main levers of science development – Ph.D. and doctorate defence, dissertation committees were closed by state. In other countries of CIS they were saved. Founded instead of thesis de-fence scientific brainpower training through master course and Ph.D. as an alternative doesn't stand up to scrutiny, the quality is very low. Indeed science develops not only thanks to public officials' activity but to separate scientists – patriots. Among them we can list the following persons: S. Zimanov, O. Sultan-gazin, Sh. Shokin, Zh. Takibaev, M. Aitkhozhin, O. Zhautikov, A. Sagynov, U. Zholdasbekov, A. Abdulin, B. Birimzhanov, A. Kaidar, T. Kakishev, S. Kirabaev, K. Ormantaev, A. Koshanov, M. Myrzakhmetov, M. Otelbaev, T. Khalmenov, A. Zhuma-dildaev and others.

All named scientists have their own scientific schools. Though the quality of our science is so low in comparison with world level but talented youth worthily continues the honoured traditions of scientists of the older generation. But support from governmental side is not enough for such beginnings.

If we speak about education in our country its level is very low. The reason of it is presence of private institutes' variety. The quality of education there is extremely low. It is very easy to get a diploma there. More than 50% of graduates do not work within speciality. The professionalism of the chosen sphere is very weak. And aquired specialties are not requested on labour market.

There are three reasons: first of all, a wrong state policy in educational sphere; secondly, an unsatisfactory institutional training;
thirdly, an unconscientious attitude and an unwillingness of students
themselves to study. Besides 90% of students study on a paid basis
and only 10% – win grants. It is a hard weight for youth from countryside. I visited Cambridge and Oxford Universities. There are
only two private universities in great Britain, and all the rest are
state. If desired it is possible to study free of charge under help of
the government. The other example, from 2014 till 2015 is in all the
regions of Germany in higher education establishments a gratuitous
instruction was introduced. There are only insufficient payments for
catering and servicing in libraries. It begs the question: If our quality
of life is better and higher than English and Germans have? Truly
speaking we turned the education into a commodity. Riches educate
their children abroad, but children of poorer families (even more intellectual) are deprived of this opportunity.

The biggest problem is a lack of engineers of high technologies
and in colleges – professional specialists' training. Under a weak training and attitude development of specialists, what moral education are
we speaking about? It would be logic to introduce a special subject of Abai's study about an appropriate man in general education
schools, colleges and universities. We do a lot in grading the system
of work of teachers, doctors, architects, economists and lawyers.

Unfortunately, modern specialists are short of human qualities
and spiritual values. It is explained by the fact that acquired education is too limited for sake of education itself it doesn't develop
conscience, doesn't discover their internal world and view. The
children's level of knowledge is closely tied to parents because what
can they give to their children when they themselves are not pre-
pared? How long can it continue? A full education of children suffers
a great damage because of a lack of efficient and available study
guides. Nowadays, instead of conscious re-ention of learned mate-

rial students need to overlearn them mechanically. Universities like conveyers graduate more and more variable desired and undesired specialists.

Truly speaking we turn to be ' diploma' society without knowledge. "Society without knowledge is a mill without wa-ter." To manage such society is not very hard. If only to exalt powers that be and accomplish them. The second way of management is to rule by means of force. "The worst man is wanting an initiative man" – said Abai. But initiative and desire are formed by knowledge. Further Abai said: "For acquisition of knowledge and science a man has two reliable weapons: the first is Muluhaza (thinking) and second is Mufahaza (consolidation and reliable memorizing)". Abai in his works the word "science" quoted very often (111 times).

The most important is to form a high conscience of people, to raise their social intellect by means of knowledge gaining. Only then a man can implement his opportunities in practice. Usually any man has the first evidences of knowledge and capabilities (skills). Their external appearance is desire. Desire is induced by ability to some-thing. A man of ability doesn't sit idle. He is in constant search and will choose a favourite doing.

Desire is a mean of purpose achievement. It could be traced by the following lines of Abai's piece of poetry:

The words of learned scholar Should reach a desired.

The poet under "desired" sees a loving, passionate, initiative per-son with a gut feeling. Only a human being can see the un-noticed, hided sides and cognize them.

How can we give a new impulse for science and education de-velopment?

The experience of foreign countries shows that today science can develop only in conditions of all-round care and support from government. A criterion of this care should be as a mini-mum alignment of our scientists' conditions with conditions of foreign researchers under an active attraction of investments into advanced technologies. Taking into account an important role of science and high technologies in XXI century, it is necessary to take cardinal measures by means of state institution foundation in this sphere (National Committee or government agency) and on the analogy of USA the National Science Foundation. Nowa-days there are a lot of academicians and academies. However, the country gets a little from them. That's why, consolidating all them together, it is necessary to found the State Civic Academy of the Republic of Kazakhstan. The state where science and education are well developed according to needs and requirements of people is strong. As in developed countries under the aegis and guidance of President it is necessary to found the Supreme Consultative Council for Science and Technology. It will promote an international competitiveness of the country. It is very important either where academic forces are concentrated, to open the science and innovation campuses. It is advisable to found the scientific schools of world-class scientists and create conditions for their fruitful work. By efforts of these scientfic institutions it is necessary to develop a State scientific and technical strategy and policy of its effective realization.

For entering the list of civilized countries it is necessary to take care of a worthy financing of science. Only a scientifically developed country can show itself on a high level. As we emphasized before in developed countries science is budgeted to 3%. We have – 0.16%. This is on 20-25 times less than in developed Countries. It can be helped. For this in 2020-2025 years to begin financing from 1.5% from GDP and gradually lead this figure to 3%-4%. It is necessary on an international level to found the scholarly traditions of scientists and increase their wages by several times. In order to interest scientists and encourage their work a foundation of **State Order named after Kanysh Satpaev** is required. It is necessary to raise status of scientists. Providing young scientists with flats and creating for them corresponding conditions we could give an opportunity of new discoveries.

By this we can prepare the scientists of the XXI century. In order to enforce the scientific discoveries and inventions implementa-ion, it is necessary to found the scientific centers, technopolises, venture and innovation funds in regions. The akims activity in their annual reports should be appraised by their contribution in science and education development in their oblast, city and region.

It is necessary to implement in higher education establishments an international certification that could raise a level of personnel training. We cannot decrease the quantity of fees at universities. Ministers who came for 1-2 years couldn't do it - try as they might, but it didn't come off because at their heads the same ministers or their "uncles, higher direction" sit. gratuitous instruction couldwere implemented at 50% for beginning and then on all 100%. By my reckoning free education requires not more than 3.5-4 million US dollars.

If we consider taking care of our country's future, it is enough to devote only 3% nds from the National Fund. Nowadays for the needs of national education 4% from GDP are devoted. It is necessary to raise it to 6%. There is a need to eliminate an administrative management in universities and transfer to self-ad-ministration through scientific councils. This would be more democratic in universities' life. It would be right if rector or director of scientific research institute will be selected by scientific council or staff members. If scientific professors and associate professors who stand at the top of science don't have the right and cannot man-age themselves then where is our democracy? It means that there is no reliance from above from the side of higher-ranking direction. It seems that authorities are affraid that under this situation they lose a principle of autocratic decision in educational foundations and a total disobedience will appear.

In words, without quality increase in higher schools, Kazakhstan cannot become competitive. For this we urgently need to raise the status of educators. It is necessary in educational foundations to successfully complete a professional standard practically. Students should be taught how to turn acquired knowledge into capital. Because our students receive abstract knowledge, which are far from reality. In secondary educational institutions implementation of subjects according to Abai's study, choice of speciality, small business and also harmony of nature and human being are the basic requirements of the epoch of globalization.

The main purpose of education is not only to give knowledge, but to educate spiritually appropriately the **man.**

Abai made all his efforts in order to bring in a conscience of his nation such philosophical meanings as "spiritual values" and "existence" (humanism, fear of god, splendour, honesty, respectfulness, etc.) The great Abai taught that **"It is necessary to learn Rus-sian. Because wealth, science and art – all these are of Rus-sians possession"**. This Abai's advice was realized on all 100% under the Soviet Union. As Mukhtar Shahanov said, that policy so pressed us that the last generations became mangurts who forgot their native language [27]. If in times of Abai there was a need to learn from Russians, but in conditions of globalization process we should strive to become competitive on world level. It wouldn't be out of place to say that indeed in the epoch of Soviet power we became familiar with world culture thanks to the Russian language and a socialistic tenor of life.

On my opinion, every man first of all ought to know his native language well. Language is a soul of the nation. Secondly, it is necessary to know an international language of market economy – English, the language of Internet. This is the language of programming and data bases preparation. Mastering languages we should make a step to society humanization. We have a state law about languages. It is a pity that though 25 years went by after the state independence getting our native language – Kazakh – didn't took its respectable place. It is necessary to admit a separate law about the Kazakh language. Such law is absent only in our state. Let's look at this from the international point of view! In such situation we are forced to say: "Protect the Kazakh language from Kazakhs themselves!" In our time we: M. Shakhanov, S. gab-bassov, A. Osman, D. Koshim led the group and worked out the project of a new law about the state language and sent it on the name of President (in 2011). We received a run around from the Ministry for Culture of the Republic of Kazakhstan. That's why it is necessary to give it a real state status by a new law. Because, as Akhmet Baitursynov said: "The loss of language is a loss of nation itself". The native language is necessary for our culture, literature, young generation, scientific brainpower development. The Kazakh language is the language of honour and our existence. Finally it is necessary for unity of the country and state

This results a necessity in careful relation to culture, science and innovations, investments from foreign companies. Only by this way we can raise our competitiveness on an international level. And the roots of competitiveness are in qualitative education and professionalism of people.

It is important to consider for future generations that if in XIX and XX centuries the struggle for world leadership was carried out basically on the field of military machinery and corresponding technologies development, what led to weapon of mass destruction creation which is able to destroy the whole world, nowadays and in perspective of XXI century this struggle more and more shifts toward informational and socially psychological sphere. The main purposes of confrontation the domination in intellectual, informational and psychological areas become.

Today the global area is first of all a competition of ideas, projects and struggle for meaning and values of human life. The real leaders are those countries, which dominate in ideological intellectual sphere which exist on new knowledge and accelerated development of science. To this I call you in order to achieve this purpose by means of decision of harmony development forming task between science, state and society. The sooner we'll decide this task, the sooner we'll close these irretrievable gaps or sooner will be swallowed by others because of national intellect deficiency which should serve to the state of Kazakhstan.

Only healthy nation will achieve a desired target.

THE WORD SIXTH

What is the level of national health and sport?

People say: "The main wealth is health". It is interesting to know what condition of health our citizens have. Does the government pay enough attention to it? On my point of view the question requires a special decision. For example, the problems of tuberculosis, infant mortality, anaemia, suicide are considered probems here in comparison to foreign countries and our country opens the list of disadvantaged countries in this sphere. Forecast is unnerving and this is very sad. Of course we cannot say that things are in a bad way. We have some achievements: the health clinics were opened according to world standards, the level of qualification of our doctors is high and annually we conduct thousands of qualitative and unique operations. However it's not enough because in remote rural settlements the elementary first-aid posts are absent. In order to receive a qualified medical aid a rural man is forced to get to city, what is difficult especially in winter time when snow complicates the vehicles' movement. The acute patients (children and old people) don't have time to reach doctor. That's why there is a high mortality.

The budget funded for the needs of medicine compounds is 3.5-3.7% fromGDP. It means that among CIS countries we take the last place. As the World Health Organization (WHO) reported on a health guard of our population we should fund not less than 6% from GDP. Only under these circumstances the health of our citizens will be under the required protection. The health budget of foreign developed countries compounds 8, 10, 18% from GDP. According to the World Davos Economic Forum estimates in 2015-2016 Kazakhstan takes the 93rd place according to the level of healthcare and primary education, i.e. within many years already our country is in the list of outsiders. In countries' rating of health condition of their population, which was based on an investigation of the Agency Bloomberg, Kazakhstan took the 111 place.

The soil of our country is rich of mineral deposits; this fact is well-known around the world. It is difficult for our state to cope with problems having wide territory and thin population, because our country is considered by many neighbor countries and not only by them as desirable **cake**, and they are ready to tear off a piece when occasion offers. Especially those countries which have a large population. These are China with 1.3 billion of population, on North – Russia with 150 million of population and Uzbekistan nearby with 32 million of population. That's why our government needs to keep both eyes open! Any insufficient mistake in internal or external policy of the country can turn into a big tragedy. In such situation if we'll develop slowly there is a probability to be economically swallowed in one moment. That's why it is necessary to increase quantity of population and raise quality of life. We need to gather rapid pace of development in all spheres of life. And run circles around in comparison to neighbor countries. Why not to take a pattern by Russia or Belorussia, appearing in the Single Economic Union, where infant capital on a newborn compounds 10 thousand US dollars.

Besides, nowadays our country has the lowest salary of medical staff, especially of staff nurses. They keep body and soul to-gether working for 1.5-2 salaries in medical establishments. The lowest salaries have cultural professionals, teachers, doctors and scientists. getting so low salaries can we preserve a healthy and intelligent nation? In foreign countries doctors and advocates have the highest wages. For example, a country doctor in USA gets a wage of 150 thousand US dollars. It means that monthly he gets more than 12 thousand US dollars.

Our professors, doctors of sciences, associate professors and medical officers would not disgrace their foreign colleagues by competence, but get wages on 10 times lesser than abroad. What would our government, Parliament, Minister say on it? Their own salaries are incomparable. Truly speaking, not all doctors who all their life serve people, are in the full of health. For exam-ple, the length of life of emergency physicians is below average. According to international practices it is necessary to raise the smallest salary to 40% from average pay in whole economy.

Azerbaijan reached this rating. And in developed countries it achieves 60%, we have only 20%.

That's why on the lowest level of international standard the min-imal wage should be raised to 40% of average monthly earnings. Only under these circumstances we can create the conditions for survival of every worker and every family. We are obliged to do it on the first step. In 2015 our average monthly earnings exceeded 127507 Tenge. If the minimum salary would compound 40% from this sum we would receive 49000 Tenge. But today it compounds only 21364 Tenge. It is on 2.4 times lesser than normative. For this reason the most dis-advantaged layer of population consists of teachers, doctors, scien-tists, workers of the budget sphere. That is the root of evil. Without adoption of a new law we will never raise the minimum salary to 40% from average monthly earnings and consequently increase minimum level of subsistence.

An employment issue of healthcare workers doesn't stand up to criticism. As medical workers themselves say, academician K.S. Ormantaev, the department of pediatrics was closed, be-cause of paid education only those that 'have' can get diplomas those who are working in medical facilities are disadvantaged healthcare ren-dering non-professional aid. In the 90-s the weak students were kicked out on 1-2 courses already, and to 4-5 courses to 20-30% of students were 'flunked' out. Nowadays we have the other trouble, students who pay for education "hang" till the graduation of institute, but get diplomas.

If we really would like to stand up for human bodies and souls, thus **we need to implement a free education by state grants and to make more severe the order of students' admission in medical**

universities.

We cannot conceal one fact. Previously in auls a three-stage aid was rendered. First of all even small aul had its own first-aid post where the first aid was administered. Secondly, in kolkhoz and sovkhoz centres worked doctors and even small hospitals were presented. Thirdly, in regional centres the patients were treated in polyclinics and hospitals. And nowadays everything is concentrated in regional centres only. For rural people it creates difficulties with transportation in all seasons of the year.

In whole for improving the health care manpower training, increase of salaries, medical facilities equipment and implementation we need to adopt another law where would be written in black and white: "the doctors caught in corruption do not have right to work in this sphere".

An offer **to fund for needs of medicine not less than 6% of budget from GPD** should meet with support from the side of state. **Otherwise we won't have a forward shift.** It is necessary to develop the country pharmaceutics, to begin production on an initial stage possibly simple in composition medicines. And then gradually implement technologies of more complicate medications. Nowadays in our country about 10% of medicines are produced in reliance to prime cost of the total volume of manufactured products. It is very little. It is necessary to hasten the construction of pharmaceutical plants and plants of medical equipment production.

Sport is an insurance of health. It is necessary to cultivate love of sport in every family, because without everyday physical training there is no strong health. We need to raise a question on governmental level about opening of sport complexes, schools and clubs across Kazakhstan available for all citizens of the Republic. A link between physical training and medicine has roots stretching back into deep antiquity. Our forefathers since child-hood cultivated love of sport to their children. Beginning from 2-3 years kids could famously ride horses, shoot from bow and knew wrestling. The sporting bouts and games were organized among young and adult men between auls. If we say by words of the great Abai: **"The whole life of Kazakh passed a-cock-horse"**. In former times to the envy of many nations Kazakhs at the age of 80-90 years became fathers. Where are such men now?

Or did we become worse? Surely in those times the air was fresh, we drank only kumys and shubat, ate only plain boiled beef. The time and morals changed today. That's why in accordance to requirements of present day we need to make adjustments. 30-40% of young people are unfit for military service.

In such a manner the meanings "sport" and "health" are of key category today, because health is a required condition not only for development and growth, but for society survival either. Statistically, the rates of reproductive capacity in our country are low. Yes, we already have our own world and Olympic champions. But it is necessary to place on the agenda a question of health promotion and **implementation of regular mass sporting events** . I'd like to give an advice to growing generation: if you want to become healthy and successful, go in for any sports, especially race, skiing, cycling, visit fitness clubs, workout facilities.

If train regularly into a lather and walk on long distances, than there is no need to worry about nation's health. Among youth a healthy lifestyle is cultivated. And that is right! Smoking and alcohol is a share of weak and spineless people. The potential of Kazakh nation is high. Besides if we took effective measures before there were no problems.

To our joy our country has a great chance to stand in one line with many developed countries, because creative nation of Kazakhstan with its highly educated and scientific groundwork should cheer up and recover liberty at last. For today there is an acute question about an **immediate implementation of new innovation developments**, only then our country will be appreciated in world thanks to highly organized and civilized nation.

It is necessary to work hard in this direction, because a man who came to understanding and is able to use Abai's study about *appropriate man* in practice can make himself and his country happy.

Admit a man by his words,
But don't make promises looking at him.
Abai

On condition of a man of aul cognize a citizen man.

THE WORD SEVENTH

What is a situation in aul? What do we need for its improvement?

It should be noted that in Soviet time villages developed very successfully. In order to understand a situation in villages let's make a short excursion to the recent past. In the Soviet period the main production units of agriculture in Kazakhstan were sovkhoz and kolkhoz farms founded in the period of new grounds' clearing. Sovkhoz represented a central village with its own production and social infrastructure where the basic population lived and several small villages called departments.

There lived about 2.5-10 thousand inhabitants. Each of them had secondary school, nursery, hospital, post office, culture centre or club, library and several shops. And in cultural meaning life of inhabitants was built. Today we have another situation. Blossoming in recent past central farm yards in sovkhoz and kolkhoz farms are ruined. A mass exodus of rural population to cities continues. From the whole infrastructure of Soviet time only schools and first-aid posts remained. The thin out buildings of nurseries, culture centres, hospitals, 10-15 thousandth stock breeding complexes demolished and sold out. Some villages became wastelands. I myself and people of my generation are bystanders of these events.

In 1991 when the country received its independence there was a lot of happiness. And when the Declaration of Independence was adopted our deputies were glad with tears in their eyes full of pride for realized centuries-long dream of our forefathers [24, 28]. The first years of independence were heavy for the country: crisis, inflation, zero economy, closed plants and factories, that's why it was necessary to adopt a row of important laws. The same situation was in other fraternal countries of the former Union. In common, changes occurred influenced a lot the look of an aul. These changes were described in detail in article of Dulat Issabekov – Aul goes to sky. Under a beautiful slogan **"Opti-mization"** all listed above social production posts were closed. Especially it is painful to see as after war gaping holes of windows of recently productive 10-15 thousandth stock breeding complexes. Only recently villages began to be restored to life again. But changes are insufficient. We still didn't reach the level of 90-s [29, 30].

Nowadays rural youth is basically unemployed what can lead to the loss of the faith in the future, alcoholism and other bad practices. As Abai said: *There is a reason why Kazakhs are addicted to bad habits, this is an absence of work. If they cropped the fields and were in trade, they hadn't time for bad?* [1]. Unemployment in villages reaches 75-80% and in remote – 85%. Nowadays, the population of rural districts numbers from 700 to thousands of inhabitants.

A considerable part of inhabited localities are placed in re-mote distance from motorways. Especially it is difficult for solitary villages inhabitants who often in winter time stay fully parted off regional centres. The bulk of rural population goes off in search of a living. The situation is as follows: on summer time they work in cities and on winter – sit at home. As a result young people tend to cigarettes and drugs or choose the way of religious extremism, thieve and hector, the cases of suicide became often. Unaccustomed way of life, slender purse in families influence a lot the health of women, that's why there is a high infant mortality.

The only category of rural men on whom the village stands are public employees: akimat staff and teachers, doctors. Akims of rural districts day and night need to solve current issues of their home folks, beginning from family internal squabbles to tractors furnishing for cleanup of snowdrifts on roads in winter time. The bulk of inhabitants regard to the category of self-employed, i.e. they don't work anywhere but live on what they grow.

The great Abai's *Words of edification* imposed absolutely new tasks on social life and living. That was a search of social truth. But till nowadays there were no social community which lifted to the top of justice. Notwithstanding that the titans of humanity beginning from Aristotle and Al-Farabi showed the way to such society the traces of social inequity are still not covered. Abai, by his saying: *We speak right and you, listener, improve yourself* claimed from listeners and readers their artistically ideological aesthetical growth. Because these categories he considered as a necessity of life and art.

Our government figures unemployment to 5-6%. This data does not correspond to the facts. With such achievements our country can enter the Guinness Book of Records. There should be a limit of reality distortion. Indeed the rates of some European states compound 15-25% and in average more than 10%.

Our government clangs all bells that 2.7 million people can provide themselves. In sober fact these figures correspond to un-employment in our country.

Rural men as often urban residents either stay out of social insurance benefits: pension contributions, health coverage, i.e. 20% of population remain on a "wayside" of society not getting set by law benefits. That's a pity to look at it, because the bulk of rural inhabitants are representatives of native nationality.

Figures represented on papers are mostly falsified, because akims show data of past years. Till nowadays a mindset of liar is stable. When will we stop lying and think only about our pockets? If an unemployed person will come to take credit, he'll be openly informed that it is necessary to give a "hat" in order to receive all documents about work availability, amount of salary, etc., or the only way to get credit is a city apartment occurrence. But if a rural man would have a flat in city, he would move there long ago. It is necessary to emphasize that credits are allowed on a term of one year. Any man who is acquainted to biology from school times would say that it is difficult for one year to turn lamb into sheep, calf into caw, foal into horse, i.e. to achieve a market-able condition. Rural man grasps at a straw and agrees in hope to improve a family welfare or to pay for his child's education. And again simple people get into a clinging trap of banking bail. let's again remember Abai's words: **How to facilitate management of people?** Here he sees a lever of political power management in hands of honest, thinking about peoples' interests and competent persons. Besides, the great thinker described a chronic "disease" of class contradictions in Kazakh society by his piece of poetry *November and December – these two months*:

A poor man tends cattle himself,
His wife is at home,
there is nothing to heat a house,
Thawing a frozen fell,
trembling with cold,
She begins to sew a woolen caftan for her *husband.*
To worker a richman will give no thing in excess.
He is ungrateful and a poor man is impolite.
The God himself counterposed them,
Long ago, not in one moment.

In these two couplets the antagonistic realities of representatives of two competing classes of that time are brightly de-scribed. This is a true picture of diverging interests of two layers of population rendered by poetic pattern.

By words of Galym Turganbaev – rural worker who man-aged three regions for 13 years, farm – for 12 years, who cares about people, first of all, many modern rural workers are young and inexperienced; secondly, public officials from Astana don't come to auls and don't receive exact data about situation that is happening ; thirdly, there is no constant control from the side of higher bodies. But even if they come with inspections, thus these visits end with full tables. And the result you can imagine. It happens commonly.

If from the side of government the large holding companies are supported with 86% of subsidies, thus villages – only with 14%. We cannot understand it! The funded money is not enough for agriculture renewal. It is unknown where the bulk of these money go, may be somebody in tops knows. It begs the question: Is there anybody who worries about a simple rural Kazakh? [30].

Regarding basic funds, especially techniques, we stand on the verge of crisis. About 70% of agricultural parks in the country are worn out. There is no amortization program and others for their renewal. But if it existed, there is nobody to realize it, because we lack engineers and specialists. As Galym Turgan-baev says, for 24 years of independence in Kerbulak region and other places farms are still not provided with engineers, technicians, animal technicians, agronomists. Where the graduates will go in this situation? Where is so called state order? The authorities absolutely don't think about it.

If farms have any techniques, thus it is of Soviet time or dis-assembled on parts and is beyond repair. The only way is to adopt a law urgently in order to attract mechanics and engineers, and if we'll be shot of them, to send youth for education from the number of our own rural graduates providing assurance that then they will return to native auls. young specialists who set to work enthusiastically after institutes run from villages within a year because of way of life despondency and low salary, young married people are not provided with accommodation, etc. It is difficult to survive for them.

How can we develop aul?

In countryside about 45% of population lives, i.e. more than 8 million people. The majority of them are representatives of na-tive nation. "On condition of aul cognize its citizen" as the prov-erb runs.

Small farms are short of new techniques and technologies for their field boundary development. They cannot compete to large farms. The manufactured products don't sell. If even it is sold it is for a trifling sum. It reasons a necessity of cooperation of small farms into large. For this we urgently need to adopt a law about "cooperation". A necessity of technical service centres will appear and a need of collectivization of agriculture from a new angle. Repeat once again, the basis of this is cooperation. Here we need a support from government. In such newly founded cooperatives the share of state (government) can reach to 20-30%. The main is to pay attention to financing enough subsidies and cheap credits for agricultural production and strictly control their receipt in places. Only in this case the investments will be made to the most basic objects, the quantity of working places will increase what will become a rough push for village development.

In order to widen small farms and farming it is necessary to provide them with new techniques that meet the last requirements. Creation of cooperatives will give a new impulse to already existing complexes. It is necessary to organize one or two centres of technical servicing and repair in every region. Possible, in these newly created unions the new working places will appear and aul will lift up its head. Along with consumer cooperations w i l l revive procurement organizations, which admit reduction of animals, agricultural products and their processing. The evidence of this serves an experience of many foreign countries: Canada, USA, European Union (especially Switzerland where in order to engage their farmers during long Alpine winters they invented production of Swiss watches). The task number one is to build a new type of technological aul. Such auls could be organized not far from Almaty in the Kazakh Institute of agriculture, the Kazakh scientific research institute of live stock breeding and in village Shortandy. For example in Singapore the base of modern agricultural technologies 10 scientifically production parks are created.

A rational approach allowed them to build 500 farms of different spheres on 1.7 thousand hectares. Why don't we use this experience?

To found new holdings. If we will continue without exact calculation thus in future within 40-50 years oil resources and other mineral deposits will be exhausted. Do you really think that our descendants will never ask from us? Today we have nothing to answer.

From everlasting Kazakhs tended live stock and made farms. The main brand of our country is not oil or gas (maybe it is simply profitable for some public officials to present our country as petroleum). The whole world imagines our country as agrarian. In the beginning of 90-s of the past century the level of agricultural revenues in regard to Gross Domestic Product amounted 27-29% and now these rates are low – 5%. Under the growth the figures to 20% would be more actual. Unfortunately, many types of food products, 40% of meat and milk products are brought from abroad. But under a wise management we should do conversely – to export to other countries. Shame of us if we cannot support our nation with the most important: meat and milk. That's why it is necessary under the support of government to create in country **Agricultural holdings of meat and wheat** and hurl all effort into protection and prosperity of rural settlements.

In this regard the words of deputy chairman of RSFSR Sovnarkom – Turar Ryskulov are epideictic, who 11 years held this post and once shared his thoughts with Stalin: "Comrade Stalin, meat is a currency. We need to store meat products and sell to Europe and on profit earned to educate young specialists who after education will work in this sphere.

The meaning of these words is still actual today. If you consider that Kazakhstan in the Soviet period for export produced 300 thousand tons of animal products. But if today we wouldn't raise a question about this spheres renewal, then it will be too late. Why not to raise the sphere which is well-known for Kazakhs sustainably?

Especially since in forthcoming 30 years a demand on animal products will increase twofold and a water deficiency – on 50-60%. This opportunity couldn't be lost.

Reconstruction of live stock breeding, corn lands and plant cultivation is not a step to past as many people think, but con-versely a perfect opportunity to move forward and leave behind many post Soviet states and not only them.

A pending task for us for further work in auls is professional employees training . I have something to say to youth in this aspect: choice of agricultural professions, work in agricultural products manufacturing and live stock breeding are not outmoded traditions, but our priority. It is inappropriate to chase after loud titles of lawyers and economists. Practicing traditional farming of our forefathers – live stock breeding and agriculture you can become rich and prosperous. As far as possible young people should be rational. In this case the aul will bloom and rise from its knees and production security of our country will be provided.

Support and help for the aul shouldn't be a debt only of rural population. This problem should be solved by government, par-iament, scientists and all of the nation. The state should do the best in order to increase the level of villages. Villages need **Asar** – a forgotten practice of past times when all inhabitants of village helped to build a house, outbuildings to their home folks. Now it's high time to remember the past and help ourselves. I offer this to concerned citizens who live in cities but were born and grown up in auls and who became high powered, educated and rich, to unite and help their auls to regain their feet. I advice to open in regions centres of aid giving where anybody can receive advice and knowledge how to take out a loan correctly, where directors and akims in administration will receive aid of business plans composition, of small cooperatives opening, etc.

It is necessary to give an expert recommendation of village development, to work out a plan and create a council of elders. Kazakh nation has wonderful features: charity and delicacy, that's why such a beginning will not get away.

Be wise, courageous and merciful,
Then you'll become special and authoritative.
Abai

What a human is, the same is his influence on society.

THE WORD EIGHTH

What does every man and his family need?

A strategic aim of society development is a quantitative development of human capital. In world practice only through human investment can we achieve a competitiveness of the country. The government should render all-round support in order to raise the quality of life of its nation in the century of cardinal transformations. Investigations showed that one US dollar invested in one man will be justified by 100 US dollars.

In the epoch of globalization Kazakhstan should develop in a civilized way. It means a peaceful life of all people and every family, provision of children with food and education at an adequate level, happy life of our society members. And authorities and administration should create for it all conditions, because people pay taxes. What do we need in a competitiveness, to reach an economical independence? We say that our economy before the crisis annually grew on 9-10%. We receive profit basically from sales of oil and other natural resources. Though we didn't free ourselves from economic dependence. Visit the bazaars, 70% of offered goods are imported. Of course, it is not obligatory that all 100% of goods were Kazakh, but we have opportunities for their production. let's take for example our auls. Let us suppose that in every family there are in average three children apart from parents. The eldest studies in university, second – in college and youngest – in school. From parents only one works as teacher or doctor. The average monthly salary is 50 thousand Tenge.

How can they feed and teach children with such salary? The educational foundations are paid, an education in university costs in average 600 thousand Tenge, in college – 200 thousand Tenge.

Where can a simple rural man find money in order to pay for their education? How do you think, is the amount of 50 thou-sand Tenge enough for food, clothes, transportation and other pocket expenses? And for marriages which Kazakh people love to visit? Every Kazakh in order not to fall flat on face will do the best, will take credit, but will perform a wedding for his beloved child. It's not important what will happen later when the time of monthly payments will come. In total the whole family will suffer.

Evidently our Kazakhs forgot Abai's words: *Be afraid of Allah, shame of people. If you want your son became a human, don't grudge livestock, educate him.*

The only decision is to raise stock. A rural man in order to grow a cow will spend not one year. And what a hard work it is to take care for animals, rural men know, what expenses should be paid for hay, feed, veterinary services, etc.

Not every man can do such heavy work and not every has an opportunity to buy livestock, that's why the majority especially youth moves to cities in search of the best share. Unemployment and idleness tend young villagers to bad habits and religious extremism. A small part of population can allow themselves to send their children for education abroad and the rest enter native paid educational foundations and one more part buys diplomas.

The education in village schools is not at an adequate level, classes provided with computers are very low. Why? There are no regular courses for raising qualifications of specialists. Besides, a big percentage of village school teachers or get education, or studied on extension departments after marriage or maternity leave. Some of them bought diplomas. What are we speaking about?! For example, in some schools in the south, depending on how much did you give to a higher command (public official from department of education or school director) the quantity of school lessons for teachers are distributed. Hence the level of salaries is different. You cannot make a step without bribes.

Abai's *Words of Edification* teach that a human life is an expression of humanism. A meaning of your life and its serenity (without regret) are tied to humanism directly. Though, there is a lot of good in life, its core is humanness.

Abstaining from a rush for wealth, to follow the principles of humanism are human dignity and feat. Saving of humanness is a top of peoples' perfection.

Today is the time of wasteful weddings, but not of rationalism and comprehensive calculation of all costs. Of course, it is necessary to conform to the rules and traditions from far past of the nation. Kazakh wedding rites are very beautiful and in order next generations didn't forget them and maintained, it is necessary to perform them with national colouring. I don't mean this. I mean that many Kazakh wedding are beyond the limits of the ceremony hosts' condition according to their budget. It worries me a lot because in chase of pomposity and prestige with a desire to perform the wedding better than somebody else, in order not to lose face, the heroes of the occasion often suffer after the wedding, when time of liabilities' discharge comes, because money on bridal spectacular performance were borrowed from friends or loaned in banks as credits. It would be nice if weddings were more creative and economic.

I hope that modern youth will certainly bring its corrections in this question and won't adopt negative features as vanity and excessive wastage. We wait that the young generation will take more seriously to the question of weddings and other grand occasions' performances. The main priority of weddings should be rationalism, unity of relatives and close people, tie of elder and young generations, great amusement and the of maintenance games and national traditions .

But if obtain further insight into the problem, thus Islam, beginning from its origin began to separate on small glides and sects, which negatively affects all Muslim nations unity. The division on Sunni and Shiah, constant conflict of "Muslim brothers", "tug of war", mess are the present pressing questions in the Muslim world. Unfortunately Muslim nations still continue to divide on smaller sects. In its time our government didn't take into consideration that this happened in different sides of our country breaks and foundation of small sects [31]. This is a result that there were no distinct spiritual conception in our country and clear religious ideology. Several years ago in Kazakhstan there were 4500 different religious glides and sects.

If calculated that the religious sects are constantly appended by two hundred of people thus it means that in near future our society will be poisoned by alien ideas. We hear the news sometimes that in different sides of our country the youth

are seriously addicted to Wahhabism and Salaphite, their members amount more than thousands of people. The government lost sight that our citizens were caught on war in Syria and in other hotspot of tension. And how many people are there who only prepare to leave the country in order to participate in fratricidal slaughters? Who can say surely that these citizens would not want to make their sacrilegious doings here after return, where quiet and peaceful?

I'll repeat once again that the government in the beginning of independence , basically solved the questions of economy, didn't take into account a religious sphere of life of its citizens, when in different places at random the religious organizations were created. Only recently they are paid more careful attention. I think it is necessary to begin with a right presentation of religious teaching foundations. For this purpose it is necessary to prepare a correct Imams' teaching who nowadays don't correspond by the level of their knowledge and moral principles: commit indecencies not corresponding a rank of religious preacher, have two or more wives, walk with a begging bowl, talk only to rich men putting the listening to different needs.

At least partially include into a teaching process the lessons of religion in schools and other educational foundations, where the principles of Islam, moral and spiritual values and national culture would be taught. I think that an expert approach to the foundations of Islam in conscience of growing generation plays strategic meaning in realization of peace and agreement between nations which live in our country.

First of all, it is necessary to give explanations of Islam, to create an **Academy of Religion in Turkestan**, to enhance the true foundations of Islam to which Mohammed the Prophet called – charity, delicacy and unlimited belief to Allah. Secondly to wake up a true patriotism in hearts of many Kazakhstan

All these and many other questions about religion will be considered in the project "Turkestan" [6].

For raising the spirit of patriotism a wide enlightment of biographies of outstanding persons is required, such as

Bauyrzhan Momyshuly, Talgat Bigeldinov, Rakhimzhan Koshkarbaev, Kassym Kaissenov, Sabyr Rakhimov and others.

Especially such influence should be made beginning from nursery, in family, school, in all secondary schools and higher educational establishments and especially on TV. Ei-ther to hold up as an example worthily the achievements of national champions and heroes well-known around the world: Toktar Aubakirov, Zhaksy-lyk Ushkempirov, Shamil Serikov, Kairat Ryskulbekov, Lyazzat Assanova, Bekzat Sattarkhanov and Mustafa Ozturk, Batyrkhan

Shukenov, Ilya Ilyin, Gen-nady Golovkin.

A special attention should be paid to deep knowledge acquisition and personal enrichment of our growing generation, to live by their needs and concerns, to decrease unemployment to a minimum among youth, to cooperate fully in all perspective beginnings. *Abai said: Children come into the world being different: some want only drink, eat and sleep; the ot-ers are thirsty to know the universe.* By these words the great Abai wanted to bring to his congeners what is good and what is bad, appealed to be aspiring and a thirst for knowledge and struggle for existence [1].

The targets of XXI century are different. This is the time of market relations and capitalism. In old times people were respected for good deeds, ambitiousness, honesty and reliability, but nowadays, if you have money in your pocket you can succeed a lot, hiding far your conscience and honour. If you don't have money it is unlikely you will be supported in hour of need, even some will make believthat don't know you at all. We need to return lost values of Soviet time, when education, proficiency, well doing and simplicity, respectability to a man of working profession and working dynasties were appreciated. In chase of survival and easy money after Union break up we didn't noticed how we became cold-hearted, greedy, spiteful to those who are poorer and simple. First of all every man has to begin from himself, to wake up after a long dream and ask a question of himself: What will I leave after myself to my descendants? *Abai said that a man should differ by such features as mind, honour and character.* I really hope that these basic human values became the main moral internals of every man. That's why people need to absorb the wise edifications of great Abai and implement them into life.

Today many young people because of pecuniary burdens take credits and occur to tricky situations. That's why the cases of suicide and many cruel offences became more often. Many people get to bank dependence because of non- acquaintance with their rights and rules of bank loan. If abroad credits are given under

2-3%, in our country they reach 15-20% per annum. Many banks and bank officials play unfair games with their clients, under pretence of different sanctions in a "civilized" manner drain already "thin" purses of simple people. In these cases the government and parliament should reconsider a credit policy of many banks of the country, in order to avoid negative consequences and by that facilitate the life of people. Why don't local administrations open close to every bank centres which will conduct an support policy of bank loans and warn about possible negative consequences, will teach people to pace oneself and will give helpful hints and advices of unequivocal use of credit money, will help to make a right business plan, etc.? Such saving approach to people won't stay unnoticed, because people skilfully applying and honourably squaring accounts with banks will receive an opportunity to rebuild their lives and in consequence to raise their welfare. I hope that these recommendations will be useful for people.

By means of wide agitation in order not to get in difficulties it is necessary to choose the right direction. If even you are going to take credit, thus its secrets should be studied from school days. In common, we need to implement a special subject about small business. In 2015 we recommended for schools and colleges the book of "Foliant" publishing house "The basics of small business" (Astana) in the quality of study guide.

I think that in this transitional period for assistance rendering to unlucky families under the support of businessmen it is necessary to found inevery region a "patron fund" which will help to revive the spiritual values of our nation. In order to educate youth in spirit of patriotism it is necessary to increase the quantity of programs with such content in mass media. The fund would be a big support for our cultural development.

25 years have passed since we gained independence. And what does every man need? It is necessary to answer this question. I will list: knowledge, health, work, food, minimum subsistence level and rest (peace).

Thanks god, the rest we have – peace. I don't speak about prosperous people. The most important now is to help poor families, which are on the lowest level of consumption. We need to stop this process. For it the government should by effective measures provide a normal living standard of people by means of minimum socially economical norms in the spheres of food, clothes, education and treatment provision. It is necessary **to develop the minimum socially economical norms for every human and entrench them in types of social contracts between authorities and society.** For this we have all opportunities. Here we need openness from the side of governmental bodies in front of people:

Today the economy is on such-and-such level, meanwhile we can provide with that-and-that, and tomorrow will be the following the growth of the economy, then we'll have a corresponding growth of needs. Meanwhile the economy doesn't stand more...; there are no more opportunities...

Making sure and comprehending such low level of minimum subsistence a man begins to move forward all alone and rely on something. At that rate people don't fall under influence of different ideologies, religious sects, extremism and terrorism and other negative factors.

And what situation do we have now? Notwithstanding of what we have – economic growth or decline – the same condition of living standards. Conversely, consumption of goods increases, living standard decreases. It's high time to tie the economy to every man. Then a man will feel his being in demand for society. As Abai said, he will desire to become a "brick" of this world; he will want to raise his abilities and skills. When you ask somebody: What do you do?, he answers you blankly: What can I do alone? We have to enhance our independence by all country. Three branches of authority without people will never raise economy. Under the common organization and unity we'll be able to enter into competitiveness with other countries. The offers for these questions are presented in every *Word*. In short, while people won't make sure in created conditions for realization of their spiritual opportunities and professional abilities, un-likely something will change in our state in essence.

In the XXI century every man including youth enters competitiveness. It is called by the time of the most creative economy, because thanks to the Internet the way to the whole world is open.

In these conditions only young people who acquired qualitative education and scientific knowledge are competitive and they can help their native land to rise. Kazakh youth should

be always ahead. For this purpose beginning from nurseries, schools and higher educational establishments, small and medium enterprises and finishing by state bodies and President we need **to implement the idea of competitiveness**.

Like in civilized countries we need to develop a professionally oriented program. From youth learning addictions, talents, skills and psychological features of our children to train them for some profession. The government should help them to receive this or that specialty. At worst getting 1-2 diplomas you can stay unemployed. If we'll consider developed countries for example, thus they receive 77% of main profit as a result of competent utilization of human capital, and 23% - from basic funds and land resources. But we all do conversely. Thus, we see that we still have a lot of opportunities that we didn't use before. The most important for us is to raise the quality of human life, to use all wealth in his interests. Any state, which does like this, will achieve a lot. In sober fact the great Abai said: *Believe yourself, your labour and mind will lead to forefront.* [2]. Aren't these words of Khakim Abai directed to each of us and state?

New technologies, engineers and small business can give a significant push for economy

THE WORD NINETH

Can we enter into competition without new technologies? Can we turn a small business to a wealth of the whole people?

Two centuries ago according to the requirements of time the great Abai talked about a necessity to conduct a socially economic reform by means of agriculture, industry, trade and science mastery renovation. In the epoch of global transformations in economic sphere it is necessary to develop distinct and optimal course without irrelevant errors and mistakes. In the conditions of present economic development we need to develop one of two ways. **The first** is liberalisation course. It means that it is necessary to erase the boundaries between rich and poor, to find the ways of contradictions' decrease between work and capital in society, to loosen dependence from foreign companies. **The second** is to foster the efforts under the support of government to accelerated development of private enterprise and formation of middle class. It means no breach of environment purity, no waste of natural wealth without acute need, to direct the main efforts on popular art development, to take care of culturally moral upbringing of growing generation. To find more favorable direction for peoples' prosperity improvement, i.e. for young generation – boys and girls, grandchildren and great-grandchildren, for their bright future, so as within 10, 20, 30, 50 years Kazakhstan could easily and with sure steps enter the rows of developed countries of the world.

It must be noted that hoping on illimitable wealth of our soil we developed the economy lop-sided, i.e. lost the chance – economy diversification. We close the stable door after the horse has bolted. Of course, many native and foreign oligarchs stood in the way. Though

Kazakhstan is independent for 25 years already it is still only an extractive state. This is a strategic mistake which will retard the country during the solution of many questions and in future.

If the above listed problems were highlighted in time our country would be light years away from others [29, 30, 32, 33].

The most difficult crisis is a technological crisis. Nowadays Kazakhstan stands on the edge of technological crisis, because the basic funds of industry and agriculture are on 46-80% in basket case, even in some spheres the percent of outdated technologies is much bigger. For example in energy industries a worn-out state of technical equipment reaches 72-75%. It can threaten tonational security. Let's remember an accident on Russian Saya-no–Shushenskaya hydroelectric power station in Siberia which brought a colossal financial and ecological damage to country, lives were lost.

The main motive force of technological progress in our country is still a question of machinery. Unfortunately this sphere develops slightly. The basic share of this sphere is accounted for by repair and maintenance department, but the production of machines, equipment, and new technologies we are almost not engaged. Today many world powers already build the VIth technological mode (VI TOR). It includes nano biotechnology, gene engineering, information and communication technology, space-based processing technology. In these spheres Kazakhstan trails by 50-60 years from many countries, even a contribution of Russia according to VI TOR in the world amounts only 2-3%.

That's why a task of prime importance of our country is a development of these spheres of economy, and, especially, we need to emphasize production of native technical equipment. For this it is necessary to build urgently new factories and plants using from one side a technological transfer and from the other – a native scientifically technical potential. ***We need to be com-mitted to the principle that if we won't process ourselves, won't manufacture, thus we won't grow and develop.*** It is clear that for such a splash we need big investment. We have a crying need to implement innovation processes into production relying on scientific pursuits and technical innovations, because as we see from the world practices the scientific priorities in technological innovations change every 4-5 years.

That's why we need to keep a wary eye on new ideas in the sphere of new technologies, to be able to implement them and bring them into circulation. Whereby we should remember our mentality, national providence, adaptability and accomplishment. Are there in our country people who are interested in scientific deductions and validity of foreign scientists? In this case we need

found an organization which will analyze and adapt innovations according to our circumstances. Let's compare: if only 6% of every native enterprises of our country are engaged in innovational activity, thus in foreign countries this rate is very high – 60-70% including Germany – 82.5%, Sweden – 75% [32]. In order to come nearer somehow to these rates we need to raise an innovation potential to an adequate level. Such projects should be realized in cooperation with scientific research institutes and higher educational establishments, with manufacturing in industrial places (on factories and plants), because the link between academic pursuits and approbation on the factory floor is on a low level. **That's why an engineering system requires a special attention according to present standards.**

According to the competitiveness index of the World Economic Forum in Davos, Kazakhstan takes 89th place in the world of innovation development of the economy. It is evidence that Kazakhstan falls behind many countries greatly and this red flag requires us to develop a whole program of narrow background training for engineers, foreman and taskmasters at the place of production.

In the 70-s in the beginning I worked as a simple technician in a Shymkent lead foundry and then as an engineer. In Soviet times the government took care about health of its people, especially workers who were engaged in heavy industry. The workers were not allowed to their working places without respirators and other personal protective equipment. Technicians of sixth grade were worth their weight in gold. Nowadays you can't find such specialists in daylight even with a flashlight.

In Kazakhstan the question of real requirement in production staff is not solved, the quantity of different specialists is not analyzed and controlled.

For example, Russia keeps such count of its graduates and upon occurrence or nonoccurrence of this or those specialty makes the list of required professions of the next year. In Soviet time a good practice existed when after graduation a leaver was

obliged to undertake work experience on factories and plants. Why not to return this good tradition? Why not to prepare our engineers, foreman and taskmasters on sites for working on international oil and gas pipelines? This problem is still not solved either. But we shouldn't forget that the world goes with big and sure steps and in order to keep pace with it we should take urgent measures.

Today's world is presented in the form of running information: computer, human, business, law, policy, security, economy, taxation system, technology, culture, etc. *Is it the birth of new informational society as one of stages of humanity development?.*

Can we make a small business a wealth of the whole people?

In the conditions of crisis when t h e economy undergoes deep transformations the core of its growth can be an accelerated development of small and medium entrepreneurship (SME). It means that we need to switch over the whole country to it, be-cause today the share of small business from GDP compounds only 18%. In developed countries this rate reaches 50-70%, and employment to 80%. As in past years in the Republic a speculative activity of entrepreneurs dominates, not innovates: 39% of SME concentrated in the sphere of trade, in industry – only 3.4%. Especially in social sphere (in education, science, health care, culture and art, craftsmanship) small business stays undeveloped, its share is less than 2%. The small and medium businesses still play extremely negligible role in the real economy. We couldn't form the system of cooperation, of small and medium businesses involvements into large companies' activity. The sore spots of small business are low technique and its involvement to innovation activity.

Even by means of these facts we see that we have a lot unused opportunities! If we say by rural language, thus the small business is a "bull that pulls arba uphill".

In this doing the main role is played by government, universities, scientific research institutes and cooperation of small, medium and large businesses. If government will help by monetary funds, tax abatement, thus educational foundations and scientific centres can provide personnel training, give scientifically proven recommendations, etc. Instead of construction of political houses in small and big cities and regional centres, it is better to open houses of small business where the entrepreneurs will be taught how to open business, small firms, how to get credit, make a business plan, the basic legislative principles, etc.

Under the condition that **we'll make Kazakh society spiritual and entrepreneurial, thus we'll become the most competitive country**. In order to realize this, the author **for the first time developed a system of projecting of forced development of SME which includes 9 big projects** shown on the diagram. [in detail see p82].

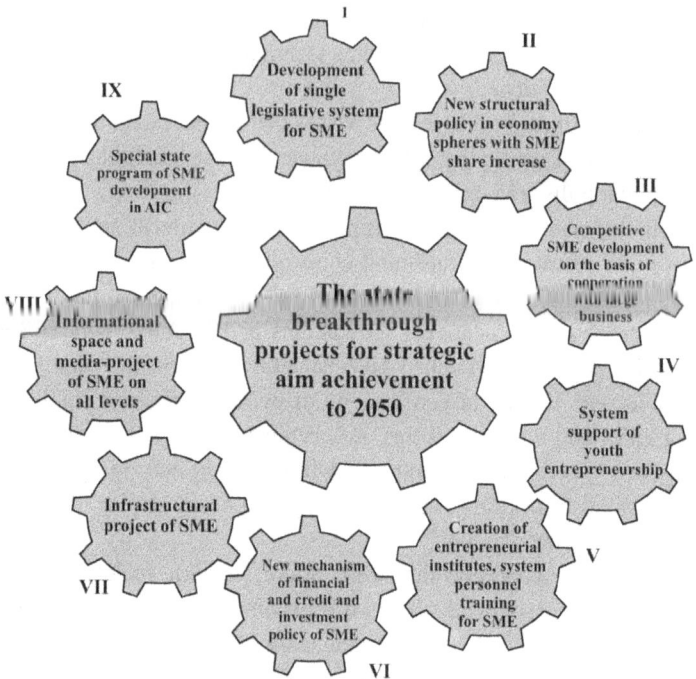

Picture 1 - **The system of projecting of forced development of small and medium entrepreneurship in RK**

If government, Parliament and society will take it for complex realization with resources' provision, thus the author is sure that by means of mass engagement of our society with small business in all spheres of our life, we would achieve a spectacular success in socially economic development of Kazakhstan. The realization of these projects can become a new driver of accelerated economic growth of Kazakhstan. All these will be only in case if we'll have success in the whole population mass involvement into small business and if we'll create for it all the required conditions. Small business should be a big deal, i.e. some kind of **national idea of the country** on the transition period to Kazakhstan establishment in the list of developed countries.

The state breakthrough projects for strategic aim achieve-ment to 2050.

Development of single legislative system for SME.

New structural policy in economy spheres with SME share increase.

Competitive SME development on the basis of cooperation with large business.

System support of youth entrepreneurship.

Creation of entrepreneurial institutes, system personnel training for SME

New mechanism of financial and credit and investment policy of SME.

Infrastructural project of SME.

Informational space and media-project of SME on all levels. Special state program of SME development in AIC.

Let's take Singapore as an example. 40 years ago before getting independence it was less developed and backward country. If at that time an annual income per head of population compounded was only 2650 US dollars, then now it exceeds 35000 US dollars. It is the level of the world developed countries. Nowadays, according to the data from the annual Davos Economic Forum Singapore enters the list of five the most developed countries in terms of global development. It begs the question: What

is the secret of such rapid development of this state? The reason is explained by development of infrastructure, support of education, science, sport, by accelerated support of small business, rooting out corruption in market economy and all spheres of production, rendering help in investments through joint fund and other measures. In order to realize such works a strict control was established.

First of all it is necessary *to adopt a law about a small in-*

novation entrepreneurship. Such an approach will lead to an abrupt jump of the native economy. In case if under the support of government the interest to innovational private entrepreneurship will be intense, thus Kazakhstan may become competitive in the whole world. Especially if in private entrepreneurship the youth innovation ideas and scientific discoveries will be of high priority, in this case the country will move off dead centre. Those young people who graduated from foreign universities shouldn't settle wherever, for example, in Silicon Valley of USA. The government should create such conditions which could attract an advanced youth to native enterprises. To open the way for young people who passed the program Bolashak who are worthy to be successors and innovators of many new developments in different spheres of society life.

It is necessary to exempt from taxation for 1-2 years the start up representatives of small business, to pare down to the minimum the endless inspections and extortions from the side of tax structures. Some, not being on time to begin their business, leave in despair giving up on the idea; the others are forced to comply with and to become as people say as quiet as the grave and the brave try to resist such rules and struggle alone. But while the laws won't change such disorders would continue endlessly. In 1992 as a scientist I wrote a book about private entrepreneurship and handed it out to decision-making structures for usage. Only after 5 years past the decree of the President about development of small and medium business was issued. I think that the achievements of district, town and regional Akimats

should be judged according to the level of private entrepreneurship activity. Relying on knowledge, professionalism, spiritually and political prowess we can say surely that exactly thanks to middle class formation we have more opportunities to lead the country forward.

We need a lot of capital expenditures in the sphere of technological development. According to new spheres of economy it is required to organize the investigations in scientific research institutes and universities (they are new materials, power resources, hybrid machines, hydrogen batteries, new energy sources, usage of different types of fuel, nanotechnology, urbanism, etc.).

When the soil feeds like mother its child,
The sky covers and protects you like father.
Abai

Who has a parity of nature and culture,
that is a respectable man.
Shakarim

THE WORD TENTH

What is a harmony of human and nature?

The harmony of nature and human is a foundation and basis of existence. Today we have left for us and bequeathed by our forefathers rich and illimitable spaces from the Altai Mountains to the Caspian Sea of our vast native land. Unfortunately, in the epoch of the Soviet Union in a result of wrong policies an uncontrolled quantity of productions of chemicals, heavy metals, lead and phosphorus were constructed which for a long time polluted primary nature. It led to irretrievable consequences and ecosystem dysfunction of the whole natural layer. As an example could be taken with the Aral crisis. Even today in chase of immediate profit many people don't want to bother that all our negative interruptions in the harmony of nature will backfire and eventually the human himself will suffer. Besides, the polygons in Semipalatinsk, on Kapustin yar and in Baikonur were built, where numerous nuclear tests were conducted. To our sorrow, the territories (2 million ha) where the tests were conducted are still unsuitable for agricultural needs and will be out of action for several dozens of years.

In the period between 1949-1991 the quantity of nuclear tests on Semipalatinsk test site reached 470. Nobody knows exactly how many shepherds, who grazed their live stocks peacefully, died in nuclear "cloud". Relying on cold hard facts a half of million people were irradiated. The regions of Semey and Aral were announced as zones of ecological disaster. The wastes of launched rockets on Baikonur still cause harm to health of people who live in nearest inhabited localities.

The Aral Sea area throughout life of one generation decreased two times. Instead of annually required 100 cubic kilometers of water the Republic receives only 34.6 cubic kilometers. In Kazakhstan on one man accounts for a little water. That's why our Republic among the CIS countries takes the last place [13]. We receive water from China, Russia, Kirgizia and Uzbekistan. We need to reconsider this problem in essence. Water stays a problem for us in this century too. In Kazakhstan we still don't have a strategic program of water supply.

Abai remembered us that natural phenomena are tightly linked to each other and are in constant development, by means of science and education we can cognize their internal secrets. By words: "Desire to know more" he appealed to scru-tinize knowledge thoroughly and find their scientific levers. The launch vehicles falls on Baikonur and in its surroundings bring a huge harm to health of local population. For example, on July 2, 2013 during blastoff at Baikonur the launch vehicle "Proton-M" fell, aboard there were 600 tons of heptyl, amyl and kerosene. From the side of Russia for actual damage 90 million US dollars were promised. Even under realization of such agreement how can we restore the actual damage? And this happens in the period of independence.

The manufacturing wastes also reached the incredible fig-ures – 20 billion tons, including 230 million tons of nuclear wastes. The country needs a creation of new sphere of such waste destruction. In Kazakhstan as in the whole world either the question of environment protection is particularly pointed. Nevertheless, in our country on nature protection only 0.5 US dollars per head of population are funded. It is a miserable amount in comparison to other European countries. Among Euro-Asian countries we take the last place. According to the global ecological rating the economy of Kazakhstan is located in an unfavourable zone. The situation threatens physical and genetic health of the population. The structure of fauna and flora is destroyed.

The problems of agriculture will not be solved by themselves. We said about it above. Because of unconsidered land development 60% of them became dry and suffered erosion. According to anthropogenous factors the condition of natural zones changed for the worse.

Such environment-oriented questions accumulated for years cannot delay any more. This calls for urgent operational measures from state. As has been said above the agricultural problems are one more bane of our country. Be-cause of wrong distribution of irrigation water some regions suffer its lack in consequence of which the cultivated lands are in distress. That's why we need an immediate budget allocation for this sphere [29, 30]. Since we take water from China, Russia, Kyrgyzstan, and Uzbekistan. The question of soil requires a special attention. A man is originator double as bystander of natural basis and in violation of humanity functioning. It means that intruding into the harmony of nature a human destroys himself paying more attention to self-actualization and personal fulfilment and forgetting about the whole Universe' development.

It shouldn't be forgotten that every man is a part of nature and he exists in global and biological interrelation with the world around. In Abai's point of view on global development a dialectic motive prevails. He considered that natural phenomena are inter-related between each other, constantly change and develop. That's why he came to a conclusion that external and internal secrets of nature could be cognized and discovered.

We should always remember: if nature exists, thus we exist.

That is what Abai wrote about it:

> *The sun is a fiancé and the soil is a long-awaited fiancée,*
> *The both are so passionate...*
> *Being sated by the sun streams,*
> *The soil blooms like a peafowl.*

That's why the future of humanity is in our hands. Whether we'll save it for descendants or will destroy. There is no other answer. Only in harmony with nature can man will be happy. The XXI century should be the age of the green economy.

In the opinion of many distinguished scientists, humanity stands on the first stage of ecological disaster. However all is not lost yet, we have an opportunity of ecosystem rehabilitation – the point of no return hasn't arrived. **Karl Marx supposed that for nature cruel treatment the nature itself will revenge.**

In XXI century an opportunity to predict consequences of anthropogenic activities and to give recommendations how to develop agriculture and industry, to conduct business not depleting the world›s natural wealth appeared.

According to the data of scientific investigations if in the XXI century we won't take prompt cardinal action for the planet's ecosystem protection thus the whole of humanity is endangered [34, 35].

Nowadays the countries, regardless of status, develop the measures of ecological disaster prevention. Such leading states as USA, PRC, EU member states, India, Russia don't observe the written Kyoto protocol of carbon sequestration in the environment. The time has come for a crackdown on greenhouse gases and their reduction to atmosphere to a safe standard. First of all, it is necessary to order new impositions on carbon wastes and strict sanctions for their negligence. Then to accelerate the process of the foundation of the world power ecological fund of the whole of humanity.

In 2009 in Copenhagen during the UN Conference the declaration of global warming circumscription in the norm of $2^{0}C$ was adopted. However, most regrettably, even UN is unable to forbid USA and PCR and other large states to follow the rules of this declaration. But when ecological crisis will come then we'll be powerless to stop it. Now, the summit of 2015 in Paris will be decidable for the fate of humanity.

I am sure that if we seriously want to immortalize human-ity and preserve nature, thus in XXI century under interrelation of society and nature we should build a common home of human civilization. As quintessence I offer a suggestion to admit the global power ecological strategy on the level of UN. It is necessary to follow the rules of power-ecological limitations in order to mitigate irreversible hazards.

The most faithful way to solve difficult situations is consumption of solar and magnetic energy, usage of hydrogen fuel, consumption of nonospheric power-ecological production.

This power-ecological revolution and new paradigm of energy consumption are directed on **the VIth technological mode** assimilation in the second half of XXI century. In order to perform these tasks the world community needs to put forth tremendous efforts.

In short **Kazakhstan needs a "broom" which will clean the environment not only out of multiyear wastes and rub-bish, but will clear soul, conscience, morality and psychology of humans** . And what and how to do – it is in our interests. Every human, every family should begin from themselves. Finally, the performance of above mentioned measures will depend on the level of societies hu maneness. Are we ready for this?

They live by mere ideas of the party,
This rottenness is unrecoverable.
I suffer for ordinary people.
Akim is a spouter, biy is a gaper.
                                    Shakarim

To justify the confidence of people is worth a lot.
It requires firmness and insistence,
patriotism and faith in future.

THE WORD ELEVENTH

Is the system of management efficient? What is the level of professional competency? What steps should be made for effective state management?

Abai said: "A man who wants to give advice and change Kazakh should have two prerequisites. The first is strong power and a man who has big authority. The second is a man who has a glut of wealth. Kazakh couldn't be brought to heel with-out bluff, bribery, by rational arguments, without lessons and flattery".
Evidently these sharp and chastising words of Abai and Shakarim were said out of desperation and pain for ordinary people. Even today some of these words could become true. getting independence our country achieved many positive results in different spheres of life, we learnt a lot, know a lot, even teach our children abroad and adopt international practices.

However disaffection of ordinary people isn't lost on notwithstanding stability, interreligious and interethnic concord. The reasons are low wages, unemployment, constant effort for dignified life of people, low standard of living, corruption, bribery, violation of electoral legislation and other negative factors.

Abai in his *Words of Edification* pays a special attention to human personality, most of all, the main governor (akim) and considers their humanness and competency the main condition of prosperity and splendor in society. The poet doesn't discover the roots of his acquirements; it is a destiny of readers and listeners themselves. Abai said:

"Bai is unmerciful, poor is disobedient,

They are counterposed to each other by the God himself"! Abai's social injustice and inequality are complicated. His cognition coincides with the views of sincere akims of middle ages.

Consequently the evils should be searched in ourselves. By my reckoning there are a lot of shortcomings in our country, a lot of contradictions in the system of management, lopsidedness in political structure, bribery and fraternity are still not disrooted. It is only too true!

We go no further than to say that how fast our economy develops! We had, have and will have many talented professionals. The only one what our authorities need is to use them. Since Abai and Shakarim could lead Kazakh society to progress by their edifications.

The XXI century requires looking from a new angle on aroused problems and starting out from them to create qualitative, corresponding to modern requirements, systems of management.

The main criteria and priorities of our development are revival of spiritual values, rooting out corruption, professionalism, creation of democratic system.

Management of state without democracy is ineffective. More specifically the present system of state management in Kazakhstan betrays itself, because have little professionals and production workers. Then again relying on practices of developed foreign countries we need to decrease the excessive stages of authority management.

For example, in our state branches of power in ministry consist of 13-14 stages: minister, Vice-Ministers, Secretary-general, chairman of committee, committee deputy chairman, department head, his deputies, department heads, their deputies, chiefs of section, chief officer, managing officer, executive and assistant. They are engaged in duplication of work of each other, controlling of each other, etc. creating the same situation in regional, towns and rural administrative establishments. But in foreign countries the number of stages in branches of power doesn't exceed seven, that's why it considered optimum in all structures of government control. People put about a rumor: "An epoch of akims and singers came". And it is remote from progressiveness and rapid development of the country, because there is no dialogue between authorities and society.

Let's remember the great Abai again. Once he said: "A proverb appeared **"the core is not in doing, but in humanity"**. It is conformable to an idea that "it's all about the people!". Do you agree to this? And what is the situation in our country? In majority fraternity, family ties and acquaintanceship govern personnel practices especially on hot seats, but their competence and business proficiency are put out of account. And the rest should offer worship to these newly-crowned public officials. Such agas are apt to pride and dictate.

As Abai said: *"My congeners, my people each of you is headed by biynullity".* Even nowadays some representatives of people are too vain glorious. Recently under the expert personnel selection, half of 23 thousand staff didn't pass the test, even among those who passed rigorous selection process some people don't cut the mustard.

Nowadays a meaning "no silver, no servant" is popular. Bribery sails before the wind in our country. Besides, that's going too far when the national act of state procurements is also adjusted to bribery. The other regional responsible executives and akims who defected to the West increased the amount of briberies to 50%. Of course, such defects of the system led to losses on billions of Tenge. And tens of millions of innocent children – the future of our Kazakhstan, suffer because of this. As already was mentioned before, in the country along with bribery, fraternity and family mutual cover-up get ahead.

If a new authority comes to power should be akim or head of power structure, he will surely attract his own "team", and we have a lot such examples, in a manner of speaking it happens all over the place. There is a bitter misunderstanding between authorities and ordinary people, misconception of interests and a difference of material component [30].

If Kazakh people won't unite and promote their priorities today, in XXI century, thus there is a probability to blend into the flow of alien history in the epoch of global transformations and frequent crises. I hope that my considerations will lead my fellow citizens, especially public officials to the right conclusion in order to prevent a history repeating the backwashes of which we still observe around.

In the words of specialist – agricultural professional, nowadays corruption is widely spread. The family ties strengthened. Recently they hid, but now everything turns open. The appointed akim attracts his own people and sometimes all of them are co generic. And the officials of power structures do what they

like if only not to come to the notice of higher-ranking management [30]. That is the "disease" of the powers that be: not to serve to people and be concerned in money-grubbing by means of bribery.

One of the diseases in the system of management is a window-dressing. When akims make their reports they hide imperfections of their regions. For whom are their beautiful phrases and "logic" figures needed!? Why do we cheat ourselves for higher management's sake!? So, are we going to carry to the point of Zhanaozen events and will solve them after with negative consequences!?

Nowadays the science and education is kept down. The budgets not only on them but on social needs also are limited. Thus, for purposes of flashiness apart from them the big funds were budgeted from the National Fund for World Expo-2017. To our discredit, not being in time to make a half of building works the heads of EXPO were caught stealing multibillions of Tenge. That is the face of top-level officials called upon to justify people's confidence.

As people say, it's a pity that officials who work in government, parliament, procuracy and police and also akims look like temporary rulers who seat their only for wealth accumulation.

Such irresponsibility of officials to people can lead to a big crisis because day by day the gap between population and officials increases.

Those upstairs refer to considerations of complaints and claims of people frivolously making little semblance. Though they care for welfare of their families and relatives. People see and know everything. It is deeply regrettable and worrying that before such bureaucrats the professionals are forced to tiptoe around and wheedle – talents, scientists, writers, bankers, entrepreneurs, teachers, medical workers, etc. Many actual inventors and scientists, who made discoveries of global scale stay out of view, are pushed aside. At the same time such people are constantl controlled by the highest ranks. After all these to whom should they complain?! Where should they go?! The only one way stays – abroad. That's why we have a big outflow of brainpower. Imagine, how can we grow and develop under such circumstances?! How many of our citizens – professionals are abroad now, like Mukhtar Magauin, Bolat Atabaev and also businessmen, etc.

Their hearts beat together with Kazakhstan, with the whole country. They would like as patriots to return and help our motherland to develop. Either there are a lot of Bolashak graduates, who stayed abroad. Frankly speaking some of them return back but cannot find work or only beginning to work because of pressing from the side of ruling circles leave the Republic. Only with their return and fruitful work here, our democratic institutes can work. But when will it happen?

The great Abai was exasperated not without reason: *"Some are volost husbands (bolyssy), the others – biys. If they had desire to learn something, to listen to advics, they wouldn't stand for election to these positions. They are publicity junkies looking down* their *nose at all. For them honesty, mind, science and knowledge mean nothing in comparison to wealth (livestock)".* Nowadays authorities and people draw apart so much; there is nothing to tell [30]. If we want to meet the requirements of XXI century, thus we should realize revolutionary changes. Not uniting a small number of people, without common national consent, we'll be immersed by other large countries.

Because by means of transnational companies such principal powers as USA, Great Britain, China and Russia have eyes on our natural wealth and do the best in order to snap them up. We understand the reasons of the most powerful nation – the Soviet Unions breakup.

What steps could be made for successful state management?
First of all, to reduce artificially bloated staff on 20-30%, to cut out 15-20% the counterproductive government expenditures
in all spheres of administration, to create a strict control from the side of Chief of State and Parliament. To spend the saved amount on the spiritual sphere and social needs of its citizens.

Secondly, to train highly qualified specialists of all grades, especially technical engineers.

Thirdly, to escalate fighting with bribery in order to prevent corrupt officials from lining their pockets with billions of Tenge.

Fourthly, to reconsider tax and expenditure policy, to increase taxes for rich people and to make small business property
of people.

Fifthly, to advance democratic transformations in Kazakhstan. The political targets of state should be distinct and predictable.

Using practices of developed foreign countries, taking into account our own peculiarities, **to conduct throughout the country cardinal modernization: political** modernization, **social** modernization, **economic** modernization, **spiritual** modernization and **scientifically technical** modernization.

According to t h e above mentioned and other questions for 25 years at various times I referred to President and Government and send more than 30 conceptual letters-recommendations. A definite part of my recommendations was added, like they say, to the armoury, and the rest part waits its turn. I understand perfectly that our system changes slowly and thoughts of scientist go far forward [33; see an amendment 1, pp. 122].

Now a politically-democratic period should begin. On this stage to enhance the influence of Parliament in all spheres of country life, i.e. to give government of state to parliamentary presidential form of government which will lead to presidential powers narrowing; then to equal powers and authority of three branches of government: the legislative Branch, the Judicial Branch and the Executive Branch.

Because pure and simple Kazakhstan is considered as a unitary state, unicameral parliament should be brought back. The totaquantity of deputies shouldn't exceed 150 persons, from them 50% should be elected from different parties and 50% accord-ing to single mandate of the majority constituencies. Deputies should consist of honoured workers, well-known professionals of their work, heroes of labour and others; to be specific, not always do ordinary people know their deputy by sight and that's why the difficulties occur under the votership questions appearance who doesn't know to whom refer. In Parliament to lower limit to (3-5%) for deputies elected according to party list. Way back when I worked as deputy I saw all listed above gaps and problems in law. These conclusions I made from my personal and professional expertise and everyday life estimations and also considering international practices [33].

I consider that t h e foundation of multiparty parliament is optimum for the present situation in the country. Because parliamentarianism is a multiparty debating environment. Only through discussions and hot considerations we can come to right and correct decisions. The country needs fair and democratic elections. The People itself should make a decision to what party to throw the handkerchief and believe in open and fair elections. I myself fell into deception of unfair elections. All manner of frame-up and machinations take place. When pluralism will be settled in Parliament where the vital questions on deputy proceedings will be decided through debates and discussions, the true decisions will be made. But nowadays the following picture is observed. Speaker says: "Who in favour – raise your hands", and deputies raise hands automatically, says: "Who against – drop" and they drop. I constantly feel somehow quite creepy at such indifferent attitude of deputies under the consideration of the most important and fateful decisions for our country. I'd like to finish this thought by Abai's words: *"If in habit of human to agree and ease up when the majority speaks, it means that he is a barbarian".*

During my work as deputy , visiting many foreign countries, I made a conclusion for myself that multiparty Parliament can expound explicitly any questions, share opinions and give ideas.

With such Parliament any country has more successful development in comparison to others with single-party Parliament. Many deputies should understand one indisputable truth that reforms are conducted not for the sake of decision-making structures, but for the sake of society's welfare and peoples' prosperity and improvement. Establishment of public control of executive government institutions would be in priority now.

If we remember Abai again, than he said: *"In the past our fore-fathers, by contrast with the modern generation, had two types of character, though we lost them... The reason of estrangement from each another is these characters: the first type is a national leader, a leader of a group of people, who decides all points of friction; the second type is freedom-loving and sensitive, the one who always will come to help his congeners. Where are these characters now? Could we lose all? Are the everlasting human companions when friendship correlates to insincerity, dishonesty, enmity, everlasting rivalry and envy?" [1].*

Two centuries already passed since Abai said it, but the cart remains there still. The quantity of people who don't give and take bribes becomes fewer and fewer. I think it's high time to cut this knot: fraternity, relationship, clannishness and corruption. At this rate we will reach a full degradation of nation.

A famous politician Machiavelli said: *"The authorities go two ways, the first – relying on law and the second – hoping on force".* Most regrettably our authorities go the second way hoping on force and money. Now, in order to return peoples' trust, it is necessary to create favourable conditions for people welfare improvement, to conduct more open discussions and so-cial analyses of all most relevant issues on spots or on the level of government which relate to all spheres of human livelihood. All themes and problems should be solved.

We need to develop and strengthen people's unity and interethnic concord in Kazakhstan. The best support will be if under the President we create **the Public Chamber**, the members of which will be people of name, scientists of different levels and advanced youth.

Their powers and authority will include careful analysis and ultimate solution of the most important questions, after what the Public Chamber can refer to the top leader with recommendations. Then many questions still haven't been solved and which didn't reach authorities could be decided. The full project is included [33].

One of immediate tasks is the sharp excessive spending cuts, **switch to new system of government, conducting a new personnel policy and a social reform;** we can receive a qualitative result of work in all spheres of society life and a beneficial human development. Only in this case the authorities will receive total efficiency from people and obtain people's wholehearted support.

It would be perfect if the representatives of authority would begin from themselves and became a guide for mentioned above innovations. In result of such affairs people will cheer up and can build the following life with sure steps, in consequence the authorities can rely on a highly organized nation.

I, as a professional of my work, call the native administrative institution to new achievements and positive changes. Though since our country received independence 24 years have passed, we still have a row of laws which were not adopted or were not completed.

Among them are:
- *the constitutional law about the Kazakh language; - the law of national security in terms of crisis;*
- *the law of property act;*
- *the law of public assistance act; - the law of minimum-wage;*
- *the law of local self governance;*
- *the law of cooperation;*
- *the law of rents on land and natural resources;*
- *the law of innovative ventures;*
- *the law of patronage;*
- *the law of energy policy act;*
- *the law of self-regulating organization;*
- *the law of exploitations' commercialization;*
- *the law of offshore companies, etc.*

These and other laws require an immediate adoption on this stage of our society development.

If we'll remember the history of our city, we know how people pull through hunger and war. That's why I can assure for certain that we'll overcome the real difficulties on the way of better future achievement.

One more scrupulous task is uprooting of bribery and corruption among all layers of society. Yes, I know that it is very difficult task, because people are used to give and receive bribes at any reason and create a team only of their own people. But if we'll have a strict law, control of performance and openness of mass media, thus we'll solve this problem successfully.

On the way of new achievements Kazakhstan should get over two difficulties within two decades. They are **the way of good public administration and complete professionalism achievement**. Parties and deputies which entered the Parliament should work out their distinct line of activity and follow the tasks performance till conclusion, give fresh ideas and solve them for the welfare of nation, attract courageous and educated people on sites (in villages, regions, towns, on enterprises and in educational foundations).

To get out of crisis and catch the process of global achievements without wars and serious conflicts is a difficult task. This problem will be solved thanks to deep self analysis by scientific approaches to it. People say: "Scratch the wound – the blood will come; don't scratch – it will pain". Tell nicely – will lose; say rude – will hurt a girl. In other words, why should I put up with inequity and suffer the "doings" of representatives of authority?! Aren't they obliged to serve people? Because all of them are candidates or doctors of sciences. After their thesis defense of this or that theme, rather than continue academic pursuits practically, conversely, all dissertation committees are closed. Now dissertations in Kazakhstan are not defended at all, though in many post soviet countries this problem is solved long ago.

Only bold ideas and their implementation to all spheres of society life will pull out our country to the rows of the richest and most developed countries. When the power structures will instil confidence in the minds of Kazakh people that only people is a singular host of our soils wealth, will prove allegiance and solidarity to people by their doings, our Kazakhstan in the near future will advance much sooner, expressing the ideas of enduring values of human existence.

I believe that our youth will help the older generation and it's ablity to realize the best progressive ideas for the sake of next generations.

Nowadays there are no communistic ideology, dictatorial regime, squabbles and dislocations, which were in Abai's epoch.

Youth, I refer to you. you are the generation of the XXI century. you don't have the weight of olden times. You have a qualitative education, know multinational languages, besides you are informed thanks to the Internet about everything, you know how and in what directions the civilization develops. That's why according to spirit you are very close to the great democrat and thinker, spiritual reformer Abai. Such congeniality to khakim Abai rests big responsibility upon you. looking up to Abai, scaling negative phenomena in the world, you should work out your own **spiritual immunity**. You all will have energy, power and

desire to face the matter out. The main is to be humane to surrounding people. I repeat at last once again: the solution of all these problems depends on efficient state management and personal professionalism of all spheres of our comprehensive life.

All Kazakhs should remember
Abai and his heritage.
Ahmet Baitursynov

Let's reread the works of the great Abai by the whole nation
and, delving into the subject of his genius ideas,
let's realize his learning practically

THE WORD TWELFTH

The great Abai's learning about "an appropriate man". Who is this man? What is his portrait? What kind of Kazakh should be in the XXI century?

Abai is a natural talent, wise man, khakim, genius person, ideal of Kazakhs. He was the personification of both East and West knowledge. Speaking more specifically, he founded his own school by means of learning and study of scientifically philosophic sources of Al-Farabi, morals and philosophic ethics of yusuf Balassaguni, basics of Sufi learning of Hoja Ahmet yassawi, Suleymen Bakyrgani and many other scientists [1, 2, 20, 46, 47].

The main thing there is the learning of Abai about "an appropriate man". Its deep meaning is an early awakening of mental predilection. In one of his rhymes Abai expressed this thought by the following words:

"It's not difficult to become scientist,
If forget childish tricks.
The whole science is in book,
If not to be lazy.

That is how he advised to make a first step to knowledge. In order to broaden his knowledge, Abai penetrated the content of conceptual notions of **"mulakhaza" and "mukhafaza", ana-lyzing them** and **made daring searches**.

As a result the learning of the "appropriate man" there appeared which guides every human to do everything with mind, to display gallantry and kindness, to commiserate and sympathize, besides do it wholeheartedly. The one who will go this way is "an appropriate man" – concluded Abai [26]. Here the main ideas from the poem «Құтты білік» ("The science of happiness") about splendour he included in the quality of basics of humanness into the conception of "an appropriate man" as ethical direction. As the component parts of this conception khakim Abai united together science, mercy and justice, emphasizing those only persons who followed these recommendations fully and kept to the rules in their deeds, could be called appropriate.

Abai's learning of "appropriate man" will effect only if we discover visible and invisible world mysteries and tie them to present life tightly. Speaking about modern life. We shouldn't forget about big changes in the world. In last century, when socialist and capitalist systems existed, the balance (parity) was kept. It was explained by the fact that USA and USSR were so to speak two sides of scales according to finances, commodities', production and military potential. And after break-up of the Soviet Union the USA began to conduct biipolar policy in their discretion by means of domination over others, using excessive dollars as a result of what the volume of American dollars exceeded in 10-12 times the amount of manufactured commodities.

The achievements of science and new technologies of the world countries were used only for wealth accumulation, thus the capitalistic society turned to society of excessive consumption and wealth accumulation which became the basis or result of the most negative factors in the world.

Speaking Abai 's language, they do only one: the visible secrets of nature, the material world gave into hands of international global companies for wealth accumulation and profit extraction.

And the invisible secrets of nature remained out of view. This refers to spiritual values, culture, history, human factor, etc. Besides, this fact was admitted by Bill Gates and other billionaires. Moneyed pack becomes richer, but 1.3 billion people in the world are hungry and cold and hardly survive. The consequences of such situation could be very incendiary. gentlemen, get over yourself! You should understand this danger! The complications of social inequity in some countries of the world led and can lead to different civil convulsions and riots, wars which we observe in different regions of the terrestrial globe.

Abai's learning of "appropriate man" is a conception, socially economic content of which is not fully discovered, but scientific value stays very high. The American economist Gary Stanley Becker considers that "a man of economy" is intended to not only make products and getting profit, but he needs to satisfy his spiritual requirements aswell. He pays a special attention to freedom of cultural, political and social views and philosophy. If this "man of economy" equipped himself with bright brain (knowledge and mind), warm heart (humanness, honesty), implacable energy (will, motivation), thus we had not so much costs in economic development of society. That's why a man of capitalistic society, free of spiritual foundations, doesn't think about any values. Mainly it is peculiar to capitalistic West. But I am tempted to say that with transfer from socialism to capitalism such awesome tendency of profiteering and soullessness after the breakup of the USSR was distributed on all countries of the CIS, and that's a pity that on Kazakhstan either.

Moral poverty in the row of states is even proved by the fact of same sex marriages legalization, etc.

We should strive to economic and technological progress like in Europe, USA and Japan, but we have no right to lose our national spiritual values.

And we have a lot of people who give preference to visible material side of the world on advice of "well-wishers" for wealth accumulation. There are a plenty of public officials and successful entrepreneurs or so called rich men who arranged their life several generations ahead. But the government and Parliament being under their thumb don't give them an objective appraisal. Otherwise, how can we understand that from the total volume of produced oil the share of our country consists of only 22%, and 78% rest in hands of foreign companies? Do we live in alien country? Evidently our policy makers forgot the words of Abai: **"Don't think about profit, think about honour"**. To our regret, for 25 years of independence under the necessitous execution of Abai's covenants , if we transferred methods of economic management and governance onto the other rails, we wouldn't get enmeshed to foreigners. Frankly speaking there are a great lot of grave mistakes and unforgettable errors.

In a word, the **"materialistic model"** of the world development which we imitate and copy stiffly is truly speaking ineffective. We create the conditions for endemic adverse lives of multibillion heaps of people. It is necessary to find a new way for advancement. That's why, considering systematic approaches of management, we need to search the answers of solution adequacy and entity of these questions. Among them the most important is to provide ideas of the invisible side of universe awakening, **its spiritually humanistic directions, advancement and** conscience **of people**. Nowadays, in the XXI century it's high time to rest upon human rational powers and spiritual values. Otherwise we can face a big dangerous disaster. Turning the process of human development onto the East and transferring its material side on the rails of society spirituality and humanism we can provide peace and rest and stable development aswell. Under the question how can we realize it in deed, we can call to Abai's learning of "appropriate man" again. Here the other question arises as a natural result: Who is that appropriate man? Do we have his prototype among us?

Whom can we take as an example and on whom can we look up to? Surely we have, they are Turkic nations and Kazakh people among them.

By virtue of their nature Kazakh people are genius. It could be traced by the great historic persons listed in this book.

Speaking about present times, as an example of Abai's appropriate man, I would name the recently gone academician **Salyk Zimanov** – an outstanding public man, corypheus of juridical science and the memorable peoples' writers **Herold Belger** and academician **Tursynbek Kakishev**. If see into their biographies thus we'll know that these doers, calling for and fighting for people's interests and its independence, left after them oral and written scientifically orientated very deep ideas and offers. The whole conscious life they devoted to Kazakh nation humanization. Even if they were not liked by some, they were favourite for our people. That is whom we can call the "appropriate men" according to Abai [24, 28]. I would like to wish youth to study their works and take a pattern by them.

I think that our immediate task is together with Abai's learning of "appropriate man" to revive the system of spiritual development of East, synthesize them and harmonize in a consistent manner with development of the world spiritual values. For this purpose by contrast with capitalistic moral we need new ideas that consider material, conscience and soul as a whole entire system. One of such ideas is 'The great Silk Road' restoration, the spiritual centre Turkistan revival, the big economic belts cration, the spiritual and logistic projects performance, etc. [5,7].

The most important is a human himself, his inner world, every family, young generation upbringing and national traditions revival. Because in new postindustrial civilization the human factor and spiritual conscience are brought to the forefront. It means a return to Abai again on a par with Confucius and Nostradamus [1, 4, 36]. Only then the humanity will understand the Abai's phenomenon.

Changes happening in the epoch of globalization are the evidence of the fact that the views of humanity are directed to East, on the region of the Pacific Ocean.

Speaking simple language it means a return to the ideas of **Confucius**, **Al-Farabi** and **Abai**. For this reason we need to revive the philosophy of East [9].

It is explained by the fact that in the XXI century the develop-ment of civilization inevitably leads to this way. The process of globalization in spiritual sphere already penetrates quickly and deep, what will conduce observance of rights, collaboration and peace in international relations. It is required to make radical changes in spiritual conscience of people and global psychology. Their transfer lies through the way of prior ideological postulates reconsideration. Thus, for example, the economy should be directed not on needs of abstract purchaser's satisfaction, but on the necessities of a concrete man. In such a manner, as a new offer, I would like to express an opinion that **"by means of the minimum socially economic standards implementation to every man"** in the sphere of human capital, we can provide prosperous and comfortable life [5].

I would like to remember none the less the words about Abai of the poet-thinker Shakarim: **"Abai was unlike Kazakh, he was a special human, very wise. Unfortunately, the living en-vironment of Ibragim agha was Kazakh surrounding, that's why he was little respected. Excluding this factor he stayed a wise man, khakim and philosopher"**. Shakaim's sayings about Abai, the well-known Kazakh writer, patriot Magzhan Zhumabaev, rendered poetically:

The real khakim, worthless your gold words,
If even thousands of years will past, delightful they are.
Such human who became khakim from router,
Your songs will forever sound in ears.

Thus today the time and fortune themselves led the great Abai, so anthemised by Magzhan, to the global stage. Our task is to fling ourselves into his learning of "appropriate man". Speaking schoolish language, people, rich men and poor should admit this human giant on all 100%. As to his poetry and edifications recognition, benevolent intentions and dreams achievement, of course, we have not much to boast of – we do too little.

Hence the negative processes logically arise from here in policy, economy, command chains, which we observe now.

The only one remains: **Let's by the whole nation learn and reread desperately and patiently his heritage, key into his creative work and perform his advices and recommendations practically.** If we can do it, only then we will raise the **"national immunity"** of our people to its highest pitch, as a competent member of humanity we will cross the threshold of the global civilization. **The saving nurse of Kazakhs should be not foreign propagandists and advisers, but the works of the Great Abai (including** *The Words of Edification***) and the philosophy of East. We have a full right to call Abai a world person and spiritual sender, who in the Steppes of East real-ized the spiritual revolution exactly.**

In such situation it would be good for every man to ask ques-ions to himself: "How can I come into the paradise of my inner world? Can I achieve it in this life? and to try to find the deci-sions of his questions.

In the measurable future, in the time of post industrial development on a par with other global geniuses, the culture of thinking, the learning of "appropriate man", "The Words of Edification" of Abai, undoubtedly can lay into the basis as one of the foundations of the future new Moral codices. For this the arguments will be enough and these Moral codices will be-come the heritage of the whole humanity – global civilization. In purposes of realization in present conditions of the idea to revive the great Silk Road, it is necessary to found **The East-ern Academy of The Spiritual Values named after Abai** in Kazakhstan, which will include the centres of Abai's heritage and East philosophy study, of the scientific personnel training for Eurasian area, what would become a big support for civilization development.

In future development the epoch of solar and hydrogen energy
will begin, equivalent to mineral fuel energy.
Vladimir I. Vernadskiy

THE WORD THIRTEENTH

What will be the life of humanity in the XXI century?

The great Abai with his ideas, as Vladimir I. Vernadskiy, have gone from Kazakh soils long ago. His view, mental world, etc. as noospheric civilization are hard understood for us. In the epoch of globalization the most difficult question is a choice of the right life journey. It regards to every human and society in whole. We cannot live singularly, without any ties, without trade relations and competitiveness strengthening and also without collaboration with other countries, retiring into shell as it was in the epoch of Abai. That's why it is necessary to consider this problem wider. This is the purpose of "the word thirteenth".

The terrestrial life form evolution, which appeared billions years ago, was accompanied by the world history logic development: **plant life → animal life → mind → human society → biosphere → naonosphere** – these are the basic stages of life development on our planet.

Struggling for existence and survival the humanity began to perceive itself and environment, striving to cognize the edicts of nature, using its opportunities, to develop it and satisfy its requirements. The humanity within its seven-millennial development for the purpose of responsibility increase for the future obtained a vast experience and extensive knowledge.

History knows a lot of crises, conflicts and wars. But never yet there was such critic situation when an ability of planetary civilization in whole was endangered and a drastic fall of natural resources required a scientific approach.

Preservation of human civilization and probability of its further successful development are impossible without study of common patterns and proportions in the production-consumption system, making the foundations of replenishment cycles and global processes management.

A necessity of working **the integral conception of transfer to post industrial civilization** is based on preconditions and circumstances of logic formation of the global historic development, which is tried to be explained by all scientists of the world and global community, considering the problem from different points of view [33-42].

It can be said without prejudice that **the objective logic of the world historic process can serve as model (standard), exclusively precise estimation criterion in understanding of the past, present and future human development**. The humanity came into the global transfer period from industrial to post industrial civilization.

Surely, nowadays we should think about what will be in the world in 2050, in 2100 years. And in future our purpose of achievement the highest organization of people in single entity will stay for survival and preservation of common civilization.

On this basis the author made an attempt to work a conception of transfer to post industrial civilization, where systematically observed all six base elements of transfer, i.e. spirituality, new scientifically technologic revolution, ecologisation of society and material world, space exploration, global security and economy in whole, what in case of accumulation can give a great break [V-section].

The scientific novelty of megaproject is contained in pack-age treatment of all constituents (i.e. base components) as a single worldview process of global world development and on its basis development of network model of the global system of management and regulation of world processes and possibility of stable world development preservation under the transfer to post industrial civilization.

The time has come to ask a global community a question **of the global system of civilization management and world pro-cesses regulation**, which in the end of XX and in the beginning of XXI centuries asserted them. It means that the case is the global world system of politic and economic decisions making.

On the first stage of the global world management for decision of mentioned above specific problems we need to carry on the reasonable conversations of the world legislative body foundation (the World Parliament), the executive body (the World government), the judicial body (the World Court), the Security Council, the World religious union only with definite powers and authority.

Whereby it is necessary to use the whole world historic experience of humanity development, including UNO, EU, g8, g20 and international organizations, institutes, and others either.

The world economy development prospects are connected to the **innovative economy** formation, which could be observed as the most important direction of the world development in the XXI century.

The founder of the modern conception of innovation is Joseph Alois Schumpeter [48]. Competition represents by itself the main instrument of resources saving and efficiency growth, one of driving forces of society development in whole. It is well-known that the classic of the "comparative advantages" theory is David Ricardo [49]. later this idea according to the stages of economy development was elaborated by Michael Eugene Porter [50], Joseph Stiglitz [39] and other world scientists.

Globalization and world crisis showed that many theories including Keynesianism and monetarism are correct only under the definite permissions and tides of revolution. Despite the nod toward the ideas of these scientists – the founders of innovations and competitiveness – in practice in chase of super profit the world transnational corporations, which control more than a half of the global GDP, often forget about the other constituents, for example, about human factor, morality, spirituality, rapid stratification of society, society ecologisation, etc.

Life changes rapidly, that's why in conditions of globalization and world crisis, Porter's models don't have significant effect in terms of objective reasons which they had before. The new economic rules appeared and other forces began to influence the markets and reorganize them. The keys from the world economy were handed to scattering of financial oligarchs, the US Federal Reserve System (which belongs to 20 private banks of USA), international transnational corporations, international financial organizations, including the International Monetary Fund, the World Bank, etc. Countries of the big seven, the big twenty, the biggest world organizations, including UNO, NATO, EU, practically let the dice roll the world economic processes, provided with dollars and having already uncontrolled emission of the "modern currency".

Now the world is confused by the questions of how to return the lost, how to resist the world crisis defiance, how to fit up the house of panhuman civilization, etc.

The strategy of construction of humanity survival in the XXI century and following ages.

Ecology Space exploration Scientifically technologically revolution Safety and security **Economy** Spirituality

The world without wars

The planetary home of panhuman civilization of post industrial world

In the basis of the market system management the development spontaneity lies. But humanity strives for consciously controlled process of the whole economy, which eliminates subjective roots of the market economy. It should be objectively conditioned, consciously led transfer to the new system of reference of economic existence, sunrise of civilized economy.

The world needs a civilized economy, and it should be-come the main principle of building of all economic process-es and the whole production cycle.

First of all, not repeating previous mistakes, we need to understand what to do with the world development strategy: Where do we go, where are we led? I suppose, we don't know ourselves where do we go and those who lead us don't know.

For the first time in the 90-s already the United Nations organization advanced an idea of stable development. But on the way of stated objectives performance the definite difficulties appeared, the world crisis of 2008 also influenced negatively.

V section the network model of the global system of management and the world processes regulation is represented, where all basic constituents of the single worldview process are shown in an integrated manner, the decisions of which will lead to a new type of planet civilization. In detail see [54].

A lot of information was written about the world financial crisis. Without offering specifics, we need to emphasize that among scientists and experts it is widely stated that it is necessary **to find a single regulator of the world currency**, in order in future we could plan the balance between the global production, consumption and monetary coverage of goods and

services. It is possible to keep the main mechanisms of currency production and regulation, as a result of what a new financial architecture will be worked out.

We made an attempt to explain the approaches of determination of **a single universal currency measurement for the whole world by means of "power", i.e. by correlation of kilowatt to currency – kW./currency**. It allows to get rid of speculative capital which is not provided by real power [13, 51].

The modern calculation of GDP in dollars is incorrect with regard to different currencies conversion rates. The unit power (for example kilowatt) in different countries of the world can "cost" different amounts in different currencies, but kilowatt stays kilowatt, no matter where does it is used (in Africa, America, Europe or Asia), and that's why the power exactly can be and should be used for currency conversion rate determination.

In case of crisis it is necessary to create **the Intercurrency Reserve Fund**.

In conclusion we need to note that UNO in its new capacity should control the "cost" of all world currencies (**filling with power**) and should exclude any possibility of currency creation without actives provision. Consequently, it is necessary to create an expert currency commission of the United Nations, which will examine correlation of all world currencies to their power provision.

What way will we choose? In 2015 the strategy of the world development of the United Nations terminates. To our opinion, a new stage will begin aimed on an innovation economy of the post industrial civilization, i.e. on new knowledge, science, high technologies, spiritual values revival, which will promote a competitiveness of all spheres of panhuman capital.

There is a hope that this project will give impulse to a new strategy of the world development. In simple terms, the innovation economy is not only production of crude materials and commodity output, but the development on the basis of new advanced ideas.

*A man who lost his moral character
makes irretrievable mistakes.*
Confucius

A spiritual revolution is a necessity of the XXI century

THE WORD FOURTEENTH

What should be the Moral codices in the conditions of society humanization in the *XXI* century?

The spiritual values, in the words of Abai, feed and lead two wings of human life and his perfection – humanism and cognition. Justice makes mind bright, heart merciful (humane). Abai in "The word fourteenth" further emphasizes and details: only from justice depends how heart takes up mind. Only what mind accepts as just comes from heart. In poem "Thought, hesitated" the poet takes heart and justice in unity and, remembering his own life, tells impatiently about his mistakes and events of un-just deeds, bitterly regretting about everything.

The process of humanity development in the XXI century according to forecasts should go the way of society humanization. For this the whole humanity, every government and international organizations, notwithstanding religious identity, language and races of nations, should become by means of mutual collaboration the initiators of integrative ideas and projects creation and new ways of development determination. Interpreting according to Abai's words, nowadays we need to change a social pattern, when a priority of material side of so-ciety prevails instead of spiritual needs.

Here an expected question appears: What does the Moral codices of humane society should be? Human abilities are unlimited. If he will do everything necessary and learn from youth, acquire good knowledge and put them into practice,

thus he will achieve intended target. He can become very rich (billionaire), to build a career, to be a great scientist, architect, etc. On this right direction he can be led astray by means of different attractive material offers, bribery, etc. It's not a secret that unfortunately many of these people hit in the trap. And a part of people save their human face and stay true to their moral principles, thus achieve significant success.

Consistency of spiritual development of society and nature works out such moral of humanity that allows managing rationally of spiritual life of human. If we'll analyze all world moral codices (religious, professional, corporate, etc.), thus their basic core is humanism, humanness, i.e. ethical principles. For example, the religious codices consider conception of life purpose, careful attitude towards health, human respect to himself and surrounding people as core values.

And the professional codices cover the level of specialists' training and linked to it for this branch the values of ethic principles. Non observance of these principles finally will lead to human retirement or expulsion from personnel. Thus, as far as valued the Hippocratic Oath performance for medical worker, the ethical norms for journalist are equivalent. The other exam-ple, in ethical codex of the giant technological company Apple, the following principles are prescribed for its staff: First off – honesty, respect, secrecy, dutifulness, scrupulosity.

Besides, the codex includes the rules of personnel behaviour in social networks and prohibition of participation in group speculations discussion, connected to company, etc. The similar norms are described in codices of such companies as Ford, Intel, Microsoft and others. It means that a great influence on these companies' success achievement can be exerted not only by the process of material values production and obeyance of laws, but by non-compliance of ethical principles.

life proves incontrovertibly that the main condition of econ-omy development continuousness or viability is an appearance of moral segment in it. I would like to emphasize that the mor-ally ethical co-dices should be not in mentioned above spheres, but in international contracts and agreements either. Because the preference there is given only to economic benefits, over-shadowing their humanitari-an and ethical content. That's why the adoption of the **International moral codex** stays a pending task, which covers the questions of such panhuman values in peoples striving of a new humane society creation, as humanness, honesty, justice and others. All these to-gether will promote a stability preserving in economic and political development and, eventually, national security protection.

Indeed, if take into consideration the present reality in Kazakh society, even if you are triply honest in work, you will achieve nothing. As Shakarim said: It is a dead aim, barren scheme. And conversely, cunning, quibblesome, freakish per-sons, by any turns of the indirect corkscrew, regardless of such negative doings (I would say, crime behaviour), for example, backslapping and cor-ruption, rise to the top of authority, but after unmasking step down from post, leaving a complete negative. Among them the heads of government, akims, ministers, public officials of different levels, representatives of business and bankers often appear, apart the others... This brings up the questions: What society do we build? Why don't we live honestly, what should all do? When will we re-ceive an answer on this question?

I think this strategic blunder and wrong understanding, which lead the society and the whole humanity to crisis, could be got over only with clear conscience and high mind of peo-ple. For this every human should feel that only victory over these negative factors will bring happiness.

In order to attain this objective, as I see it, it is necessary to keep the following conditions:

First, it is necessary to raise **the level of spirituality, conscience and attitude development of our people. We**

need reasonable efforts of a new conscience of society members' formation. They shouldn't think only about survival, but by means of their abilities perfection to switch to new stages of material and spiritual development. **A spiritual revolution is a necessity of the XXI century.**

The second, the principle of transition from quantity to quality. Against the background of unsatisfactory knowledge, presence of 2-3 diplomas and unemployment, we need **to improve professional excellence**. Only then our competiveness on the international level will be increased. That's why the government and Parliament should create for it all conditions. In the XXI century in the human quality measurement the Abai's learning of an "appropriate man" should be used as the most advanced idea.

The third, according to acquired professional knowledge a human should have **spiritual power, patriotic feelings, psychological readiness – very strong will.**

This comes as a result of everyday meticulous work. Thanks to such measures a human conscience raises on the highest level.

The fourth, every human should adequately use his powers against the world challenges, which appear everywhere. The most important, instead of breaking head over the question of how to manage the others, every human should cognize, **know himself**. Because respecting himself he will know the price of respect to others and they will return the compliment.

The fifth, the spiritual development of human is tied not only to religion. It is a frame of life, only an attempt of society humanization. After all we don't account for our material wealth to the god, conversely, we report about the level of our spiritual values and conscience.

A man can take pride in his success of wealth. Though his spiritual poverty brings his success to nought. And this man stops to be an "appropriate man". The wealth put to wrong use will lead him to misfortune. But a spiritually rich man is not able to make harm, because an inner condition of his soul will not allow it. For this reason it would be perfect if we in the higher educational establishments **educated "morally sta-ble citizens"**, on a par with professional knowledge plying. It would be well to pay a special attention to self- cognition, po-tential opportunities discover, culture, clean habits and quality of inner world of our educated.

The sixth, in order to perform all these, **a man should con-trol himself, be able to handle himself.** It means that a man in order to achieve a desired goal, to be called an "appropriate man", should behave himself coldly and stably, save external and internal factors, be able to control his deeds. Surely, these factors are founded on the highest moral values and ethical norms of people. Without morality we lose everything. We need to apply maximum efforts in schools in order to form character of youth, ability to think correctly and readiness to fight with negative factors. It is necessary to get out of easy ways of daily bread earning according to orders from above. This noble work requires big efforts, desire and constant control.

Here it is appropriate to remember the words of Abai that in order to achieve some result in any doing from time to time give an account to yourself. Meeting all these requirements a man forms as a personality. Then, achieving in his develop-ment a definite level, he becomes, as Abai said, an "appropriate man". No matter what people think, without qualitative education a spiritually un-formed human will give nothing valuable in his life. Because, according to Abai's opinion, he didn't become an "appropriate man" yet, he has little patience and moderation to estimate his thoughts and spirit. If a man keys into Abai's learning of an "appropriate man" wholeheartedly, he will come to a conclusion "I will change myself, achieve a desired objective", thus he couldn't be stopped by anybody on this way. Eventually, **a man who saved his moral characteris able to lead himself, his country and whole humanity to good deeds, and a man without morals makes irretrievable mistakes.**

Predicting future it is possible to say that if humanity developed with high morality and conscience, thus it could avoid violence, wars and big conflicts. In order to achieve this we need to change radically the system of education and upbringing. It is necessary to put at the heart of not materially consumer concernment of people, but an inoculation in their conscience the morally ethical valuables. Surely, this is a long and hard process.

Though while the spiritual requirements of every human won't draw to a head in fact, unlikely the life conditions will improve. Without this any man hereafter will stay deprived of rights and a slave of false collectivism. The authorities by means of wrong information win from him an approval of their deeds, through different levers force him to believe fables. This situation could be called **"forcible belief in shameless lie".** If such situation will continue in that spirit, it will lead to dictatorial regime. We observe it in row of countries in different points of the world.

According to Abai, justice includes three interrelated between each other cognition: **"appropriate man",** zhauanmart-lik, **imanigul.** Justice is unique feature of the poet, which comes from the bottom of his heart.

Power and mind find the way

Both for runaway and for any runner. Who has justice and mercy,

That is closer to native and alien.

These two features of human – mercy and justice – make a man "appropriate".

There is a hope that in civilized development as a result of the VI-VII technological modes a big change will happen in the world – scientifically technological revolution. **In future the epoch of**

conscience evolution, spiritual revolution and society human-ization will happen. And the humanity serving them will rise on the top of its spiritual growth. Only then people will reap the fruits of the world development.

And to this time we have 1-2 centuries, if the world war won't break out. And it tightly tied to human factor. In this spoffish time the humanity armed with Abai's learning of "appropriate man", insightful works of **Confucius and Nostrada-mus** and other world geniuses, unlikely will go on universal slaughter and self destruction. What more could one ask for?!

Not predicting far future will be occupied with near difficulties.

THE WORD FIFTEENTH

Instead of conclusion, we have a question to the future.

Indisputably, it is impossible to discover the content of all Abai's "Words of edification". We only tried to explain his most important thoughts, to link them to present state and show the levers of application under the decision of advanced questions. Life changes fleetly, what ideas and prognosis will be in the epoch of globalization and world crises – that is on what the intellectual and material resources of humanity should be directed. It is necessary on the world level to change radically in society development the human factor exactly.

Most of all we are concerned with the question: What will happen tomorrow? What does the future hold? Apart the yes-terday's and today's difficult situations. In the epoch of the world globalization **the humanity transfers from industrial development onto post industrial period.**

To our opinion it is necessary to pay a special attention to market economy, which will be replaced by ***innovative econ-omy*** of post industrial civilization. Such paradigm should be based on new knowledge, science and high technologies, on competiveness of human capital, which is able to change the whole system of spirituality and values of society members.

Nowadays both capitalism and socialism precede Renaissant reformations. The time of post industrial civilization came. Whereby an exit into noosphere by means of space exploration and hereto related new systems of communication of considerable importance in development. Here at the interface of capitalism and socialism the third way of humanity development should move to the front – the period of post industrial civilization, based on innovative economy. The author calls it "***innovationism***". It means a new way of transfer to new type of social relations. The history itself proved more than once that any economy which is not based on spiritual values and humanistic principles, finally, is subjected to crises and disarrangement. In its turn in changeable century of globalization **the idea of society globalization can become a factor of na-tions and states rapprochement.**

After the mentioned above measures performance by means of revival and application of multiyear historical values the massive opportunities for spiritually cultural humanity development and radical changes in global scale appear.

This will be a giant stride forward in humanity development. The main task of humanization idea is to change the level of thinking, conscience and in total the whole inner world in compliance to new civilized society requirements of the XXI century. A titanic work of the global confrontations and contradictions liquidation yet lies ahead.

It is necessary either in order to revive harmony of society and nature development to eliminate grave mistakes in deployment and production of primary resources and mineral deposits. It follows from here the decision of problems solving, solicitous attitude to resources, new ideas of projects of new development creation. These issues must be dealt with expeditiously, it is very important to draw from consistency of historic development. It follows from here that the decision of spiritually cultural development of society problem stays an overriding priority.

Answering a question "What new type of society should be in the XXI century?, it is necessary to take into account the following two factors.

First of all, to use logic (experience) of the global historic development ably and cautiously, and also spiritually cultural values of every country and region, true native history. In or-der to cognize future we need to know the past history well: what changed for many years and what disappeared, what stood without changes (differences).

If refer to Abai's words, we can predict future, analyzing visible and invisible riddles of the universe.

Secondly, the new consistencies in the XXI century, first of all, **transition to post industrial humanly nonospheric civilization.** Its first stage is an assimilation of the new techno-logical mode. It is necessary to invest actively the innovative technology, science, techniques and human capital.

The time of new strategy creation in global world order has come.

In comparison to more favourable life conditions in preceding millennium, for new civilization, new culture the bigger tolerance and secular pluralism are important.

In the author's opinion, with regard to the world history development the basic component parts of society humanization and spirituality revival in the XXI century are:

- *history of past, condition of present and perspective of future;*

- *transformation of world psychology, increase of hu-man ability to think from a new angle;*

- *revival of spiritual and moral values, plea for collabo-ration and mutual understanding of the world religions, in-cluding Islam, Christianity, Buddhism, Confucianism, etc.;*

- *quantitative growth of the world population and in-crease of life quality in the process of creative human capital development;*

- *harmonious society development (the epoch of hyper-democracy;*

- *spiritual revolution, machine intelligence appearance.*

In conclusion I would like to say that thoughts rendered in this book, raised issues, mentioned levers and ways of their solution appeared not for one day. They appeared in consequence of long-standing searches in my conscious experience, their analysis and public speeches on different forums (articles, reviews, reports and books) from all kinds of rostrums and in the sphere of redneck masses, as ex-member of the country's Parliament.

These are the acquirements benefits of my experience abroad, work on plant, in short, of my 50 years of life experience and fundamental scientific works. This idea inspired me during my parliamentarian practice (four times I stood for election to deputy) and after meetings with people of different professions and layers of society. Especially recently I began to go deeper into history, culture and pay a special attention to spiritual values of our people, learn life journeys and works of many great persons of the great steppe, talk to them in thoughts and "get" their advices. "Sharing" my views of future with Abai and Shakarim, I expressed my personal estimations in written form and bring to your notice. **If I speak too sharply, then I apologize.** However new times and world crisis require such critic, because through it we can open the door to the future. The conventional wisdom says: "Without critic there is no error correction". If this book contains any shortfalls I think they are redeemable. Because I am Kazakh and my mindset is the same, the committed in work errors are correspondent, everything is in Kazakh manner.

In conclusion I would say: considered in this book problems are not decided yet. yes, it's not real. But I made the best of my ability and tried to make my contribution in undoing such tangled knots in social sphere, economy and policy, in order to prompt people to think about it. All my life I worked and work in the interests of my country, for happiness of every family and its security. If my thoughts and offers, my deeds in time will meet with approval and bring anything to the table in the process of Kazakhstan entering the list of the world civilized countries, it means that I worked not for nothing and I will consider that my life mission is performed.

Before writing this work I consulted with myself for a long time. Learning the works of the great historical persons of ancient times and of those whom I was happy to see and hear, the edifications of political and scientific doers of present time, I decided to write their names in this book.

They are: Dinmukhamed Kunaev, Kanysh Satpaev, Mukhtar Auezov, Alkey Margulan, Salyk Zimanov, Baiken Ashimov, Assanbai Askarov, Umirzak Sultangazin, Shafik Chokin

Shakhmardan Essenov, A. Abdulin, Tursynbek Kakishev, gerold Belger, Murat Aitkhozhin, Omirbek Zholdasbekov, Sauk Takezhanov, Karatai Turyssov, Marat Ospanov, Nurlan Bal-Gimbaev and others.

To all these mentioned people I express appreciation, wish your families health and happiness! Not consulting with them and not applying their spiritual values it's unlikely I could write such work. Once again many thanks! Let their Aruakhs fly above the Kazakh people and help in its good intentions.

Three mentioned couplets of Shakarim's poem have an in-credible emotional meaning for every family.

It is notable that under the world crisis in Europe and other countries beginning from 2007 it was recommended to read the works of Karl Marx and everybody began to study them. Because Karl Marx as nobody else discovered the core of the problem and regularities of the world financial crisis. If we faced the **society humanization**, thus I would advice to read and analyze the works of Abai. We need to do it turning our face toward Abai in the XXI century, in order we could take from his books truth, relying on his learning of "appropriate man", apply the postulates of honour and nobleness for changing ourselves, our inner world. If we'll observe the past centuries, thus we'll find that before Abai and after him there were intellectuals and corypheuses. I hope that we'll have in future either. It seems that Kazakhs already don't have the unexpressed words. To our sorrow, words do not meet the actions. This is our "disease", our mentality. And the great Abai all his life worked for changing such mindset, conscience and way of thinking.

In the process of present globalization in the world, in order to answer different challenges, we need to refer to Abai again. If we won't perform his ideas, we are destined for unending retardation from others. The time has come to study extensively, attend scrupulously to his "Edifications" in practice. I would like to express it in the following words;

Intelligences lived and performed before us, Who gave their all for own Kazakhiya. There is no word unspoken,
Where are the people who implement this idea? For twenty four years of independence
There were more words and fewer deeds.
If you'll carry on this way up until, my bloater,
You'll be swallowed; I don't see the other fate. Open your eyes, don't sleep, wake up, Kazakh!
In order to prevent any scorns of any enemy,
With his eyes on your wealth and lands
There are so many thievish men, we cannot count.
Globalization prowls like a hungry wolf,
It does not care you independence.
Let's turn to Abai from now,
His "Edifications" are the fortress yours and mine!

I have one question for future: "The humanity in the second half of the XXI century and in the XXII century will rise on new stage. What stage is it?" It is a civilization creation of human noosphere, space exploration.

It begs the other question: **"How can we transfer to noosphere humanization and to the first type of the world civilization?"** I'm sure: these questions will be answered by young scientists, who absorbed all achievements of native and world science, literate and competent, working on the prob-lems of the world civilization development, the future Al-Far-abis, Dulatis, Chokans, Abais, Shakarims.

Eventually, the Kazakh Republic should achieve the top of the world civilization. let's assist it in this noble mission, my dear fellows!

LIST OF REFERENCES

1. Abai Kunanbaev, Qara sozdery. – Almaty: Oner, 2006.-124 b.

2. Abai, 1, 2 tomes – Almaty, Zhazushy baspasy - 1995 3. Mukhtar Auezov, The way of Abai – Almaty, 2006.

4. John Hogue, Nostradamus, The complete set of prophesies – Moscow, 2002 – 864 p.

5. Orazaly Sabden, XXI gasyrdagy adamzattyng omir suru koncepsiasy – Almaty, 2014 – 72 b.

6. Shakarim Qudaiberdiev. Shygarmalary. – Almaty, Zhaushy, 1988. -560 b.

7. Orazaly Sabden, «Turkistam ongiri» rukhany – zhana tekhnologialyq klasteryn quru. Qazaqstan qogamyn izgilendiru zholy. – Almaty, 2014 – 104 b.

8. Turar Ryskulov, The set of works in 3 tomes – Almaty, Kazakhstan, 1997.

9. Sergey Oldenburg, Confucius. Buddha Sakyamuni. – Moscow, 2012 – 192 p.

10. K.M.Baipakov, A. Azimkhan; All roads lead to Turkistan: monuments, persons. –Almaty, 2013.

11. Mohammed Haydar Dulati, Tarih-i-Rashidi – Almaty, Turan, 2003. – 616 p.

12. Qazaqstan tarihy kone zamannan buginge deiyn. Bes tomdyk. – Almaty, Atamura, 2010.

13. Orazaly Sabden, A. Armenskiy, I. Kopylov and others. life control on Earth Planet. –Almaty, 2012. – 628 p.

14. "Qanysh" enciklopediasy, – Almaty, "Qazaq enciclope-diasynyn" redakciasy, 2011.

15. Dinmukhamed A. Kunaev, About my time – Almaty, Deuer, 1992. – 312 p.

16. A. Abdulin. geology of Kazakhstan – Alma-Ata, 1981. – 186 p.

17. Qazaq encoclopediasy. 10 tomdyq. – Almaty, Kazakh-stan, 2008.

18. M. Magauin, genghis Khan, Four-volume work – Al-maty, Deuer, 2011. – 608 p.

19. Chokan Ch. Valikhanov, The selected works – Moscow, Science, 1986.

20. Al-Farabi, The historico-philosophical tractates – Alma-Ata, 1985.

21. Chingiz T. Aitmatov, Cassandra›s Brand. – St. Peters-burg, Alphabet-classics, 2007.

22. Jacques Attali, The short history of future. – St. Peters-burg, 2014.

23. Nursultan A. Nazarbaev, Eurasia zhureginde. – Almaty, «Zhibek zholy» baspa uii, 2010. – 308 б.

24. S. Zimanov, The complete set of works, 10 tomes – Al-maty, Media – Zan corporation, 2009.

25. Zholdasbekov O. Mazhinalar mekhanismderinin teori-asy. – Алматы, Fylym, 1979.

33. Orazaly Sabden, 22 tomdyq economica tandamaly en-bektery. – Al-maty, 2012.

34. A.I. Subetto, The noospheric scientific and spiritually moral foundations of humanity survival in the XXI century. As-terion – St. Petersburg, 2013.

35. V.I. Vernadskiy, The scientific thought as a planetary phenomenon – Moscow, Science, 1991.

36. N. Makiavelly, The sovereign. The thinkings over the first decade of Titus livius. – Minsk.

37. l.N. gumilev, The ancient Turkmans –Moscow, 2014. 38. John Maynard Keynes, The Economic Consequences of
the Peace – 1919

39. Stiglitz J. Freefall: America, Free Markets and the Sink-ing Economy Norton: 2009.

40. yury V. yakovets, The global economic transformations of the XXI century. Economy -384 p. 2011.

41. David Director Friedman, The next 100 years: prognosis of events in the XXI century – Moscow, ЭКСМО, 2010.26. Myrzakhmetov M. Abai-tanu 1-2 kitap, – Астана

42. Michio Kaku, Physics of the Future – Moscow, 2012.«Деловой Мир», 2010-1180 б.27. Shakhanov M. Olender, balladalar, dastandar, ander. – Almaty, 2012.

43. Eltutqa. El tarikhynin aigili tulgalary. M. Zholdasbekov, Q. Salgaruly, A. Seidimbek. – Astana., «Kultegin», 2001. -357 b.28. Herold Belger, The selection – Ruan, 2014.

44. «Turkistan» khalyqaralyq enciklopedia. Bas red. A.29. g. Kaliev, The agrarian problems at the turn of the cen-tury. Republican State Enterprise The scientific research insti-tute of economy, agroindustrial complex and rural development – Almaty, 2003.

30. Turgambaev g. Aqiqat zholynda. – Almaty, 2008. – 480 p.

Nysanbaev. – Almaty., Qazaq enciclopediasy. 2000. -656 b.

45. Turil lhalyktarynyn tarihynin murazhaiyy. – Almaty., 2003. 53 b.

46. Babalar sozy. – Astana., «Foliant», 2015

47. Derbisali. A. Qazaq dalasynyn zhuldyzdary, Tarikhi filo-logialyq zertteu, A., 1995.31. lama Sharif, The Kazakhstani truth newspaper – 10.08.2011.

48. Joseph Alois Schumpeter, The Theory of Economic De-velopment – Moscow, Direct-Media, 2007.32. A.K. Koshanov, The selected works in 10 tomes. – Al-maty, economy, 2014.

49. David Ricardo, The beginning of political economy and tax assessment. – Moscow, ЭКСМО, 2007.

50. Michael Eugene Porter, Competitive Advantage – Mos-cow, Alpinabusiness BOOKS, 2008.

51. Orazaly Sabden, A. Armensky Sustained economic growthin the EurAsEC countries on the basis of laws of devel-opment. – Almaty, 2011.

52. T. Koichuev, Thinking over sensible subjects – Bishkek, 2015 – 180 p.

53. A. Askarov, Osiettei olmeityn sezim qalsa... Almaty, 2007, 144 b.

54. Orazaly Sabden, A. Ashirov, The conception of human-ity survival strategy in the XXI century and food security – Al-maty, Economy, 2015 – 200 p.

55. Orazaly Sabden, The Kazakhstani truth newspaper – De-cember 4, 2015.

ADDENDUM

The list of letters and recommendations to President and the Government of RK from 1990s till 2016s.

1.About the republican program of personnel training abroad (1990)

2.About creation and organization of the National Scien-tific Fund activity (November 13, 1991)

3.About creation of the Supreme consultative council of science and techniques under the President of the Republic of Kazakhstan (July 1992)

4.About integration of science, education and personnel training (No-vember 23, 1993)

5.About the governmental program correction (1994)

6.About the new economic policy conception (February 1995)

7.Conception of the new economic policy (Advices of Ka-zakhstan, January 1995)

8.Zhana economicalyq sayasattyn tuzhyrymdamasy («Kh-alyq ke-nesy» 13.01.1995.)

9.About the state support of native manufacturers (1995) 10. About the economic reform acceleration in Kazakhstan

at the threshold of the XXI century (November 1997)

11. About the state monopoly of wines and spirits produc-tion and the KAZAKHSTAN SHARA By national corporation creation (May 1998)

12. About the economic reform acceleration (May 1998) 13. About the National Agency of Science and Technology

creation (April 2006)

14. Stabilization and growth of Kazakhstani economy com-petive-ness (Almaty, 2008)

15. About the innovative development of Kazakhstani econ-omy and role of science (Almaty, 2009)

16. About the human capital competiveness in the Republic of Ka-zakhstan (2010)

17. Economy 2020 – the new way and the Kazakhstani eco-nomic miracle (2011)

18. About the national scientific center of fundamental and applied researches creation (2011)

19. About some directions of organizations' perfection and territorial development management (2011)

20. The Public Chamber of the Republic of Kazakhstan is a chamber of big hopes (2011)

21. To political modernization of the country: new approach and new project of its realization (2011)

22. law about the State language of the Republic of Ka-zakhstan (2011).

23. «Turkistan oniri» rukhani – zhana tekhnologialyqklasterin qury turaly (2012)

24. The note about the pension age of women (22.05.2013) 25. The note about the science reform (open letter 06.03.2014) 26. The note about the fate of science (open letter 06.11.2015) 27. It's time to gath-er the forces of all the Kazakhstan people
in front of big challenges (15.01.2016)

28. «Public Chamber» the need for an effective state control (13.05.2016)

29. Development of Kazakhstan's virgin lands of the XXI century - as the revival and strengthening of the country's history (24.05.2016 г)

II SECTION

THE GREAT HISTORIC PERSONS

Al-Farabi
(870-950)

Mohammed Haydar Dulati
(1499-1551)

Abylay-khan
(1711-1780)

INTRODUCTION

The humanity in continuous struggle for survival began to study and acquire the surrounding world and itself. It strived to cognize the laws of nature development and to use them and its opportunities of everyday requirements satisfaction correctly. In such a manner, in its development of two thousand years' duration it obtained vast experience and knowledge. The Mus-lim nations, population of which nowadays numbers 1.3 bil-lion people and lives on big areas of Eurasia, Africa, Australia and other continents, Turkic-Speak-ing among them, made a tremendous contribution in civilization development through many centuries. The indelible marks within this framework on the territory of Eurasia the forefathers of Tur-kic-Speaking na-tions left: Scythians, Saka, Huns, Turkic Khanate. Till nowa-days the whole world is favorably impressed by left after them cultural artifacts: rock carvings of animals, variable utensils, adornments and giant kurgans, where their chieftainry slum-ber. The names of Tomyris and Attila, who went down human history by their acts of valour, are widely known.

So, the famous Saka queen Tomyris governed vagrant tribes – Saka (in greek records they were called "Massagetae"). Dur-ing battle with the great Persian King Cyrus from Achaemenid dynasty Tomyris kills him cutting off his head and puts it in bota bag with the words: "Though I survived and won you in battle, you ruined me indeed, capturing my son by trickery. That's why as I promised I ply you with blood to satiety!".

And gold plated grave known today as "gold man". Attila conquered the Roman Empire. The West European compos-ers wrote operas about him; in many European countries his monuments were erected.

Genghis Khan and Emir Timur founded the huge empires from coast of the Pacific Ocean to Vienna in Europe. The main wealth was accumulated on this area. These empires were the most powerful on the Euraslan continent. Even the Roman Empire admitted the authority of Attila over it and rendered tribute for a long time. The European countries were helpless before his troops that time. They were severed by internecine wars. If it hadn't been for consequences of the following three factors: remoteness of this dominion (the Eurasian continent), incredibly frigid climate and advance of an epidemic (plague) throughout the whole Europe, thus under the further con-quest in what direction would the European civilization go? (Picture). The modern history created a new "headache" for Europe. The public unrest and wars that happen in Middle Eastern countries and Africa caused big migration processes. Basically migrants consist of Muslims and Turkic-Speaking nations. Such penetration to the European Union can cause an international integration process. It remains to be seen what waits us in future.

In this flow we need to know what are the merits before the whole humanity of our great historical persons, state and pub-lic doers: **Queen Tomyris, King Attila, Yer Tonga, Tonykok, Arystanbaba, Al-Farabi, Yusuf Balassaguni, Manas, Ni-zami Ganjavi, Hoja Ahmet Yassawi, Makhmut Kashgari, Genghis Khan, sultan Baybars, Emir Timur, Ulugbek, Alisher Navoi, Mohammed-Khaidar Dulati, Korkyt, Abai Kunanbaev, Ataturk, Bektash Veli, Chokan Valikhanov, Gabdolla Tuqay, Turar Ryskulov, Mukhtar Auezov, Berdy Kerbabaev, Rassul Gamzatov, Chingiz Aitmatov and oth-ers.** Taking into account their heritage left for us, if the panthe-ons in Turkistan will be monumentalized, the memorial comp-lexes would give an impulse to further civilization integration development and arouse interest from the side of foreigners increasing the flow of travelers and tourists to our country. And we would get an opportunity to show this all to them.

In second part of this book the short summaries of the great historical persons are represented. They were taken from the following works (10-12, 17-20, 43-47).

I don't doubt that the facts and data in book will help our youth to think over its future and understand correctly the layers of native history, strengthen patriotic feelings of growing generation. I think, the heroic feats performed by our forefathers will cause a desire of young people to take example by them, as the great Abai said: "If even you'll not become like him, do an imitation of him". In the epoch of globalization to be in touch with global development, to apply ably the spiritually cultural values of every country and every region is a great necessity, an everyday task of all of us. Eventually, the complex of these tasks will cause its salutiferous **effect of the new world strategy creation on our planet.**

QUEEN TOMYRIS, TUMAR – (TOMYRIS) (approximately 570-520 years B.C.) – famous

Saka Queen, who governed Scythian vagrant tribes (Saka) in distant ages. In greek originals her nation was called Massagetae.

The name of Queen Tomyris came to the world prominence and stood in history thanks to her land-slide victory over the great Persian King Cyrus from Achaemenid dynasty (558-530 years B.C.), who had a bash at the Central Asia conquest, titled as The King of Asia, who didn't know defeats. The queen of Massagetae tribes Tomyris (531-528 years B.C.) was brought up in the spirit of her time -brave and battailous. Legend has it that between Saka and troops of King Cyrus the deadly and murderous war was waged hitherto unheard-of and unseen in history. Eventually Massagetae, applying ingenious ploys of embattling, cut the multitudinous troops of the Persians to piec-es. The main fighting forces of enemy headed by their King oc-curred in no way out – in condition of full isolation. The best part of Persian troops and Cyrus himself fell on the battlefield. His body was beheaded and at the order of Queen Tomyris the head of her archenemy was doused to leather bota bag which was filled with blood. As legend has it the Queen in revenge for her son treacherous killing kept her word and sinking the head of Cyrus in bota bag said the following: "Though I survived and won you in battle, you ruined me indeed, capturing my son by trickery. That's why as I promised I ply you with blood to satiety!"

According to Herodotus, the Persian King Cyrus died at the hand of Tomyris during the battle. This history about the great woman-warrioress, along with the name of Queen Tomyris, is passed on from generation to generation and immortalizes. That is how Queen Tomyris thanks to her heroism and mind left her indelible image of the great strategist and wise governor in the history of Saka nation.

KAGAN YEDIL or ATTILA (on ancient Turkic language, latin – Atti-la, was born in 406 year – died in 453 year) – distinguished historical figure, who took a special place in the history of humanity. Chieftain of the legend-ary west nations of Huns. Descending from royal lineage he acquired good education and for many years studied in Rome. This is an outstanding historical character in the history of humanity, who united under his domination Barbarian tribes from the Rhein to the Northern Black Sea region.

The father if yedil (Attila) – Munzduk was of royal lineage of Huns. Because the society of Huns was considered as bel-ligerent, Kagan yedil (Attila) from an early age, as the other descendants of Huns nation, was brought up under the laws of those times: was taught archery and horseriding. In the times of Attila reign his empire achieves its highest level of development and prospers thanks to his wisdom and bravery.

In the period between the first and second campaigns Bleda died (brother of Attila) and from 444 year till death in 453 year Attila ruled powerful Hun empire single-handedly, which repre-sent a consocation of different Barbarian tribes, living on north of Danube (including right coast) on the wide territories from the Black Sea region to the Rhein.

In 451–454 years Attila conducts war with the Western Ro-man Empire. In 452 year, defeating Italy, he conquered such cities as Mediolanum (nowadays Milan) and Ticinum (nowadays Pavia). Rome agreed on peace treaty in return for annual tributes and scots payment.

For 19 years of governance Attila expanded the boundaries of Hunnish empire several-fold. He went down in history as the great warrior of East and conqueror, who founded gross empire. Possible that's why the Western chronographers rank the name of Attila together with the names of the great persons of human-ity development history, such as Alexander the Macedonian and Julius Caesar.

Six centuries after the European states began to mint the gold and silver coins depicting Attila. In culture and art of many European countries we can find the musical compositions, poems and plays dedicated to Attila.

YER TONGA – legendary his-to-rical figure. The vision of Alyp yer Tonga, as a great historical character, Abu Raikhan al-Biruni, Makhmut Kashgari, Mohammed Khaidar Du-la-ti, Hamza Issfakhani, Rashid ad-Din and others described him brightly in poems and prose in their times. On their opin-ion Alyp yer Tonga was the figure of na-tional scale. In all literary writings and historical sketches Alyp yer Tonga was represented as talented chieftain, who showed his great features of strategist under the battle between Turan and Iran.

An outstanding poet of Persian nation Firdausi (940-1030 years), evidently, studied epic "yer Tonga" from cover to cov-er. In his world-known writing "Shah Namah" he could inter-lace be-tween each other legends, historical sources, glorifying songs and lamentations of Turanian King, chieftain and famous warrior yer Tonga artfully. There is one circumstance which should be tak-en into account: in "Shah Namah" Firdausi has several chapters which describe the campaigns of the Turanian nation's sovereign Afrasiab (i.e. Alyp yer Tonga).

In the epoch of Islamic literature development its significant rep-resentative and outstanding poet yusuf Balassaguni (the XI cen-tury) also read the epic "yer Tonga" in original and used it in his poem (dastan) "Kutadgu-bilig". In writing of yusuf Balassaguni "Kutadgu-bilig" a chapter dedicated to the legends of Alyp yer Tonga is called "The features worthy to be praised and of profit of good deeds". "The lamentations of The great yer Tonga" legend was extant at our days without changes by means of Makhmud Kashgari's glossary "Collection of Turkic dialects" ("Diuani lugat at-turk"). It describes good deeds, no-ble origin, wisdom and pre-science in governance of Turanian nation, auspices to common people and benevolence, bravery and outstanding features of the grand Commander yer Tonga. The main idea of "yer Tonga" is protection of Turanian nation against foreign enemies, plea for unity and solidarity of Turkic nations, glorification of Mother land's honor and celebrity.

TONYKOK (646-741 years) – prominent figure, founder of **The Second Eastern Turkic Khanate**, of Oghuzian tribe descent, corypheus, who made a big contribution to ter-ritorial expansion and Turkic population increase when he was a vizir (adviser) of three venerable Kagans of the Turkic Khanate.

The history doesn't know the other person like Tonykok who thanks to his mind, judiciousness, power, spiritual strength, pre-science left a large footprint on sands of time and became famous in nomad history, admiring and amazing chronographers by the intravitam stone epitaph of monument foundation, which narrates of merits, hospitality, aspirations, bravery, feats and achievements of his nation. He was honored of the highest rank of the Turkic warrior – Apa Tarkhan title, i.e. "Political governor of the Turkic troops". Vasily Bartold (1869-1930) in his researches of runic relics compares Tonykok to the famous French statesman, talented diplo-matist, Royal adviser Talleyrand-Périgord (1754-1838).

The stone runic epitaph of Tanykok narrates the following: "The Turkic Bilge-Kagan (wise governing kagan) spiritualizes the Turkic-Sir nation (Esirians) and the Oghuzian nation". At the order of the honored steppe figure Bilge Tonykok an inscription on stone was stamped, which estimated and narrated about his role in the history of independence getting by Turkic nation and the Turkic Khanate establishment as a separate nation.

In the history of China development it is narrated clearly that when Bilge Kagan returned Tonykok to horde in 716 year he was 70 years old already. From that time he was always with Bilge Kagan helping him by wise advices to hold the Turkic Khanate together and protect from external invasions and threats. Chron-ographers noted that Tonykok lived into old age and died a natural death. According to sources his death occurred approximately in 741 year at the age of 95.

KORKUT, KORKYT-ATA – fa-ther of kobyz, akyn, composer and great thinker of the whole Turkic people. Korkyt-ata is a historical fig-ure, who left a rich musically literary heritage to descendants. There are different guess works in science of Korkyt-ata's stages of life. Though the majority of research-ers came to a conclusion that Korkyt-ata was born approximately in the beginning of the IX century and lived by the side of the Syr-Darya River in Oghuzian Kipchak tribal alliance.

In historic writing of Rashid ad-Din "Dzhami At-Tarikh" ("The Collection of Chronicles") genealogy of Korkyt-ata was originated from Kaiy tribe, while in "The genealogy of Turks" of Abilgazy it is narrated that he was originated from Oghuz branch – bayat, died at the age of 95. Abubakir Divaev and many other scientists, researching the life of Korkyt-ata, came to single con-clusion that his grave is located not far from Syr-Darya shores. However as for the rest they differ in opinion. So, for example, in researches of Auelbek Konyratbaev it is said that Korkyt-ata died in the beginning of the XI century, while in works of Alkey Mar-gulan the years of life of Korkyt-ata fell on the VII-VIII centuries. In the history of Kazakh philosophy Korkyt-ata is represented as philosopher-humanist, who took his place in the culture of the global thought as scientist-thinker and creator of Turkic world view foundations, corypheus and public man, who enhanced the unity of people. From legends of Korkytata it is known that he was great at three types of art. First of all, he was baksy (shaman) beyond compare of Oghuzian Kipchak birth. Secondly, he was the first who made kobyz and played kyui on its strings, by means of which the sounds of nuture were rendered. Thirdly, he was renowned storyteller; his songs and tales are the historical literary heritage, which express the Oghuzian Kipchak life. Korkyt's birth was also linked to miracles and legends from the Turkic nation's folklore. Korkyt was a forefather of songcraft, zhyrau-storyteller, baksy, kyuishi, legendary occult fortune-teller of the Turkic Oghuzian tribe.

As legend has it, Korkyt-ata all his life fought against death. For example, *he, saddling his fast-running camel Zhelmaya, goes forth in search of Zher-Uyuk – the promised land, where the human life is beyond death power and where human can find im-mortality. But wherever he goes, wherever he is, here, there, and everywhere he sees people digging grave. To his question:* **"Whos grave is it?"***, every time he receives an answer:* **"Korkyt's grave"***. Thus, existing vulgarly say-ing:* «Қайда барсаң да Қорқыттың көрі» (**"Wherever you'll go – everywhere is Korkyt's grave"***). Not finding Holt from death on Earth, absolutely tired of es-capement, Korkyt lays a carpet on waves of Syr-Darya and falls asleep. Then death overcomes him by means of small snake that swam out from water , from* it's *bite he died.*

The researchers drew a parallel between the philosophy of Korkyt and a well-know Sumerian epic "The poem of gilgamesh".

Comparing gilgamesh's heroism and self-denial, putting the clock back on millennia, they found common in their attitude to life and death; the purpose is to find immortality for people.

"The Book of Our Father Korkyt" is the first written literary epical issue (monument of literature) of Turkic nations, which expressed their way of life, history, customs, world view and characters. This manuscript was created in the XV century. To his de-scendants Korkyt-ata left the great heritage in type of kyuis for kobyz – Korkyt, Zhelmaya, Targyl tana (piebald heffer), yelimay (Oh, my Motherland), Korkyt kyui, Konyr, Voy Ushar.

MANAS is the main batyr of "Manas" dastan (poem). "Manas" dastan is a tradition-al epic of Kirghiz nation. This epic is an example of the oral folk arts, which was passed on from generation to generation, from mouth to mouth over the ages and survived in memory of people. "Manas" consists of more than half a million of verses and considered one of the most extensive epics in the world, and according to content depth and image variety doesn't disgrace such world-known epical poems as Homer's "Iliad" and "Odyssey", 20 times as much by volume than they both together and two times bigger than the "Mahabharata".

65 types of different written variants of epic's passi are known. The famous scientist-enlightener Chokan Valikhanov made the first sci-entific writing of epic's passi and translated into Russian the signifi-cant fragment "The dinner (meal) of Koketay Khan".

There is a theory that batyr Manas is buried on the North of Kir-ghizia in Talas region near the Alatau Mountains. The mau-soleum, where supposedly batyr's mortal remains are buried, is located in 40 km. from Talas city. This place became the pilgrimage for many travelers and tourists. From 1995 year in these parts the traditional Kirghiz games and competitions on horses began to be conducted. The mausoleum's frontage contains writing-edification: "This is the majestic mausoleum of the most celebrated woman Kenizek-Khatun, the daughter of Abyk emir". In the content of dastan (epic) this writing is explained by the fact that Manas's widow Kanikey made this false writing specially, in order to protect and save the burial of her dearly beloved huband from demolition and destruction. At the same time, accord-ing to certain origins, approximately in 1334 year the building, which bears the name of "The Mausoleum of Manas", was built. On the place of already destroyed by years mausoleum now-adays stays the Museum named after Manas.

ABU NASR AL-FARABI (*Abu Nasr Mohammed ibn Mukhammad ibn Tarkhan ibn Uzlag al-Farabi, 870-950 years*) – world-known thinker, philoso-pher, sociologist, mathematician, phys-icist, astronomer, botanist, linguist, logician, music theorist. **Wiseman and scientist, who was called the Second after Aristotle, teacher of the world culture and science.** He was born on the Syr-Darya riverside in Otrar city, which was the center of Turkic nations in ancient times. Arabs called Otrar as Farab.

He made a tangible contribution to all spheres of science and art development of that time, leaving for future genera-tions a plentiful source of knowledge and researches as cultural heritage. Relying on ideas of the Ancient East thinkers and Greek philosophers, first of all Plato and Aristotle, he interpreted them from a new angle. In his work "The tractate of required conditions for philosophy learning" he expressed his point of view of nine conditions of Aristotelian philosophy, claiming that achievement of desired goal depends on that who desires it. Human should improve himself from spiritual point of view, "only thinking sense and cognizing the true course of nature, a man can reach perfection", summarized Al-Farabi. Al-farabi's tractate "Fassul almadani" (The words of edification of statesmen) is dedicated to social and political life, peculiarities of social structure, problems of society. Nowadays the library of the Kazakhstani Academy of Sciences keeps about fifty works of Al-Farabi. Among them are writings still unexplored and untranslated (tractates), covering some spheres of science: "The book of addendum-annotation to Al-magest", "The methods of geometric lines construction", "Astrology", "Kitab al mussiki al Kabir".

The last years of his life he spent in Misr (Cairo), Haleb and Damascus (in ancient times Sham in Syria). In Damascus (Sham) he spent the rest of his life and died at the age of 80. He was buried behind the so called Small gates (Bab as-Sagir). The great son of Kazakh steppe Al-Farabi left in heritage the huge treasury of knowledge – the works on Turkic, Arab, Persian.

In the history of the world science and culture the name of Al-Farabi is highly significant and honorable. His works promoted not only the development of Turkic and Kazakh philosophy, but became a bridge for coming together the cultures of East and West. Al-Farabi's apprentice-followers who continued his work became the leading scientists of studious habits from Central Asia, such as Abu Ali ibn-Sina, Beruni, Boszhani, Omar Khayyam.

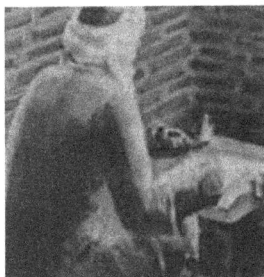

ARYSTAN-BAB – holy man, the first teacher of Hoja Ahmet yassawi. His name, as of spiritual advisor and Sufi teacher, is widely spread in the vicinity of Otrar, Sa-yram and yassi (nowadays Turkestan). The prominent Sufi representative Suleyman Bakyrgani praised "Khorasan is the center of all babs, Sanssyz bab is in India, the head of all babs is Aryslan-bab". Kazakh shamans (Baksy) in their appeals to the sanctified asked from them support and healing with the following words: "Tumen bab in Turkistan, ask support from you, Sanssyz bab from Sayram, thirty babs (forefathers) of Otrar, the main is Arystan-bab".

As legend has it, in Emir Timur's sleep a holy man appeared in dreams, who said that first of all it is necessary to build a mausoleum above the grave of Hoja Ahmet yassawi's teacher, and only then build a mausoleum for his apprentice. So, at the order of Timur the lame in the XIV century a building was constructed above the grave of holy Arystan-bab, which, unfortunately, didn't came down to us.

The name of Arystan-bab is often met in Hoja Ahmet yassawi's writing – "Diuani Hikmet". It is interesting that the ninetieth hikmet is dedicated to the words-edifications of Arystan-bab, to which Hoja Ahmet yassawi refers, directing the following words to readers: "Arystan-bab said", "listen to the words-edifications of Arystan-bab". This hikmet is an evidence of Arystan-bab's holiness, who called on all people to saintly life, putting them in the right way. All valuable insights about Arystan-bab are mentioned exactly in this hikmet.

Arystan-bab's deeds, which became legend and example, are the only witting about him and, unfortunately, today we don't have any data about his life and activity. The hikmets of Hoja Ahmet yassawi describe the life of Arystan-bab in the following way: "His life was full of hardships and severities, his bednight was hummocky and rough". The writings of Karl Zaleman, Abuba-kir Divaev, Vasily Bartold, Mikhail Masson, Alexander Semenov, J. Spencer Trimingham, Irène **Mélikoff** provide some details of Arystan-bab. Arystan-bab was the greatest figure, who made a contribution to the Islamisation not only of Otrar surroundings, but the whole Turkic-Speaking world. In the Otrar region the mausoleum, hotel and other cultural institutions named after Arystan-bab are located. His burial is also located there.

YUSUF BALASSAGUNI (was born approximately in 1015-1016 years) – famous poet (akyn) of the Central Asia. The motherland of yusuf Balassaguni is Balassagun city (the other name is Kuzorda) in Semirechye.

Yusuf's father was poet (akyn) either. He sang and played kyuis in khan's palace in the capital of Karakhanids' state Balassagun. It is known that Yusuf's father turned his son to his lifework and

Yusuf began to serve in waiting. We have very little information about his life. He made a significant contribution to development of many spheres of science, such as mathematics, medicine, astronomy, astrology, art, literature, linguistics, etc. The name of yusuf Balassaguni is forever tied to the history of the world literature and culture thanks to his great writing-dastan (poem) "Kutadgu Bilig" ("The gratifying knowledge). This poem was donated to the state of Karakhanids' founder (942-1210 years) – "khan from khans" – Sulaiman Arslan (908-955 years). That's why khan by his own order titles Yusuf Balassaguni with the status of "Hasshadjib" – "the great vizir" which is identical to the present rank of the State Councilor.

Three variants of dastan (poem) are extant. The first one

which was written in 1439 year in the old Uyghur alphabet is located in Herat city (kept in the royal library in Vienna). The second variant was rewritten in Egypt in the first half of the XIV century in Arabic type (kept in Kediven's Fund of Cairene library). The third variant, which was found in Namangan city, was also written in Arabic type and considered to be the most complete variant of "Kutadgu Bilig". This manuscript is kept in the fund of the Institute of Oriental Studies of Tashkent city.

Among the manuscripts more than 600 poetic quotations were found, which were handed in the form of rubais – quatrains. Putting together the distinctive features of three found manuscripts, scientists could compile them into the full scientifically proven version of "Kutadgu Bilig" dastan.

The "Kutadgu Bilig" poem was created in the Middle Ages in a common for all Turkic-speaking nations' literature language, which was formed and functioned on a vast territory of the Kara-khanid Empire. The translation into Uzbek K. Kerimov made (1971 year), into Russian – N.grebnev and S. Ivanov (1983 year), into Kazakh – A.Egeubaev (1986 year), into Uyghur the poem was translated by several interpreters (1984 year). The "Kutadgu Bilig" poem in some specified sense played the role of constitution ("The law of forefathers") in peoples' life of that time.

HOJA AHMET YASSAWI (1093-1166 years) – scientist, holy man. It is considered that Hoja Ah-met yas-sawi was a descendent of the Hodge lineage (кожа) – the representatives of "white bone" – «ақ сүйек». His father was a famous in Ispidjab (nowadays Sayram city) holy man, descendent of

Azret Ali Sheikh Ibrahim. Mother – Aisha (popularly called Kara-shash ana); she was the daughter of Sheikh Mussa Hoja. Certain origins contain the information that Hoja Ahmet yassawi had a son – Ibrahim and a daughter – gauhar Hoshnaz.

Hoja Ahmet yassawi's lineage continued thanks to his daugh-ter gauhar. If in the IX century in such cities as Otyrar, Ispidjab, Balassagun, yassy, Sauran, Sagynak, Shash, Sutkent, Zhent, Kudur, Otluk, Ozkent and in other cities of Mawarannahr the activity of Islam companions had political nature, thus from the beginning of the X century on the way of Islam establishment the educational centers began to form and finally formed – madrasah, based on principles of spirituality and morality.

After the religious knowledge acquirement from Yusuf Hamadani in Bukhara, Sheikh Ahmet yassawi returned to Turkistan (yassy) and began to preach the Sufi religious ideas, which were widely spread in those times in the Central Asia.

The prime spiritual guide and teacher of Hoja Ahmet yassawi was Arystan-bab. In Kashifi's writing "Rashahat-ul ain-il hayat" it is narrated that Hoja Ahmet yassawi within 16 years was an ar-dent disciple and obedient of Arystan-bab, who taught him zahir sacraments (exotery) and batin (esotery) and explained him the meaning and significancy of these Islam revelations. The main work of Hoja Ahmet yassawi – "Divani Hikmet" also mentions his teacher Arystan-bab frequently. In "Divani Hikmet" the in-teresting facts and valuable data regarding culture, literature, history, ethnography, economy of Kazakh people from ancient times could be found. For the first time "Divani Hikmet" was published in 1878 in bookish form. Then it was republished in Istanbul, Kazan, Tashkent. One of these variants of 1901 was published by Tynyshtyk-uly especially for Kazakhs of Kazan.

Hoja Ahmet yassawi's apprentices were: the first is the son of Arystan-baba – Mansurata, the second – Saiydata Horezmi, the third – Suleyman Bakyrgani. The most famous and eminent in consequence became the third – Bakyrgani, popularly known as Hakimata (Kash-ifi, "Rashahat-ul ain-il hayat"). Regarding the apprentices of Hoja Ahmet yassawi, Mehmed Fuat Köprülü said the following: "In works of life and deeds of Sufies, along with Sufies of Iraq, Khorasan and Mawarannahr, Sufies' collective name was also mentioned – "Turkic Sheikhs", under which the Sheikhs of Sufi tariqah of Hoja Ahmet yassawi were implied.

In the end of the XIV century the famous emir Timur the lame built a mausoleum on site of Hoja Ahmet yassawi's burial in Turki-stan. Eventually Hoja Ahmet yassawi himself became a spiritual en-lightener of the Turkic nations, and his mausoleum – a small Mecca.

NIZAMI GANJAVI, Ilyas ibn Yu-suf Nizami (17.8.1141, gyanja city – 1209, lbid.) – Azerbaijanian poet. The main works were written in Persian. ganjavi is his pseud-onym. His father lived in Iran, then he moved to gyanja city, he educated son in traditions of Tur-kic nation. Nizami courageously criticized struggle for throne of the gov-ernors of Iran, Caucasus, Turan in the XI-XII centuries and praised the life of common people. His first writing – "Hamsa" ("quintuple") consisted of five poems (das-tans), such as: "The treasury of se-crets" (1173-80), "Hosrov and Shirin" (1181), "Mejnoun and leilah" (1188), "Seven beauties" (1197) and "Iskander-name" (1203).

From his writings the separate parts of lyrical song's collec-tion are extant. It is "Divan" which consists of 6 kasidas (kasida is an ode), 116 ghazels (ghazel is the lyric verses), 2 kitas (kita is a mono-rhyme form of poetry) and 30 rubais (rubais is a quatrain). Nizami's dastans differ by compositional construction, attractive-ness of story line, beauty of language and high idea of justice. "The treasury of secrets" is religiously philosophic poem, which consists of 20 passi, in which the poet appeals governors to justice and to become defenders of their people. If the poem "Mejnoun and leilah" was written by the virtue of the ancient Arabian legend story line, thus in the basis of "Seven beauties" the legend of Bahram gur shah was implied. The poem about Bahram gur was based on his seven wives' narratives, who described the strug-gle of emperor with evil and his devotion to justice. In his book "Iskander-name" or "glory" the poet represents Iskander in char-acter of wise and just emperor. Nizami's writings made a massive impact on creative work of many Eastern poets. So, in the XIII century a lot of works appeared which echoed his poems. Some of such poets, for example: Amir Husrau Dehleui, Alisher Nawai, Ahmad Jami and others. If in 1383 year the Kipchak poet Kutba from Sarai Berke wrote "Hosrov and Shirin" poem, thus the ger-man poet goethe wrote "The Empress Turandot" poem, based upon the poem of "Seven beauties".

Nizami's poems were widely spread in Kazakh steppe from the moment of their creation. In the ground of "Iskander" poem of Abai Kunanbaev and in Shakarim's creative work the story lines of Nizami's works are reflected.

MAKHMUD KASHGARI – Turkic scientist, author of famous writing "Divani lugat at-turk" ("Col-lection of Turkic dialects"). Full name – Makhmud ibn al-Hussein ibn Mohammed. Place of birth – Bar-skan city on the shore of Issyk Kul lake of present Kirghizia (accord-ing to certain origins on the Shore of Chu River).

The father of Makhmud was a famous leader, emir of Barskan, in consequences of Kashgar, which became a political and cultural center of Karahanids' state. Here Makhmud acquired his education and lived for long years. The exact dates of his birth and death are not known. There is no any information about his life, neither in researches nor in sources of those times. It is known that in order to complement knowl-edge received in Kashgaria he set forth to Bukhara, Nishapur and Baghdad, and perfectly acquired the knowledge of Arabic and Persian languages. He is well-known as a gifted philologer, chronographer, ethnographer and geographer of his time.

Makhmud Kashgari was the first linguist who created a course book of the Turkic language, the scientist who cor-rected grammar and developed philology of the Turkic world, increasing the status of language.

In the history of Turkic languages study he was the first who applied the method of comparison and formed the basis of dia-lectology of the Turkic languages. This comparative analysis of the Turkic languages in the quality of researching common method formed some kind of a single school for all Eastern linguists. In "Divani lugat at-turk" a rich Turkomans' history, geographic location, literature and art, peculiarities of ethnol-ogy are discovered. It reflects the information about histori-cal figures, scientists, writers of those times, original poems and proverbs and sayings of the Turkic nations. Moreover, Makhmud Kashgari compiled a full map of the Turkic world of those times with indication of all new large cities locations, such as Kashgar, Balassagun, Taraz, Ekioguz and others, and communities including the names of ancient cities of the Turkic world. That's why it could be called some kind of the first en-cyclopedic guide. A special attention in Makhmud Kashgari's writings a surviving map attracts, as the oldest in the world. His works were translated into Uzbek, Kazakh and Uyghur.

GENGHIS KHAN (Tur-kic – genghis Khan, Mon-golian – genghis Khaan, the real name – Temujin) the first founder of centralized state in Asia, an outstanding military and State figure of his time. He was born in the family of the head of ancient lineage bahadur yessugey. Thanks to his military talent and parlaying weakness and separate-ness of his enemies in 1183-1204 years in struggle for power he cut to pieces the troops of the head of Merkit clan – Tohta and clan of Nayman Tayan khan, capturing the vast areas, and became a mogul of a variety of tribal unions.

As a result of these victories and a row of economic mea-sures performance, during the quriltai (statutory meeting) in the year (1206) of Barys (snow leopard) the steppe aristocrats acclaimed him the great khan of all tribes genghis Khan (from Turkic word "sea" – "теңіз").

Genghis Khan was aclaimed the second khan after his father yes-sugey. He was acclaimed as genghis Khan in order he pro-tected the Mongols.

In internal politics he strived to compel the state manage-ment to one center, divided the Turkic Mongolian tribes on military administrative units "thousandths" (because upon the request of khan each of them was obliged to provide 1000 warriors). These units together with their pastures as property genghis Khan passed to his relatives and noyans (command-ers).

The great khan organized the written proceedings. In 1206 year he confirmed the rules of common right "The great yas-sak" (trib-ute paid off in furs). In order to suppress outbreaks inside the country he established the personal guards (keshich) consisting of 1000 people.

He established the strict army control, for slightest petty offenses the guilty and hen-hearted soldiers were condemned to death. In military strategy and tactics for enemy defeating Genghis Khan applied the following methods: detailed survey, cutting enemy to pieces, sudden attack, leading enemy into error by means of entrapment deployment from special forces, manoeuvres' performance by means of numerous horse cavalry, etc.

In 1200 year Temujin together with Tugyryl-khan confront-ed Tayshauyts. During the campaign he was wounded by an arrow to shoulder. The majority of Tayshauyts were killed in battle, and a part of them yield themselves prisoner. This was the first big victory of Temujin.

In 1202 year Temujin committed a campaign against the Ta-tars. Before the campaign he declared a prohibition of trophies' sharing during the military operations. In vicious fight Temujin got a victory. On the morrow of the battle he convened a council. There the decision was made to kill all Tatars with height below the belt, except children.

To this decision Temujin came after murders of Mongolian governors (including his father yessugey).

In 1207-11 years genghis Khan conquered Siberia and Eastern Turkestan (Buryats, yakuts, Oyrats, Kirghiz, Uigurs).

In 1211 year he opposed against Qin Dynasty, in 1215 year he captured Beijing city. In 1217 year the Northern China fully passed into the hands of genghis Khan. And in 1219 year the Korean kingdom bended the knee to him.

The Mongolian troops' campaigns to Northern China and Korean kingdom were leaded by the great chieftain – Emir Mukyli gauin Zhalairi. After China the part of genghis Khan troops conquered Semirechye in 1218-1219 years, and in 1219-1221 years – Kazakhstan and Central Asia.

The captured lands genghis Khan divided on uluses (khanates) and distributed between his children. In possession of Jochi the territories from Irtysh to Ural Mountains were in-cluded, on south of the Caspian Sea – the surroundings of the Aral Sea, among Central Asian areas – the Northern Khoresm and Syr-Darya coast;

Chagatai: Mawarannahr, Semirechye and Kashgaria; Ogedei: the Western Mongolia and the region of Tarbagatay.

Then the father's ulus – Mongolia itself was passed down to them. Genghis Khan died during the one of invasions to Tanguts.

The successors of Genghis Khan continued his military campaigns with little intervals.

SULTAN BAYBARS, Baybars son of jamak (1223–1277) – the fourth sultan of Mamluk State, who governed in Egypt (1260–1277), of Bakhrit dynasty descent of Turkic tribe. In historical writings he was called Baybars. He was of Kip-chaks lineage descent. However there is no shared vision about Kip-chak Baybars origin, some sources point out that he was Kipchak from Khoresm, Derbent, the other refer to his Mangistau roots.

The last researches of Baybars genealogy erode differences of his origin and produce arguments in favor of his roots from Kip-chak tribe of the famous lineage of Berish, he was the great family's descendent. In the popular romance "Baybars", which ranks with "The Thousand and One Nights" of Arab countries, the exact names of Baybars's parents are given – the father is Jamak and the mother is Aynek.

In youth Baybars have been sold into slavery on Damascus's bazar for 800 dirhems, subsequently to his belonging to new owner Aydakin Bundukdari he was named after al-Bundukdari. Thanks to his special features Baybars was noted by the Egypt sultan – Salikh Najumiddin from Ayub lineage and was appointed to chief of one of the parts of his personal lifeguard. Thus Baybars became al-Salikhi by the merit of his new benefactor. In campaign against crusaders Baybars governed the Egyptian army. After Egypt conquest he becomes an Egypt governor under the name of Baybars al-Bundukdari al-Salikhi. After getting into the saddle Baybars directs all his army's forces and power on counterattack against Crusades.

Sultan Muzaffar Sayfuddin Kutuz proclaimed Baybars the viktor of his army and directed him to Syria to repel the Mon-gols' onsurge. In the battle over Ain Jalut the Mamelukes under the chieftaincy of Baybars won victory over the Mongols. From 1265 year he conquered the fortresses of crusaders-franks one by one. After that he made march to the Small Armenia (1267 year), against the Seljuks of the Small Asia and gradually put them under control.

Baybars spent a lot of efforts for madrasahes construction, reconstruction of causeways and fairways. Till nowadays in Cairo a mosque stays which was built by his order and calls "The Mosque of Baybars".

In 1277 year Baybars was killed by his vizir who poisoned him. His body was buried in Damascus on the Bab-al-Barid burying place. Sultan Baybars could turn the state of Mame-lukes into the great power and protect Egypt and Syria from Mongolian invasion and Crusades.

EMIR TIMUR (TIMUR THE LAME, TAMERLANE), years of life 1336-1405 – Central Asian chieftain and conqueror. Emir Timur is of Barlas lineage descent, the empire of Timurids founder, was born not far from Kesh city (nowadays Shahrisabz in Kashkardaryinskaya oblast of Uzbekistan). Barlas lineage re-lated to

Turkic-speaking tribes, descendents of which nowadays belong to Uzbek nation. With Genghis Khan's troops invasion the Barlases moved from Mongolia to Central Asia.

Timur was the beg, the leader of one branch of Barlas. In the following he drew over the rest begs on his side. He was a ringleader of a rebellion against the governors of Mogulistan – khans of Chagatai Khanate. There has been talk that in youth Timur headed a band of robbers, the main craft of whos was robbery and grabbing of caravans, which moved alone the great Silk Road. He was a great beg and could create an in-dependent state of Chagatai descendents. Not being a direct descendent of genghis Khan he couldn't pretend to a title of khan, but bore a title of emir. For many years emir Timur con-ducted war against Toktamysh khan.

Emir Timur, Kutbuddin Timur gurkap, Sahib Kyran Agzam Zhanat Makan (9.4.1336, Hoja-Ilgar Kesh, born in Turkistan – 18.2.1405, died in Samarkand) – chieftain, State figure. The son of beg Taragay, biy (judge) of Barlas tribe. Initially Timur the lame was a governor of Kashgaria (1361).

In 70-s years of the XIV century he became globally famous by his outstanding features of governor and conqueror. In the Ottoman Empire and Central Asia was known under the name of Timur the lame, the Iranians knew him as Timur-i-leng, the Europeans – Tamerlane. Emir Timur compelled such states as Khoresm (1372), Eastern Turkestan (1376), Herat (1381), Khorasan (1381), Kandahar (1383), Sultania (South Azerbai-jan, 1384), Tabriz (1384). Iran and Afghanistan also entirely resign to his control.

After numerous overwhelming campaigns he crushed the golden Horde. Emir Timur in 1370-90-s years using smart a friction between khan Tokhtamysh and yedige, made more than 10 destructive campaigns to Desht-i-Kypchak, Ak Orda and Mogulistan. The crush of the golden Horde by Timur the Lame created favorable conditions and promoted independence getting for Russian state. In 90-s years Azerbaijan, Dagestan, gurcustan (georgia), Iraq entered the state of emir Timur. In 1398 year India was conquered. The Mamelukes of Syria and lebanon (Palestine) were compelled. The other countries of Western Asia also admitted the power of emir Timur. In sum-mer of 1402 year during the battle near Ankara emir Timur crushed the main military forces of the Ottoman Empire, cap-turing the Turkic sultan – Bayazid. In result of continuous wars emir Timur built up a powerful empire – the state of Timurids. Its total area reached 14 mil.km.^{2}. Emir Timur died in 1405 year in Otrar city during the march to China. He lived 68 years, 10 months, 9 days. His mortal remains were buried in mausoleum of gur-Emir in Samarkand. Emir Timur had four sons: Jihangir (1356-1376), Emir Sheikh (1356-1394), Miran Shah (1366-1408), Shahrukh (1377-1447). Emir Timur's de-scendents were the great scientist Ulugh Beg (1394-1449), the Moghols' em-pire founder - Babur (1483-1530).

Emir Timur left on Kazakh soil after himself an imperish-able memory – the sacred mausoleum of Hoja Ahmet yassawi.

ULUGH BEG *(Mirzo Ulug'bek),* (1394-1443   years). On March 22, 1394 year in emir Timur's lineage a boy was born – Mohammed Taragay. After a while he was provided with a second name-pseudonym Ulugh Beg. His father Shahrukh was the third son of emir Timur. Being some time a gov-ernor, Shahrukh promoted the science development. From childhood Ulugh Beg was keen on poetry, history, astronomy and mathematics. His devotions were the results of travels with the great grandfather Timur through countries with rich culture and de-veloped science.

Thus, Ulugh Beg still in early age toured such big centers as Armenia, Azerbaijan, georgia, Iran, Turkey, Afghanistan. Addi-tionally to Ulugh Beg's becoming scientist the collected by his father Shahrukh large library in Samarkand promoted.

Ulugh Beg had an intimate knowledge of the Classical greek sci-entists' works, such as Plato, Hipparchus, Ptolemy. At the same time he learned in-and-out the works of outstanding sci-entists of Central Asia, who lived and created before him, such as Khoresmi, Farabi, Ferghani, Biruni, Ibn Sina, Nasir al-Din al Tusi.

However his surrounding basically ruling upper circles of society didn't support young Ulugh Beg in his beginnings as scientist. After Timur's death his empire moldered on two parts. The first is Khorasan, the second is Mawarannahr. The second part of empire acclaimed still young 15 years old Ulugh Beg its governor. It is noteworthy that many cities of the present South Kazakhstan region (Otyrar, Taraz and others) belonged to Ulugh Beg exactly. The court vassals did their best in order to increase Ulugh Beg's interest to the military arts and diplomatic activity study, trying to suppress the grounds of scientist and direct him on his great grandfather's deeds continuation. Failing to coun-ter their influence in the beginning of his governing Ulugh Beg made several marches (1425-1427 years), some of which had a successful outcome. In such a manner he proved that there was the blood of warrior and wise chieftain in his veins.

Nevertheless Ulugh Beg devoted much attention to the cul-tural objects' construction – beautiful buildings in the cities within his control: Samarkand, gijduvan, Bukhara, finishing the construction of partially constructed buildings which were began by his grandfather Timur. His dedication to art and thirst of knowledge grew every day and instead of conduction of mur-derous wars he strived to cognize the world sacraments and to distill the secrets of universe.

The most important his doing in the function of politician was the construction of astronomical observatory in Samarkand. This sublimed Ulugh Beg as a scientist, who performed a great feat for the sake of future. This observatory wasn't a whim of a giddy-headed governor ravenous for fame, but, conversely, be-came a great gift for science from a scientist who could foresee the importance of created for future of descendents.

The construction of observatory and its provision of all re-quired instruments and equipment were charged to Al-Kashi. The observatory was constructed within three years, but served only 27-28 years. Thanks to these scientists the observatory al-lowed to make experiments and researches of astronomy.

ALISHER NAVOI (Nizameddin Mir Alisher) – the great poet, thinker, statesman of the Turkic nations. He was born on February 9, 1441 year in Herat city. After the death of his father 12 years old Navoi was taken under wing by Babur. In 15 years Navoi was already known as poet, who wrote in Persian and Turkic. He studied logic, philosophy, mathematics in Herat, Mashhad, Samarkand.

He learned the works of his predecessors Firdausi, Nizami, Dehlavi, Khoresmi, Saif Sarai and contemporaries such as Atai, Sakkaki, lutfi, Jami.

Serving creative work he wrote the works which entered the collection of "Hamsa" books: "The righteous confusion" (1483), "Farkhad and Shirin", "Mejnoun and leilah", "Seven planets" (1484), "The wall of Iskander" (1485). In the XV cen-tury Navoi's writings were published and performed not only in Mawarannahr and Khorasan, but in Iran, Azerbaijan, Eastern Turkestan, India, Egypt, later his works were found in the libraries of Europe and

America. From the middle of the XIX century the poet's writings began to attract the attention of Eastern scientists.

Navoi's writings were translated into many languages. The selected works were published twice in bookish form in Ka-zakh (1948, 1968). In 1950 the novel of Aybek "Navoi" was written in Kazakh. The Kazakh scientists also made their con-tribution in Navoi's creation research (Mukhtar Auezov, yes-magambet Iss-mailov, Rakhmankul Berdibaev, K. Seydekha-nov). An anniversary of the great scientist was celebrated in 1948 and 1969 years under Soviet Union.

In 1488-1504 years he wrote a lot of works regarding the following spheres: historical biographic ("The history of Kings of Iran", "The biography of Sayid Hasan Ardash-er", "The biography of Pahlavan Muhammad"), didactically philosophic works ("The language of birds", "The breath of love"), literary- theoretic ("The scales of sizes"), linguistic ("The quarrel of two languages"), socioeconomic ("Vak-fiya"), religiously common ("The history of prophets and wisemen", "The light of Isla-mism", "The meeting of sophis-ticated men"). He combined into the collection on Persian 12 thousand song-rhymes lines under the name of "Divan Fani". The poet died on January 3, 1501 year in native city. The great Abai, inspired by Navoi's poetry, continued his creative heritage. The poet Nessipbek Aytov published a book in Kazakh consisting of ghazels of Alisher Navoi.

MOHAMMED HAYDAR DULA-TI, (1499-1551) – outstand-ing statesman, famous chronogra-pher, litterateur. The descendent of emir from ancient Dulat lineage from Semirechye, Mohammed Haydar Dulati is the author of the works

"Tarih-i-Rashidi" and "Ja-hannama", which concluded the valuable data of Mogulistan and near-border states. His full name is Dulat Mohammed Husseynuly Myrza Mohammed Haydar.

His forefathers were the out-standing statesmen of South East Kazakhstan and Eastern Turkistan, which were the territories of the state Mogulistan. On the areas of their uluses they occupied the posts of begs, tarkhans and governed their legatary domain – Manglay-Suben. His natu-ral father Husseyn was a son-in-law of Moghol khan – Zhunis and governed in Tashkent.

In struggle for power he was killed by Abulhair-khan's grand-son Mohammed Shaybani-khan. His mother Hub Nigar-khanym was the daughter of Zhunis khan. According to his mother's lin-eage Mohammed Haydar Dulati was a cousin of the great Empire of Mughals' founder in India – Zahiraddin Mohammed Babur. Af-ter the death of his father Mohammed Haydar was under care of Babur for some time. After a lapse of time at the Babur's initiative he went in tow to the other cousin – Said-khan. He participated in the war against Abu-Bakr from Kashgar organized by Said-khan. gaining the reputation of polymath, Mohammed Haydar did the work of army and state, and also educated the son of Said-khan and hereditary prince – Sultan Rashid.

In 1533 year after the death of Said-khan, feeling threatening danger and impending death from his educatee's hand, Moham-med Haydar was forced to leave the native land of his forefathers and go to India. There he fought together with the son of Babur khan Humayun against Sher-khan. For the second time conquers Kashmir by peaceful means and occupies awrang. The great Mo-guls governed Kashmir from 154 to 1551 years. In Kashmir the famous writing of Moham-med Haydar "Tarih-i-Rashidi" was cre-ated.

Mohammed Haydar Dulati left very valuable information re-garding the medieval history of Kazakhs. "Tarih-i-Rashidi" con-tains a lot of data about the Kazakh khanate formation, which narrated the po-litical events in Semirechye and Eastern Desht-i-Kypchak, highlight-ed the big political events in Mogulistan, told about the wars with

Shaybani khan. "Tarih-i-Rashidi" is some kind of encyclopedic guide in which the valuable data are collect-ed and the historical events are described of the countries of Cen-tral Asia, Eastern Turkestan, India, and also the complete history of Mogulistan and political processes which happened in the state.

Dulati knew very well the history of Kazakh khanate and Mo-gulistan formation, at the same time, he was well informed about the political events and participated in them figures of that time. He himself was a bystander of many described in his book events. Possi-ble, that's why he left a lot of reliable information about the history of Kazakhs of the Middle Ages, especially regarding Dulat tribe. The writing also contains wide information about the his-tory of Kazakh khanate formation and establishment, the follow-ing stages of its de-velopment, relations of Kazakhs with Kirghiz and Uzbeks.

Mohammed Haydar Dulati was buried in dependent to him in his time Kashmir, in "Mazar-i Salatin" burying place in the main city Srinagar (Sri Nagar – the holy city). The quincentenary of the scien-tist was celebrated under the frame of UNESCO in 1999 year in "The Mausoleum of Sultans". "Tarih-i-Rashidi" was translated into many world languages.

ABYLAY-KHAN – (1711-1780). His real name is Abilmansur. In the fifth degree his forefather was yes-sim-khan, who gave fully completed central-ized state structure to Kazakh khanate ("Есимханнын ескі жолы", i.e. "The ancient way of khan yes-sim"), in the fourth – Zhangir-khan "Salkam", who distinguished himself as chieftain and batyr in battles with

Jungars. Ablay is the name of Abilmansur's grandfather, known as cruel monomachist.

In its turn from Abylay-khan the two lineages of his grand-children – Kenesary and Chingis begin, who made a U-turn in relation to the imperial policy of kingdom. If we'll search more remote ancestors of Abylay khan, thus his genealogy could be linked to the younger son of Jochi – Tuqay-Timyr. Without such genealogy, i.e. if he wasn't Chingisid, he couldn't be a supreme khan of all Kazakhs (even Timur didn't call himself khan).

The years of Abylay khan's life are 1711-1780. In childhood he was an orphan, there is a fact that under the name of Sabalak in 10 versts from Tashkent in Karakamys region in 1725 year he grazed camels of Tole-bi. Abilmansur became popularly known at the age of 20 when after entering militia organized by Abul-mambet (also descendent of yessim-khan and Zhangir-khan), who united all three zhuzes for protection from Jungars, under the battle cry "Abylay" won the Jungarian batyr Sharysh.

After the victorious fight Abulmambet called Abilmansur over: "Who are you and what is the cry "Abylay" you have?". Abilmansur: "I am a grandson of Abylay and by means of cry (uran) called to his spirit". Then Abulmambet embraced him with emotion and referred to people with the following words: "Some time I heard that there is an only son of Baky Vali, so that is he before us, if you'll approve thus he should become the great khan". After the approval from the side of 90 the best representatives of three zhuzes Abilmansur got elected the great khan. But though Abulmambet passed the khanate to Abylay with his own hand, properly complying with formalities of ris-ing on white felt, he sits on throne at the age of 25.

This situation was brightly described by Bukhar-zhirau: "In twenty years you sail up into the clouds like a brave hawk, high and proudly your star raised, luck and success accompanied your deeds. In 25 years a bird of happiness sat on year head, enthroning you". The traditions changed with him, when the great khan kept headquarters in the Elder Zhuz, at the same time governing it directly. Abylay khan decided that as the main bur-den of war against Jungars is bore by the Middle Zhuz, thus it is logical to leave the Middle Zhuz governing in the trust of the great khan and to place headquarters there. Bringing himself to this step, Abylay khan, rendering all the signs of respect and honour to Tole bi, as to spiritual leader of the Elder Zhuz, ob-tained from him consent for khan's headquarters location in the Middle Zhuz. But even more important than personal courage and his ability to unite the authoritative leaders of zhuzes, was Abylay's activity as diplomatist and politician, who found the line of balance between two large neighbors – China and Rus-sia, and following the aggressive threat removal from the side of Jungars to its logical end.

After the crushing defeat of the last from the side of China in 1757 year Abylay was not slow to take advantage of this situ-ation and, as a matter of fact, finished the destruction of Jun-gars. His diplomatic mission to Beijing in 1757 year was com-monsensical, where he went personally with Abulmambet's son – Abulfaiz and came into Celestial Emperor's allegiance as a "vassal nawab", what actually safes his full independence, but adds an obligation to pay the set tribute. In 1765 year he con-cluded the agreement with Russia, but he didn't accept the deci-sion of the imperial government from October 22, 1778 year as lawful – to confer him the title of the great khan and didn't came to the grand ceremony, where according to scenario he should be granted with corresponding act, fur coat and sabre.

Abylay considered that on the title of khan he was chosen by people and that is why he is not obliged to swear allegiance to Russians. If even China didn't trench on his khan's dignity, thus the ceremony of oath to Russians infringes on the Kazakh nation's sovereignty – that was the position of Abylay.

As a matter of fact he could unite in one whole all the Kazakh soils, including Tashkent, and the following plans he integrated with cul-tural economic advance, considered union with Rus-sians as the basis of Kazakhs' transfer to settled agriculture and trade activity. These plans of Abylay met resistance. As before, the centrifugal grounds, impacting the Kazakh nation's fate, affected ruinously. As far back as during the military campaigns of 1725-1726 years it was possible to do away with Jungarian threat, if Abulhair not left a battlefield and not came to North-West.

Abylay khan is well-known not only as the powerful khan, but as a gifted kyuishi either. He is the author of such writ-ings as "Ақ толкын", "Ала байрақ", "«Бұлан жігіт", "Дүние калды", "Жетім торы", "Қайран елім", "Қара жорға", "Қоржынқакпай", "Майда жел", "Сары бура", "Шаңды жорық".

He moved to the Elder Zhuz and in December of 1780 year dies in Tashkent. Abylay was buried in the holy place of Kazakh nation – the mausoleum of Hoja Ahmet yassawi.

MAKHTUMKULI – Turk-menian poet of the XVIII century wrote under the pseudonym "Fra-gi". The years of birth and death are not known, but there are a lot of data about him in written ori-gins and folk tales. By their refer-ence we can suppose that Makh-tumkuli was born in the end of the 1720-s years or in the beginning of the 1730-s years in Turkmeni-stan, the region of Kara-kala. His father was the famous poet and religious thinker Dowlet-Mammet Azady (1700–1760), who cause a serious impact on son.

He grew on the riversides of gurgen and Atrek, in places where for a long time the Turkmen lived (Makhtumkuli him-self descended from goklen tribe). Initially he went to village school, where his father worked as a teacher, but dowered with brilliant talents and insistence, Makhtumkuli completed a course of primary school earlier and began to help his father in housekeeping, tended cattle, cultivate land.

There is no information how many works Makhtumkuli wrote (autographs were not saved, even the titles of poems published in collections were not given by the author, they were entitled by compilers). Nowadays the volume of his writ-ings counts more than four hundred units (rhymes, small lyric and epic poems), the total amount of which exceeds ten thou-sand versicles.

Many ideas and philosophies in Makhtumkuli's works were drawn from writings of his father, who was not only the au-thor of lyric rhymes and didactic poem "Behisht-nama", but of unique for Turkmenian literature tractate in verse "Vagzi-Azad" (1753–1754). The thoughts of happy and just state establishment, ex-pressed in this tractate, were developed by Makhtumkuli. He paid a lot of attention to the questions of patriotism and love to native people; also he used strongly marked satirical motives, which were reflected, for example, in the rhyme "Please", which became an in-tegral part of folklore. Makhtumkuli's writings are popular and ren-dered by musicians and storytellers, baksy (thanks largely to them the mas-ter's rhymes were saved) thanks largely to a new poetic language, which was chosen by him.

He refused difficult for understanding literary language, which abounded with barbarisms, archaisms (arabisms, far-sisms, cha-gataisms). His rhyme was close to folk speech, it wasn't built on Arabian and Persian metrics, but it was based on popular syllabic style. This is precisely why Makhtumkuli's works were acquired by people; significant part of his verses became proverbs and sayings. At the same time the peculiar to Eastern poetry relative abstractive views are a huge part of his poems.

As legend has it and according to travelers' stating Makhtum-kuli couldn't stand the scenes of misery which happened on his native land and died in the end of the 1780-s or in the be-ginning of the 1790-s. He was buried on Dovlet-Mamed Azadi burying place near his father. The graves located in Northern Khorasan in Ak-To-kay serve as the place of worship and embarkation.

CHOKAN   CHINGISOVICH VALI KHANOV – the great Kazakh scientist- Orientalist, historian, eth-nographer, geographer,   folklorist, in-terpreter, journalist, traveler was born in 1835 year in the Kushmurun fortress close to Kostanay. Chokan's childhood passed in patrimonial es-tate of his grandmother Aiganym in Syrymbet. Chokan's father is Chingiz, aghasultan, grandfather is Valikhan.

His great-grandfather was Abylay khan. At the age of 12 Chokan enrolled at the Siberian Cadet corps in Omsk city, which was considered in that time the best educational foundation in Siberia. In the Cadet corps Chokan learned enthusiastically, and in a matter of two-three years caught up and surpassed his age mates in knowledge. In Chokan's world view formation a signifi-cant part played his friend and classmate g. Potanin, teachers N.F. Kostyletskiy, litterateur V.T. lo-bodovskiy. In 1852 year Chokan acquainted with Orientalist I.N. Berezin and at his request wrote an article "Khan's iarlyks of Tohtamysh". This was his first scientific work.

Already when Chokan was 14-15 years old teachers told that he will become a scientist. In 1853 year Chokan graduated the Cadet corps and in the rank of cornet went into service as an aide-de-camp of the governor-general of Western Siberia g.H. gas-fort. young and smart beyond his age educated Kazakh was noted by Russian intellectuals, who by some quirk of fate lived in Omsk, writers and poets Apollon N. Maykov, Fe-dor M. Dostoevskiy, Vasily S. Kurochkin, Orientalist scholar Karl K. gutkovskiy and others. Chokan Valikhanov took par-ticipation in the fate of exiled writer-petrashevets, the future classic of Russian literature Fedor M. Dostoevskiy and pro-moted his premature release from exile.

Serving the governor-general Chokan studied history, eth-nography, literature and culture of the Central Asian nations, travelled around the Central Kazakhstan, Zhetysu, Tarbaga-tay, collected materials and wrote articles about the history of steppe areas, customs and traditions, religions of Kazakhs. In 1856-57 years Chokan Valikhanov made scientific exploratory and ethnographic expedition to Zailiyskiy Kirghiz and to auls of the Elder Zhuz, Kuldja, where he got acquainted to the his-tory of Dzungaria. In these trips he wrote the well-known "The Dzungaria reviews", "The Sketches of Kirghiz", about "the genres of the Kazakh native poetry", "The Diary of a trip to Issyk Kul", "The Stories and the legends of the Big Kirghiz-kaysatsk Horde" and other works, which became the basis of completely new light on Kazakhs, their culture and litera-ture. These sketches and articles were highly appreciated by the Russian scientists.

The other result of these trips was the fact that Chokan got acquainted to some chapters of the great Kyrgyz epic "Manas", wrote them, analyzed, translated into Russian, showed that "Manas" is an outstanding work of the Eastern oral tradi-tion of Kyrgyz folklore.

In 1858-1859 years Chokan made the main trip in his short life to Kashgar. Under the name of Alimbay merchant, shav-ing off the head and changing look, Chokan together with his companions got across to Kashgar, where lived five months. He was able to unravel a mystery of the English traveler Ad-olf Schlagintweit's death, who came to Kashgar from India for several months before him and who was killed from the hand of local feudal yakub-bek.

Chokan drove out of Kashgar many interesting statistical and historical data, which were published in "The Sketches of The Russian geographical Society" in type of two articles "The Dzungaria reviews" and "The Description of Kashgar or Altyshaar». Altyshaar, or correctly Altyshahar, i.e. "The six ci-ties", in those times was the name of the Eastern Turkistan, an unknown to the European geographical science state.

Upon his return from Kashgar to Omsk, Chokan was met as a hero, who researched terra incognita; he was encouraged and sent to Saint Petersburg, where he had a meeting with empire, who distinguished his merits to the Fatherland. Unfortunately, in Saint Petersburg Chokan was only few months and by reason of illness went back to native places. After his return to steppe, Chokan decided to retire from service and even came forward as a candidate to the head of a volost, in order after becoming a governor, to try to better the lot of his people. But, unfortu-nately, the local authorities garbled the election results... Cho-kan, offended by injustice, left to South to his relative Sultan Tezek, where died after a while from aggravated tuberculosis.

In 1904 year the Russian geographical Society published the book of Chokan Valikhanov and in its introduction acad-emician Nikolay I. Vesselovskiy wrote the following: "like a bright mete-or flashed above the field of orientalism the de-scendent of Kazakh khans and at the same time the Russian army officer Chokan Chingisovich Valikhanov. The Russian Orientalists solidly admitted him as a phenomenal figure and waited from him the great and important revelations of the Turkic nations' fate, but his untimely demise shut us out from hope..." For a short life Chokan Valikhanov was able to write the significant works. His literary and scientific creations compose of five voluminous tomes.

ABAI KUNANBAEV – the great poet, writer, public man, founder of the modern Kazakh written literature, reformer of culture in spirit of approximation with Russian and European cul-tures on the basis of enlightened liberal Islam. Abai was born on August 10, 1845 year in the Ch-ingisian Mountains of Semipala-tinsk region (according to present administrative division) from one of four wives of Kunanbay, the elder sultan of Kark-aralinsk of the county prikaz.

Abai's family was hereditary aristocratic, his grandfather Oskenbay and great-grandfather Irgizbay dominated in their lineage as governors and biys. In the way of fireside comfort and home education he was lucky, because both his mother Ulzhan and grandmother Zere were extremely charming and gifted women. In an easy state of mind of his mother precisely given by his father name Ibragim were changed onto endear-ing Abai, which means "circumspect, thoughtful". Under this name he lived all his life and became famous.

Beginning in early childhood initiation to oral folk arts and home schooling with mullah Abai continued his education in ma-drasah of Akhmed-Riza imam. In equal measure he studied in Russian school and to the end of five year training he began to write verses. From 13 years old age Kunanbay began to fit Abai to an administrative activity of genearch. He was forced to penetrate into the intergeneric quarrels, squabble, intrigues, and gradually he received disappointment with administrative and political activities, what resulted his withdrawal from it at the age of 28 and complete engagement with self-cultivation. But only to 40 year he realized his mission of poet and citizen, in particular, putting under the verse "The Summer" his name (earlier he ascribe his writings to his friend Kokpay Dzhan-tassov). At that moment a significant im-pulse in discovering the Abai's great abilities made the exiled Rus-sians: yevgeny P. Mikhaelis, Nifont I. Dolgopolov, Severin gross. Abai's appeal-ing to the Russian culture, which suffered in the XIX century its period of "Storm and Stress" in literature and art, was more than natural, because in oriental traditions the poetic word was appreciated very high.

The poetry of Pushkin, lermontov, goethe and Byron was close to Abai. In his translations into Kazakh Abai subtly got a spirit of poems across and adopted them to mental outlook of his congeners.

MUSTAFA KEMAL ATATURK; gazi Mustafa Kemal-pasha (Turkish Mustafa Kemal Atatürk; 1881 – November 10, 1938) – Ottoman and Turkish re-former, politician, states-man and commander; founder and the first leader of the Republican People's Party of Turkey; the first president of the Republic of Turkey, founder of pres-ent Turkish state. Makes the list of 100 the most learnt figures in the history. The pseudonym Kemal he received in military academy for quantitative skills.

The name Ataturk (father of the Turks) was provided to him by the great national assembly of Turkey in 1933. He acquired an ed-ucation in Thessaloniki, then in military academy and gen-eral Staff Academy in Istanbul and obtained a rank of captain and an ap-pointment to Damascus. He used his status in army for political agitation. In the period between 1904 and 1908 or-ganized sever-al secret societies for fight against corruption in government and army. During the revolution in 1908 was di-vided in opinion with

the leader of the young Turks – Enver Bey and withdrew from political activities. He participated in the Italo-Turkish war of 1911-
1912 and in the Second Balkan war of 1913. During the World War
I commanded Ottoman forces, which defended Dardanelles. After
the war he didn't admit capitulation and division of the Ottoman
Empire ac-cording to Sevr treaty of peace. After the greek armed
forces landing in Izmir in 1919 Ataturk organized the national re-
sist-ance movement throughout the whole Anatolia. The relations
between Anatolia and sultanic government in Istanbul were severed. In 1920 in Ankara Ataturk was chosen a chairman of the now
great national assembly.

Ataturk recreated army, expelled greeks from Asia Minor,
forced the countries of Entente to sign more just lausanne
agreement (1923), annihilated sultanate and caliphate, found-ed
the Republic (1923). Ataturk was elected the first presi-dent in
Turkey in 1923 and ran for office again in 1927, 1931 and 1935. He
conducted the policy of Turkic state and society modernization on a
Western model, reformed the system of education and eliminated
the Institutes of Islamic law.

After several attempts of outbreaks he was forced to dis-solve
the oppositional Progressive Republican party (and in 1930
the Free Republican Party, which replaced it) and to switch
onto more authoritarian methods of governance, necessary for
efficient reforms implementation in tradition-al Turkish society.
Thanks to Ataturk in 1928 in Turkey the gender equality was acclaimed, women got electoral rights. In the same year instead of
Arabic alphabet the latin was implemented, and in 1933 – the
family names on a Western model. In economy he carried on a
policy of nationalization and foundation on a national capital. The
external policy of Ataturk was directed onto the full independence
getting. Tur-key entered the league of Nations and established
amicable relations with neighbors, first of all with greece and
USSR. Ataturk died in Istanbul on November 10, 1938.

GABDULLA MUHAMED-GAR-IFOVICH TUQAY (1886 – 1913) – Tatarian national poet, liter-ary critic, publicist, public man and translator. Mir-zhakip Dulatov and E. Buyrin, in Soviet time Zhakan Syz-dykov, Tursynkhan Ab-drakhmanova and others were the first who trans-lated the songs of Tuqay into Kazakh. Mukhtar Auezov, Sabit Mu-kanov, Temirgali Nurtazin, Saydil Talz-ha-nov, Zhakan Syzdykov, Berkut Iskakov and others wrote articles on the basis of their researches of Tuqay's works.

Mukhtar Auezov highly appreciated the writings of Tuqay and not-ed their spiritual similarity to Abai's poetry.

Tatarian literary scholar R.Sh. Bashkurov in the book "Токайдың орыс әдебиетінен аударғандары" (Kazan, 1958, 16-17-pp.) com-par-ing the principles of translation of Abai and Toqay found general resem-blances. Under the works' translation the both found an ideo-logical conception, deeply rendered spirituality to reader. However it doesn't mean that the principles of translation of Abai and Tuqay were always similar. They have differences in aesthetic views, in targets. Tuqay making translation of the Friedrich Schiller's song "The child in the cradle" (from Russian version made by Mikhail lermontov before) added a lot from himself. He used a lot of artistic accents, idioms and phraseological locutions. This poem was also translated of Abai's own free choice. Abai tried to discover an essential idea. However they both – Abai and Tuqay went to com-mon purpose by separate ways.

Comintern and was appointed deputy governor of the Centrally Eastern department.

On summer of 1924 Ryskulov was appointed authorized repre-sen-tative of the executive committee of the Comintern in Mongo-lia. After his return to Kazakhstan in March of 1926 he worked as

TURAR RYSKULOV was t h e head of press department of the Kazakh regional committee of born on 26.12.1894 in the Eastern Talgar volost of Vernenskiy uezd of Zhetysuskiy oblast – died in 10.02.1938 in Moscow city), party and state figure, one of organizers of the Soviet power in Central Asia and Kazakhstan. He studied in Rus-sian-Kazakh school, Pishpeksk ag-ricultural school, teachers' institute of Tashkent. He participated in the national-liberation rising of 1916, was arrested by the administration of tsar, but in the absence of evidence was set free.

In 1918 he was deputy chairman, then chairman of the ex-ecutive committee of Aulieatinskiy uezd. In September of 1918 Ryskulov was appointed to the post of healthguard people's com-missar of the Turkistan ASSR; chairman of the Muslim bureau, which was found on the decision of the second conference of the Turkistan communist party (March 14-31, 1919).

On January 21, 1920 he was appointed a chairman of the Cen-tral Executive Committee of Turkistan ASSR. He paid a lot of at-tention to the local population's rights defense, the return of soils, which were occupied by settlers, for what he was under the lash from the side of Moscow.

On February 4, 1924 by the decision of the Central Commit-tee of the Russian communist party of the Bolsheviks Ryskulov was sent to work in assembly with the executive committee of the the Bolsheviks All-Union Communist Party, then as the editor in chief of the "Еңбекші қазақ" newspaper.

On May 31, 1926 by the decision of the All-Union Central Ex-ecutive Committee he was appointed the deputy chairman of the people's commissar of the Russian Federation, and at the same time the chairman of the government commission on the con-struction of the Turkistano-Siberian railway (Turksib).

Openly argued against the idea of the Kazakh regional com-mit-tee chairman of the Bolsheviks All-Union Communist Party Philipp I.goloshekin about the organization in Kazakhstan of the Small Oc-tober Revolution. Ryskulov offered to Iosif V. Stalin the specific mea-sures of the complete collectivization consequences elimination and saving the population of Kazakhstan from hunger. He tackled the issues of public education, considered an overarch-ing objective peoples ini-tiation to spiritual values. Recognizing a significance of nationally Russian bilingualism, he paid a lot of attention to education of chil-dren and adults in native language. On May 21, 1937, being on leave in Kislovodsk, Ryskulov was arrested on the charge of pan-Turkism as an enemy of the people. He died in Moscow jail.

On December 8, 1956 by the decision of the military colle-gium of the Supreme Court of Kazakh SSR he was rehabilitat-ed. Rysku-lov's character is rendered in the works of the Kazakh writer Sher-khan Murtazy: "Қызыл жебе" (1, 2 books), "Жұлдыз көпір", "Қыл көпір", "Тамұқ". The name of Ryskulov was ac-quired for a country region of Jambyl oblast and the Kazakh uni-versity of economics (Al-maty city).

KERBABAEV BERDY MURA-DOVICH (1894-1974) Turkmenian belletrist, the only founder of the Soviet Turkmenian literature. He was born on March 3, 1894 in Kouki-Zeren aul, nowadays of Tedzhenskiy region of Turkmeni-stan.

In 1923 he began to publish as a sa-tirical poet. In 1927-1928 he stud-ied on the Oriental faculty of the leningrad's university. At the same time his two poems were published:

"The maiden's world" (1927) and "The bonded, or The victim of adat" (1928), in which he stood for the confirmation of So-viet rules of morality and getting rid of vestiges of the past.

From 1930 he was at work upon the first revolutionary his-tori-cal novel in the Soviet Turkmenian literature. The first part of novel "The decisive step" was published in 1940. The full writing in Turkmen was published in 1947, and in 1955 was republished in reviewed version. In 1948 Berdy Kerbabaev be-came a laureate of the USSR state prize.

In the days of The great Patriotic War he wrote a short nov-el "Kurban Durdy" (1942), a poem "Aylar" (1943), the playes "The brothers" (1943) and "Makhtumkuli" (1943). In 1942-1950 Berdy Kerbabaev was a chairman of the Writers' Union of Turkmenistan.

After the war in his works the themes of socialist construc-tion and stories from the life of kolkhoz aul prevail: "Aysoltan from the country of white gold" (1949, USSR State Prize, 1951), novel "Nebit-Dag" (1957) about the life of oil workers. In 1965 a histori-cal novel "The miraculously born" was is-sued about a Turkmenian revolutionary and state man gaygysyz Atabayew.

In 1960-s Berdy Kerbabaev makes translations into Turk-men the works of Alexander S. Pushkin, lev N. Tolstoy, Max-im gorkiy and of the other Russian and Soviet writers and po-ets. His works were translated into Russian and were published in Moscow.

He was the Member of the Academy of Science of Turk-me-nian SSR from 1951, the hero of socialist labor in 1969, the Re-publican prize winner named after Makhtumkuli in 1970 and he was awarded on three Orders of lenin.

Kerbabaev died in Ashkhabad in 1974.

The creative work of Berdy Kerbabaev could be related to liter-ature of big style, which appeared in literature of the Sovi-et period in Russian and in the languages of USSR nations. Its feature is prev-alence of the big literary forms (romance, novel, poem), gravitation to analyze the fates of heroes through the prism of great historical events, when all small and private re-cedes into the background, taking a way to crucial tasks solu-tion and big personal discoveries.

AUEZOV MUKHTAR OMARKHANOVICH (28.09.1897 – 27.06.1946) – an outstanding writ-er, public man, scientist, Doctor of Philology, Professor, Member of the Academy of Science of Kazakhstan (1946), Honored Scientist (1957).He studied in aul school. His grandfather Auez, a friend of Abai Kunanbaev, made a great influence on the future writer's world view for-mation. In 1908 year Auezov studied in Kamaliddin's madrasah, then on preliminary courses of Rus-sian school. In 1909 year he lost father and his uncle Kassymbek took him for bring up, who sent him to a Semipalatinsk municipal five-classed school on county study allowance (1910-1915). In fifth class of school Mukhtar wrote his first work "Dauyl" ("Dur-ing the storm).

In 1915 year he enrolled at a teachers college in Semipalatinsk. Political upheaval in Russia (1917), Alash movement formation (1917) and Soviet power establishment (1917) changed his life. Auezov organized the union of "Alash youth", promoted different hobby groups opening, wrote articles for "Alash" and "Saryarka" newspapers.

On September 16, 1930 he was arrested by the bodies of the Joint State Political Directorate. They brought a variety of charges against him, among which the underground countermeasures or-ganization against Soviet power and participation in armed revolt preparations for its overthrow; rally against deprivation of prop-erty from riches; for-mation of national-bourgeois organization "Alka"; writing of works which praise prerevolutionary life and daily graft of Kazakh nation. you might as well say that Mukhtar Auezov by all his life and creative experience was arranged for a big epic tale creation about Abai. Already the first book "Abai", published in Kazakh in 1942 and a little later in Russian, amazed all by its wonderful vividness, artistic innovativeness, inimitable creative decisions. With publication in 1947 year of the second book of "Abai" novel, in which Abai's outstanding ability to spir-itual growth, active action and his proximity to people were fully discovered, the writer's popularity increased.

Taking an active participation in literary, cultural, and public life, the writer and scientist diligently fought with wrong lapsided views, ideas, criticizing them from the high civic and scientific positions. It happened, for example, in 1951-1952 years, when around the creative heritage of Abai, his poetic school, the fierce disputes occurred. Mukhtar Auezov wrote the third and the fourth books. The whole four-volume epopoeia was named "The Way Of Abai".

After the epopoeia "The Way Of Abai" was fully published in Kazakh and Russian, its translations in many foreign languages followed. The novel became one of the only works of the world literature the main heroes of which came into consciousness of millions of readers.

On summer of 1961 he went to Moscow for treatment. On June 27, 1961 he died during an operation. He was buried in Alma-Ata on the central burying ground.

In the name of Auezov the Institute of literature and Arts, the Kazakh Academy Theater of Drama, streets and schools in Al-maty, Astana, Semipalatinsk and many other cities were called. There is a house-museum of Auezov in Almaty. Studying life and creative heritage of Auezov many painters and sculptors devoted their works to him. They are Kanafiy Telzhanov, Moldakhmet Kenbaev, Sabur Mambeev, yevgeny Sidorkin, yevgeny Vuchet-ich, Rashit Nurmukha-metov and others. Throughout the republic there are his monuments. The Kazakh television did a movie about the great writer consisting of 12 episodes (the author A. Toybaev). Auezov's writings were republished more than once and trans-lated into many world languages. By the decision of UNESCO in 1997 the whole world celebrated the 100th anniversary of Auezov's birth.

DINMUKHAMED (DIMASH) AKHMEDOVICH KUNAEV

(Kazakh: Дінмұхамед (Димаш) Ахмедұлы Қонаев, January 12, 1912, Verniy city, the Russian empire – Au-gust 22, 1993, Alma-Ata city, Kazakh-stan) – Soviet state and public man, the first secretary of the Central Com-mittee of the Communist Party of the Kazakh SSR from 1960 till 1962 and from 1964 till 1986 the member of the Politbureau of the CPSU CC (April 9, 1971 – January 28, 1987), triple hero of socialist labor (1972, 1976, 1982).

The author of more than 100 scientific works. The Member of the Academy of Science of the Kazakh SSR (1952). The Member of the CPSU from 1939. The Deputy of Soviet of the Supreme So-viet Union of the USSR of 4-11 convenings (1954–1989) from Al-ma-Atinskaya oblast.

He graduated the school № 14 in Alma-Ata; the Moscow Insti-tute of gold and Non-Ferrous Metals (1936). In 1936-1942 held key posi-tions in Altayskiy, Ridderskiy, leninogorskiy mines. In 1942-1952 he was a deputy chairman of the Council of People›s Commissars of the KazSSR, the Council of Ministers of the Ka-zSSR. In April of 1952 he was elected president of the Academy of Sciences of Kazakhstan. In 1955-1960, 1962-1964 the chairman of Council of Ministers of the KazSSR. In 1960-1962, 1964-1986 the first secretary of the Cen-tral Committee of communist party of Kazakhstan. Within 45 years of his governance on senior leader-ship positions, almost 25 of them Kunaev was the first governor of the Republic. He significantly con-tributed the socioeconomic and cultural development of Kazakhstan. The mining production of the Republic achieved a high level, the new production regions of Kazakhstan were formed, the new cities and major population centers were built.

In the years of his governance of the Republic Pavlodar-Ek-ibastuz fuel and energy complex, Karaganda state regional power station-2, Buktyrma hydro-electric power station in East-ern Kazakh-stan, Pavlodar tractor plant and many other industrial enterprises be-gan to work.

The Mangystau oil-fields were mastered, rail-way construction got development, digging and production of titanium, magnesi-um and synthetic rubber began, at a quick rate different spheres of elec-tro-techniques, machinery and chemistry developed. The Mangystau, Zhezkazgan, Torgay regions formed. A special atten-tion Kunaev paid to Kerbulak flatland development, Kapchagay water storage basin and the Big Almaty Channel construction. At the same time an industry in the Republic still stayed to be a raw material base of the Soviet Union. An intensive development of military-industrial complex in the USSR influenced the economy of Kazakhstan. The major plants in Almaty, Ust Kamenogorsk, Petropavlovsk, Uralsk, Stepnogorsk specialized in military prod-ucts manufacturing. The military training areas and enterprises harmed significantly ecology of the Republic. Kunaev supported the well-known people of science, literature, art and intelligent-sia. During Kunaev's governance in 1977–1982 the fundamental five-volume scientific work of the history of Kazakh-stan in Ka-zakh and Russian was published. Kunaev made effective meas-ures for prevailing territorial boundary of the Republic protec-tion, its entirety. Kunaev returned to Kazakhstan the cotton regions on South, which were given to Uzbekistan earlier, he argued against the initiatives of the Center (Moscow) of the german autonomy creation in Kazakhstan, handover of Mangystau to Turkmenistan. For years of his governance the capital of the Republic Al-maty city (at those days Alma-Ata) turned to highly developed industrial, cultural and scientific center; the Palace of the Repub-lic, KazgUgrad, recre-ation center Arasan, sports complex Medeu and many other beautiful buildings were constructed. From 1985 Mikhail S. Gorbachev began reformation of the Soviet political and economical system. On De-cember 16, 1986 during the un-scheduled plenary meeting of the Central Committee of the com-munist party of Kazakhstan the Central

Committee representative of the CPSU g.Razumovskiy disclosed a decision of Politbureau to relieve Kunaev of his post and to appoint to the position of the first Secretary of the Central Committee of the communist party of Kazakhstan gennady V.Kolbin. This appointment provoked a wave of popular discontent, what resulted the December events in 1986. The central governance accused Kunaev in this meeting organization. On June 26, 1987 Kunaev was excluded from the group of the CPSU Central Committee, then from CPC Central Committee.

For the whole history of the Kazakh party organization Ku-naev was the third Kazakh who was its first party secretary. Ku-naev was a man of "system", he believed in "socialistic choice" and "communistic idea". Kunaev is the author of many scientific works dedicated to the problems of socialistic and communistic building, the questions of theory and practice of field surface min-ing development (about 200 scientific works). In the name of Ku-naev the Institute of Mining Affairs, a row of schools and streets of the country, the university in Almaty city were called. On Octo-ber 13, 1992 in Almaty "The International Fund of Kunaev" was created. On January 12, 2002 in Almaty the house-museum of Kunaev was opened. On August 15, 2003 in Akshi aul of Alakols-kiy region of Almaty oblast, where Kunaev spent the last years of his life, a memorial plate was established. He was awarded eight Orders of lenin, prizes and medals.

RASUL GAMZATOVICH GAMZATOV – an outstanding poet of the XX century, who made a substantial contribution to the Dagestanian literature development, what brought it worldwide fame. He was born on September 8, 1923 in a county of Tsada Hunzahskiy region of the Dagestan

Autonomous Soviet Socialist Republic in family of public poet of Dagestan, laureate of state (Stalin's) prize of the USSR gamzat Tsadasy.

He studied in Araninsk secondary school and Avarian teacher training college, after graduation of which worked as teacher, stage manager of the Avarian State Theatre, head of department and personal correspondent of the Avarian newspaper "The Bol-shevik of Mountains", and desk editor of Avarian broadcast of the Dagestanian Radio Committee. Rasul gamzatov began to write poetry in the age of nine. From 1937 year his verses began to be published in the republican Avarian newspaper "The Bol-shevik of Mountains". The first book of verses of gamzatov in Avarian "The Flaming love and Fervent Hatred" was issued in 1943, the second "The War Hangover" – in 1945. The member of the Writers' Union from 1945.

In 40-50-s of the XX century gamzatov's collections of prose and verse were published: "My soil" (1948), "The songs of Mountains" (1949), "The song of the most precious" (1950), "The native spacing" (1950), "In our mountains", "The moth-erland of highlander" (1954), "The soldiers of Russia" (1954), "The Dagestanian spring", "The upland road", "The lyrics" (1955), "My grandfather" (1955), "My girl-friends", "The word of elder brother", "The children of one house" (1956), "About you my thoughts" (1956), "The new meeting" (1957), poem "Saadu" and the prize poem "The year of my birth" (1952) – state (Stalin's) prize of the USSR.

In the years since dozens of poetic, prosaic and publicistic books of the poet in Avarian, Russian and many languages of Dagestan, Caucasus and the whole world were published: "The cranes", "At the hearth-rug", "The folk tales", "The wheel of life" (1987), "About the stormy days of Caucasus" (1989), "In midday fever" (1993), "My Dagestan", "The two shawls", "Judge me according to love codices", "The sonnets", "The con-cert" and many others, which became widely known among lov-ers of his poetry. Therefrom "The cranes" and "My Dagestan" were published in Kazakh.

Rasul gamzatov stood for election to the posts of deputy to the Supreme Soviet of Dagestan Autonomous Soviet Socialist Republic, deputy chairman of the Supreme Soviet of DASSR, presidium deputy and member of the Supreme Soviet of the USSR of 6th (1962), 7th (1966), 8th (1970), 9th (1974) and 11th (1984) callings, member of Dagestanian regional committee of CPSU. Within few decades Rasul gamzatov was delegate of the writers' meetings of Dagestan, the Russian SFSR and USSR, committee member of the USSR lenin and State Prizes, So-viet Peace Committee board member, deputy chairman of the Soviet Committee of Asian and African nations' solidarity, edi-torial board member of the magazines "The new world", "The national cohesion", newspapers "The literary newspaper", "The literary Russia" and other magazines and newspapers.

On November 3, 2003 a heart5 of poet stopped. He died in Moscow and on November 4 was buried in Makhachkala on a burying place in the Tarki-Tau mountain side.

CHINGIZ TOREKULO-VICH AITMATOV (Kir-ghiz Чынгыз Төрөкулович Айтматов; D e - cember 12, 1928, Sheker, T a - las can-ton, Kirghiz ASSR, RSFSR, USSR – June 10, 2008, Nurn-berg, germany) – Russian and Kirghiz writer, diplomatist, Hero of the Kirghiz Republic (1997), peoples writer of the Kirghiz SSR (1974), hero of socialist labor (1978). He is laureate of the lenin Prize (1963) and of three state prizes of the USSR (1968, 1977, 1983).

In 1948 year Aitmatov graduated veterinary training school and in 1953 year – agricultural institute. He worked as zootechnician for three years. Either in local newspapers and magazines his first literary experiences appeared. In 1956 year he entered the highest literary courses in Moscow. After his return to motherland he edited the magazine "The liter-ary Kyrgyz-stan" and worked as newspaper "Pravda" report-er in Kirghizia. In 1958 year in "The New World" the story "Djamilya" about "illegal" love of married Kirghiz woman written on behalf of teener was published. On next year al-ready it was translated into French by a well-known writer louis Aragon. Aitmatov became internationally renowned

In 1963 year for the book "The Stories of Mountains and Steppes" (along with "Djamilya" it consisted of "The First Teach-er", "The Cammel's Eye" and "The girl With the Red Scarf") Ait-matov got the lenin Prize. The main feature of these writings is correlation of moral, philosophic problem-atics with poetics of the traditional East. The folkloric and mythological themes play pivotal role in the story "good bye, gulsary!" (1965–1966 years).

Especially they are strong in the story-paroemia "The White Steamboat" (1970 year): tragical story of a seven-year-old boy which goes parallely to story about Horny mother-doe – god-dess of lineage, the deifying epitome of goodness. In the story "The Brindle Dog, Running Along Seashore" (1977 year) the writer transferred action into mythic earlier days on the shores of Okhotsk Sea. The fishermen suffused with belief in supreme forc-es sacrifice themselves in storm for the sake of a child survival.

In 1997 year the book-essay "Құз басындағы аңшының зары" written together with Muhtar Shakhanov sees the light. Ei-ther written by them play "Сократты еске алу түні немесе миғұла терісі үстіндегі сот" was put on the stage in the the-ater named after Gabit Musrepov in Kazakhstan.

In 70–80-s years Aitmatov took active participation in socio-political life of the country: he was secretary of the Writ-ers' Union of the USSR and the film makers' union of the USSR,

deputy to the Supreme Soviet of the USSR; after the reformation period he constituted the executive council, led the magazine
"The International literature". From 1990 year he was on a diplomatic operation.

He died on June 10, 2008 year in the hospital of the ger-man
city Nurnberg, in clinic where he underwent medical treatment.
He was buried on June 14 in the historically me-morial complex
"Ata-Beyit" in the countryside of Bishkek.

III SECTION SCIENTISTS REVIEWS

THE BOOK FOR EVERYBODY

THE BOOK FOR EVERYBODY

I have to admit that O.Sabden's book *Abai and future of Ka-zakh-stan* surprised me a lot in a positive way of these words.

In this book O.Sabden supposes that the XXI century will become the century of society humanization. In this case knowl-edge of Abai's creative work increases multiply because he re-flected deeply and extensively our spiritual values there. We can make sure in this according to M.Auezov's novel *The way of Abai* and thanks to theorists of Abai. I think that the author's main objective is to show the ways to civilization by means of Abai's heritage.

O.Sabden's uniqueness is that he makes search of mecha-nisms for Abai's actual ideas realization herein offering the raw of new recommendations and projects, in particular –the global currency regulation, the world processes management and regu-lation model, the humanity's mode of life character in the XXI century. Surely such projects are the results of deep thinking and scientific investigations.

From the raw of extremely private opinions the most I like is his *The 12 edifications of Abai* where the great thinker ad-vances a theory of *the proper personality*. This theory according to O.Sabden's opinion could be efficient if we determine their actual commonness by means of visible and invisible secrets of nowadays world and he offers his views of their determination. The author proves that the capitalistic formation turned to a for-mation of uncountable consumption and wealth accumulation and we shouldn't imitate this negative phenomenon.

The world can be calm and develop stably under the spiritual priority orientation of the world civilization of East and turn moral and intellectual development of humanity from material rails to spiritual. It is necessary to activate the learning of Abai in complex with the spiritual development of East. To examine them together with global thoughts of civilization. Of course such author's idea requires correspondent investigations.

The book sais: In the future period of post industrial develop-ment under the moral codes of society humanization creation it will be necessary to use the thoughts of Abai along with the thoughts of the world geniuses, his learning of *appropriate man*, because they are similar to common to humanity ideas.

O.Sabden offers to create The Spiritual Academy named after Abai in Kazakhstan where The great Silk Road lays which will serve as the center of special investigations of Abai's heritage, Eastern philosophy and personnel training for Eurasian area what will promote the civilizations development. This fundamental offer surely could serve as an orienting point in future.

Further the author makes an attempt on the basis of *The 14 edifications* of Abai to show the basic principles of moral code of the XXI century as an answer on the question – What the moral code of the XXI century should be? They are the intellectual and spiritual science, humane consciousness and upbringing, transfer from quantity to quality, upgrading of professional skills, human and spiritual force, patriotic feelings, mental skills and willpower, human self control and self-management.

An individual who follows such moral code can promote self advancement, advancement of his country and the whole humanity. Only in this case human can self-improve in nowadays world. But an immoral human can make unforgettable errors.

We believe that thanks to the VI-VII century new technological m-odels the big new changes, scientific and technological revolution could be made, because the evolution of consciousness, spiritual revolution, time of society humanization come on, wherein the humanity rises on the top of its spiritual development and only there it can enjoy the fruits of peaceful development. It can hap-pen within 1-2 centuries if the world war would not appear what also depends on human factor. The humanity, which will follow the learning of an appropriate man and the civilized thoughts of geniuses such as Confucius and Nostradamus, would not make such catastrophic actions.

I think each word of O.Sabden contains deep thoughts and offers which ...

Abduali Kaidar - Academician of NAS of RK

KAZAKH – THE SON OF ITS NATION – ORAZALY!

After reading the book of O.Sabden I saw once again that Abai was the genius from geniuses. The author considering Abai's edifications from economic point of view uses each of them logically concluding by them his every thought.

In this small book the author could contain his reasoning about 15 edifications and thoughts, about 30 great historical persons. And a result we received a wonderful pocket or desk book. Though it's not big but it raises very large-scale problems. The development of Kazakh society on global level, cognition of spiritually valuable cultural wealth of Kazakh people lead the reader to a conclusion that O.Sabden is a real son of his nation.

After reading this book I was admired by Abai's heritage where the ways of nation's prosperity and its bright future were predicted insightfully.

Reading of O.Sabden gives birth of new thoughts. His book can serve as a program of our country's way of development determination. It is more objective and useful in accordance with

Abai's thoughts projects adopted from foreign countries for which huge sums of money were paid and which often stay un-performed. Sometimes we need to admit that we began to boast and we like very much when somebody praises us. But under our criticism we become maximalists. In the book of O.Sabden on the golden mean of negative and positive in this regard we find the balance, and also it contains the mechanisms of ideas' performance. In a word the book beats bull's eye.

The book is performed on the world level, it reasonably and decisively correlates ideas of the great Abai with ideas of the world geniuses such as Confucius and Nostradamus, determines their commonality, thereby acquainting the world community with Abai's thoughts. The author would gain greatly if he pub-lished his book on foreign languages. Separate conclusions, con-sequences and offers of O.Sabden sound on the level of global thinkers and even exceed them. The evidence of it is the positive opinion of S.A.Timashev – one of the world philosophers, the Nobel laureate about O.Sabden's work *The conception of human living (existence) strategy in the XXI century.*

I would like to emphasize one more cute idea described in the author's book. This is the idea of the Turkistan zone foundation as a new spiritually technological cluster and turning the Turk-istan city into a spiritual capital, building of a Spiritual Academy. The global historically geographical museum, advanced technologies, tourism, logistics, new villages. These are not only offers, but the specific recommendations with financial calcula-tions. According to expert-builders this project is estimated on 8 billion USD. Either the author shows the sources of means which don't burden the nation. Such megaprojects are worth of authorities' support. Nowadays such projects don't have ana-logues. I am strongly convinced that if not today but in future they will be certainly performed.

This book determines to innovatory thoughts, it is actual and useful for country and nation, especially for creative youth.

Tursunbek Kakishev - Critic, scientist, academician.

A NEW WORD OF ABAI

The recent years Abai's *Edifications* attract people's attention widely and galvanize to creative searches for country's prosper-ity. And today under the change of society they are still actual and are able to make readers think of epoch and its members.

These new thoughts I met in O.Sabden's book – *Abai and future of Kazakhstan*. O.Sabden is a big expert and thinker. A lot of time he worked in the Republic's Parliament and was an eyewitness of old and new points of views and beliefs strikes being near the highest-level leaders of the country. In this long-ing he courageously put his abilities in the independent society establishment.

The independent Kazakhstan succeeds as a firm state, but the searches of its development are not finished. As scientist, thinker and rational citizen O.Sabden shows concern of his country's fate.

O.Sabden considers modern universal problems from the per-spective of Abai's learning. Besides, in the book along with Kazakh society the author covers a wide range of global issues; he is con-cerned of the questions of how and where the world moves? Where-by what will the Kazakhs receive, in what condi-tion the wealth of Kazakh soil, how they are used for people's needs satisfaction or if they are distributed among the pockets of those who have access to them? What the Kazakh national valuables are and on what level they are today? These and other analogue problems disturb the author and he looks for their an-swers. He tries to share his thoughts with readers and Kazakh community. Along with these issues he brings to the forefront the questions of education and science, healthcare and sport, conditions in villages, human harmony with nature, etc.

The author searches the answers on these questions not only in Kazakh society's life, but in development of the whole hu-manity. His thoughts are interesting and make people think.

The book represents a raw of information about the great per-sons from Kazakh-Turkic media. **Beginning from Queen To-myris and King Atilla this big list contains the great repre-sentatives of** eldest generations such as Yer Tonga, Tonykok, Arystanbaba, Al-Farabi, Yusuf Balassaguni, Manas, Nizami Ganjavi, Hoja Ahmet Yassawi, Makhmut Kashgari, Geng-his Khan, sultan Baybars, Emir Timur, Ulugbek, Alisher Na-voi, Mohammed-Khaidar Dulati, Korkyt, Abai Kunanbaev, Ataturk, Bektash Veli, Chokan Valikhanov, Gabdolla Tuqay, Turar Ryskulov, Dinmukhamed Konaev, Mukhtar Auezov, Berdy Kerbabaev, Rassul Gamzatov, Chingiz Aitmatov and others.

He raises the questions of their heritage necessity for present generations, finding there the answers on many modern problems, and considers that they are able to incite the thoughts of young people. This process can become the Kazakh nation's contribution to panhuman civilization. They can provide entrance of Kazakhs to the rows of developed nations and contribute in a new strategy of the world development creation.

And according to these criteria the work of O.Sabden is an innovation.

Serik Kirabaev - Academician of NAS of RK

ABAI'S LEARNING IN TODAYS WORLD

The XXI century is the world of globalization, the century of civilization improvement. In new century new technologies unknown before develop, a common human society renewal happens. In these conditions there are shouldn't be any doubt in thinking people aspiration to comprehend happening, ways of the whole society development, mode of life in new society. Consequently I think appropriate to find the answers on O.Sabden's questions through the prism of the great Abai. Of course nowadays the fate of Kazakhstan is tightly linked with the world process of globalization. The fate of national develop-ment was the object of detailed thinking of the great poet-thinker Abai and Alash doers.

In his time critically showing the contradictions of Kazakh society, Abai deeply cognized its correlation to the rules of dia-lectics. He searched the answers on such questions as: How to grade up to the countries where culture, education, entrepreneur-ship, business media are highly developed?, How to gain them upon?.

Abai's learning is still relevant because a new society develop-ment gives new problems. And in his new book O.Sabden tries to an-swer the questions of how and where we'll appear in the XXI cen-tury, can we enter the list of civilized countries, what opportunities do we have of national wealth usage and human capital in order to increase people's prosperity; and expresses his own original opinion of their positive solution by means of new ways. There is no doubt that the author's attempt to comprehend Abai's world view from the scientific point of view, to link it with global civilized thoughts is a requirement of today's world. The academician O.Sabden admits that nowadays an optimal usage of national wealth, provision of econom-ic and technologic correlation, safety of national genetic resources, and its making consistent with the process of education, science, and healthcare development are our priorities and their performance is a national objective. Only under these conditions it is possible to enter the list of 30 developed world countries by the author's opinion.

Undoubtedly, our country is globally admitted by its rich nat-ural resources. O.Sabden's offers to transfer them to national propri-etorship and thereby to correct sudden decisions of these questions will create powerful potential national companies conformable to public opinion. Of course, it is inappropriate to think that decision of these questions is possible in near future, because widely rooted divi-sion of powers and investment inter-est are still powerful. The prob-lem of property questions deci-sion in this sphere is undoubtedly linked with many difficulties and contradictions. For today the only way is to increase share fractions of national property (of course, by means of gradual purchase).

Alongside with that one more problem is settled unjust sys-tem of profitability division of rich national resources sources where their real common over-priced cost is not taken into consideration and directly exported in composition of primary products for the benefit of foreign companies. Here the prob-lem is that the prime cost of each mineral deposit should be de-termined on scientific ba-sis and get on just division in type of absolute differentiated rent. In conclusion of separate field the volume of common profitability will constitute 60-70% from the cost of natural resources. If honestly use the volume of natural resources, it can and should constitute the main body of state budget. The question of profitability was already raised by other scientists and economists, but this process is still far from its right decision. The same situation is in Russian economy.

No doubt it is axiom that the level of science being a part of essence of every independent country determines its intellectu-al potential, its place in spiritual competition on international level. O.Sabden's offers to unite in entire system the rambling sci-entific enterprises and to enforce their state management are ap-propriate. We are the witnesses of what O.Sabden fundamentally studies for a long time: the questions of science organization, its efficiency and concentration rise; and he makes suggestions which are promoted on a governmental level. The questions of science management and its budgeting also become the object of

views interchange between the author and wide audience.

O.Sabden's warnings of the condition of our villages where 44% of Kazakhs live shouldn't leave anybody cold, as Abai's either.

In fact in decision of Kazakhstani villages problems an in-disputable way is works coverage and provision, in particular, by or-ganized work and organization for these purposes of pro-duction, consumer cooperatives, joint ventures, sleeping part-nerships, etc; whereupon surely according to every sphere the variants of positive decisions, questions will be found, as ag-gregations' budgeting, increase in labor productivity, efficiency of corporate farms. It will be fair to emphasize that O.Sabden in his scientifically proved work of publicistic genre promotes duly and proper very actual problems, how and in what direc-tions technique and production will devel-op, what is in tune with problems which require adequate decision in conditions of increasing industrialization in Republic. Actually, as the author mentioned our country is at the threshold of techno-logic crisis. In modern time a key of work productivity intension achieve-ment is innovative technology. Nowadays, the development of country even in conditions of economic crisis is provided by means of victory provision in competitions by means of 35% of in-vestments involvement in new technology. That is the sup-posed way to form middle class and thereby achieve the stabil-ity of population prosperity. The problems of small and middle business development by means of intensive industrialization should be corresponding with working class of new level pres-ence, composition of class of new level, management engineers. According to O.Sabden's opin-ion the creation of society fully provided with modern technology of highest level and entering the list of 30 developed countries by means of production share increase to 50-60% of gross product (gP) is a strategic limit.

It is necessary to note that the work of well-known public doer, significant scientist-economist O.Sabden – *Abai and fu-ture of Ka-zakhstan* is confessed by society as socially economic program which should be performed by the government of the country. Problems rose in the book point to future high objec-tives and can serve as significant base and orienting point, there is no doubt.

Amanzhol Koshanov - Academician of NAS of RK

WE RARELY SEE SUCH WISE BOOKS

When I took the book of O.Sabden for the first time I thought: Why the scientist-economist bothers the great Abai? What did he want to say when the authors themselves not understanding Abai's heritage deeply during their articles writing use old mo-tives and declama-tions?

Turning over page after page of this book I felt new original thoughts of the author identical to Abai. Only when Oreke like Abai began to state his innovatory original ideas in *15 edifica-tions* I understood the root of the matter. I think that an advance notice represented as supplement to the book's title – *The mech-anisms of Abai's edifications realization in the XXI century* has a deep meaning. Thus in genius thoughts of Orazaly a wise idea lays which is directed to cover in conjunction with surrounding of the whole material world and invisible spiritual world as was said in the 7th edification of Abai: *...Not discovering visible and invisible secrets of universe, not explaining all to himself, a man cannot become human.*

But the Europeans got into consumption. They faced some diffi-culties, denying acquirements of invisible worlds, getting mixed up with false material and atheistic cognition and as a result became a society of consumption. And now they cannot find exit out of this cute problem. They need sources of spiritual treasure, as a theory of *appropriate man* of Abai, which pro-motes humanity education in spiritual direction. Nowadays the whole world thought of the universe cognition passes funda-mental changes. The falseness of atheistic and material world views was revealed. The world chose a new cognition based on quantum physicians' learning which says that cognition is a beginning of the World Understanding, creation. The new age admitted the german Nobel Prize in Physics winner's – Max Planck – statement that the world is governed by the su-preme conscience. The whole world is linked by its invisible force.

From this point of view the author in his book's fourth chap-ter – *The fourth edification* asks reader very difficult question: What was the level of our spiritual values, on what level is it now and how can we improve it?. The answer is given by O.Sabden himself: The spiritual values should be put before the rest. And further he builds up this idea through the learning of Abai and forces his reader to be deep in thought.

The book represents interesting projects which contain orig-inal and actual thoughts, worldview tendencies. For reader the cognition of the book itself is a critical transfer through the world of the great Abai, through the modern worldview of the global society, because they contain very actual thoughts and conceptions of the author himself. Their acceptance and implementation are on civil conscience of the government.

Either they enrich the worldview of young people and can serve as the base of their world outlook.

The innovative kind words become mental food. However such wise books are rare.

The unique novel nature of this book is its author's attempt to cognize Abai deeply from the modern point of view and so-cial-ly economic problems. It is absolutely unexpected and new in the world of up-to-date thought.

Nowadays almost all humanitarian sciences are in crises, be-cause all their idea theoretical bases cannot bust out of athe-istic materialistic worldview's false net. The author of this book in this question so to speak shows us the necessary worldview field and offers the ways of optimum decision of actual modern problems.

__Mekemtas Myrzakhmet__ - Academician,
Laureate of State Prizes of RK
Dr. phil., Professor, Abai scholar

THE READER'S THOUGHTS

The new book of famous as in the country and abroad scien-tist, Doctor of Economics, academician O.Sabden – *Abai and future of Kazakhstan* attracts attention of wide circle of readers. It concen-trates concrete views on today's world, solid thoughts of different politic and economic spheres, analyses on high sci-entific foundation a modern worldview in its especially criti-cal period of development and makes an attempt to determine the escape ways from this situation, calls upon readers to joint thinking.

O.Sabden discovers the hidden context and meaning of thoughts in the great Abai's edifications. Through the chosen by the author fifteen edifications of Abai the most actual problems are examined which bother the advanced thinkers and doers of the whole humanity. The book is far from eloquence, but rich of thoughts.

The author's ideas *The change of the world psychology*, *The world management reforming* which were represented in *The first edification* contain his appeals to the new civilized political, economical and social changes.

The author makes true comparison of West and East, of two ways of development. He emphasizes that the conscience eter-nity which was born on East received a huge and widespread development on West and then came alive again on East and became a common heritage of mankind which combines spiritual world of the whole terrestrial globe.

Thinking of globalization O.Sabden points that in conditions of this process a danger for small scarcely populated countries is in evidence where technologies and productive forces are not developed and which rely only on natural resources. The author offers them to develop international collaboration, to keep na-tional values such as history, culture, language, religion, mental-ity, traditions and strive for peace and conciliation. All these are tighten to Abai's thoughts and establishes succession. The sci-entist considers that only science and education can save from negative impacts of the world globalization. Abai's approval that – Science is both light and welfare and we should pay a lot of attention to it – is fair enough. However there is a question – If there is enough attention to this moving the society force from the side of government? – it is a problem already. The au-thor says that education and science turned to commodity and he warns society about the risk to lose *an appropriate personality* according to Abai.

The book consists of fifteen edifications of the author which all are interrelated. Here the questions of healthguard, family, nature, auls are tightly linked with Abai's thoughts. An objectiv-ity of critics, recommendations and conclusions of the author inspire confidence that his book will find its worth of a better cause. I think that the worldview fund is appended by one more valuable book.

Tanen-Myrza Tokhtarov - Public man.

SCIENTIST – ECONOMIST – ABAI SCHOLAR

Each Abai's word inspires, gives power, promotes love to kind, preserves from negative. It is right that academician O.Sabden chose Abai's learning in order to check out today's world from the great poet's point of view.

Realizing Abai's wisdom which says about work and education, peace and unity, the author of separate ideas of humanization – academician O.Sabden who is a gold base of our country, revived the historical memory of the great Abai's generation with due regard to generation of today's independent country. All these are facts which we achieved thanks to strong national spirit.

This is the evidence of spiritual power and wealth of both – the great Abai and the author of this book. Surely the mental values cannot appear without spiritual wealth and deep thoughts. That's why O.Sabden writes: *We need thoughts which are able to awake the whole nation. We can find them in the great Abais edifications, in heritages of the great historical persons, con-sequently developing them further.* Here the scientist means an actuality of Abai's philos-ophy cognition and his learning of ap-propriate personality. Either the author considers that one of mechanisms of our country's entering the list of 30 developed countries is knowledge of languages, in particular – English, what is conformable to our President's

N.A.Nazarbaev direc-tion.

O.Sabden's book *Abai and future of Kazakhstan* is valuable for young generation upbringing in the spirit of national values. Can it assist in social contradictions regulation and union into single nation by means of Abai's learning? The world is change-able, but people's intellect and spirituality are stable, Abai's hu-mane principles are strong and actual for all times. O.Sabden searches compatibility between wisdom of Abai and of today's world and activates it, what serves as an orienting point in society development and appeals it to look up to global development.

Abai said: *The word of scientist is for those who strive for the best,* and I think that O.Sabden is exactly such person. Besides, O.Sabden refers to *appropriate men* (according to Abai) of such prominent peo-ple as academician Salykh Zimonov, people's writer gerold Belger.

On pages 12, 13 of the book O.Sabden shows the ways of Abai's learning of *appropriate personality* cognition in accor-dance with the philosophy of East and the world civilization de-velopment. And in *The fourteenth edification* of the book the au-thor asks: *What the material code of society should be in the XXI century.* His own answer on this question O.Sabden gives ac-cording to the principles of Abai's learning. *Eventually morally developed man can lead for-ward himself, country and humanity. But a man free of moral char-acter risks to make unforgettable errors* – the author writes. It is well-known that in market sys-tem the society often faces negative phenomena as consequenc-es of unforgettable subjective errors. Ac-cording to the author's opinion they could be avoided. That's why he offers to organize The spiritual academy named after Abai, The scientific training center and The center for heritages of Al-Farabi, Abai and East-ern philosophy study which could make significant as-sistance to the world civilization development.

By this work O.Sabden made a great contribution to science. In conclusion of his work O.Sabden writes: *Read and won-*

der the exclusive amazingness of Abai – the spiritual leader of nation, whose edifications serve truly to spiritual civilization with-in two centuries already.

I wish O.Sabden to continue creative activity of generations' up-bringing ,which care of nation and are able to become leaders of nation.

*Asly **Osman** - Chairman of association*
The honour to state language, Cand. phil. Sc.

THE NEW APPROACH TO ABAI'S EDIFICATIONS

Economist and scientist O.Sabden taking into account the in-ter-est of wide audience to Abai's heritage, published the book – *Abai and future of Kazakhstan* in which he fairly noted: *The aim (of this book) to show the peculiarities of new approach to Abai and point its difference from traditional.* It means that we used to criticize short-falls in society by means of Abai's principles, but we need to try to point by Abai's eyes the mechanisms based on science and practical life in search of answer on the question: What should we do?.

The author considers that it is worthy to admit realities. In this plan we cannot say that the author's discontent is ground-less. Further O.Sabden writes: *In past 24 years old route togeth-er with successes there were a lot of slogans, appeals, bragging and lack of system, productivity, truth.* The scientist is anxious of future.

In his fifteen step-type edifications the scientist was gradually committed to two principles: The first is What did you achieve?, and the second is to search answers on the question - What to do? and con-tinue recommendations. The final purpose of the scien-tist is to point for the country – Қазакелі the way to civilization, to direct it to hu-mane society. In his first edification O.Sabden showing the world dangers for humanity expresses his own thoughts in the following way: *The first on the agenda should stay the question of new ways search which appeal to change peoples' conscience and world psychology, to revive spiritual and moral values, to establish order in families.* In the second word of the book the author estimates the country's achieve-ments: factories, real estates and searches the ways of the world crises overcome. He wonders: *We are the richest country in the world, but live poor – Why?.*

The author considers that not esteeming the status of intellect and justice the global life and stable happiness are not possible.

This thought is reflected in the following words: *Sometimes we forget to live by the rules of natural society humanization, ac-cording to global historical ways of development. These rules could be realized only under the condition of their correspond-ence to moral norms.*

We are rich with spiritual and moral wealth which passed his-torical trials, but unfortunately, nowadays we lose their values. I think that the author offer to study students of higher educational establishments Abai's learning of *appropriate man* is relevant, because it can become moral code not only of Kazakhstanis', but of the whole Turkic world.

For this purpose the idea of spiritual capital creation in Turk-istan was put. This idea was either proved by the author with a certain source of budgeting.

Some attention in the book was paid to the problem of science development in the country. According to the author's opinion the science of Kazakhstan rolls back instead of development. The author appeals to reconsider immediately the question of organization and provision of science development and offers to turn this process to the governmental rails.

On the base of Abai's thoughts the author touches the ques-tion of healthguard and sport development necessity.

A special place in O.Sabden's book took the problem of un-employment, low salaries, low poverty line, and soaring corrup-tion.

Concluding the book for realizing of all said the author ex-press-es a big hope on authorities. Though we see that the system and different formed public relations are the result of natural and historical development of society, however a huge impact on all these only the authority has. In Abai's edification he also em-phasized that authorities and wealth are the most efficient means which are able to change society.

I believe that O.Sabden's book *Abai and future of Kazakhstan* will become table-book in each house. Without doubt this book of scientist which contains the problems of improvement in all spheres of society will be properly appraised by the whole com-munity.

Zhabal Shoiynbet - Director of research-and-development center of Abai study Kazakh National Pedagogic University named after Abai, Cand. phil. Sc.

Maxat Alipkhan - Research officer

THE BOOK WRITTEN BY THE SCIENTIST OF THE WORLD LEVEL

The scientist O.Sabden published the book *Abai and future of Kazakhstan* proving his uniqueness. Before it he offered megaprojects of the world governance and Turkic world unity. And now in new book the scientist who thinks on global level describes his 15 recommendatory edifications on the base of the great Abai's thoughts. The book is actual because of raised eco-nomic problems of modern Kazakhstan and advised actions on future: development of new technologies, solution of villages' problems, etc. There is no similar book. It is necessary to learn it because it highlights not only the ways of Kazakhstani devel-opment, but also can influence the whole Turkic medium and global development. Nowadays O.Sab-den's ideas are globally popular. Recently I spoke in the grandstands of the United Na-tions where presented the book of O.Sabden – *The conception of humanity living strategy in the XXI century* to the UN repre-sentative. It is well-known that nowadays the countries of West suffer from spiritual crises. But humanity and spirituality are still in priority in our country, though unfortunately, they also begin to lose value. That's why the new book is very valuable, because on the base of Abai's edifications it appeals to revive the past rich spiritual and moral values.

As a chronographer I can note that the author in his book though uncircumstantialy, but truly remembers the names of the great persons of the times of Saka, Huns, Turkic Kaganate, khanates and Kazakh khanate. He holds their merits in the world civilization up as an example.

In the book's chapter *The great historical persons* a wonder-ful idea was expressed. *Genghis Khan and Emir Timur founded the huge empires from coast of the Pacific Ocean to Vienna in Europe. The main wealth was accumulated on this area. These empires were the most powerful on the Eurasian continent. Even the Roman Empire admitted the authority of Attila over it and rendered tribute for a long time. The European countries were helpless before his troops that time. They were severed by in-ternecine wars. If it hadnt been for consequences of the fol-lowing three factors: remoteness of this dominion (the Eurasian continent), incredibly frigid climate and ad-vance of an epidemic (plague) throughout the whole Europe, thus under the further conquest in what direction would the European civilization go? The modern history created a new "headache" for Europe. The public unrest and wars which happen in Middle East-ern coun-tries and Africa caused big migration processes. Basically mi-grants consist of Muslims and Turkic-Speaking nations. Such penetration to the European Union can cause an international inte-gration process. It remains to be seen what waits us in future.*

Further the author gives a long list of great historical persons, state and public doers beginning from Queen Tomyris and King Attila. This big list includes such significant representatives of elder generations as **Yer Tonga, Tonykok, Arystanbaba, Al-Farabi, Yusuf Balassaguni, Manas, Nizami Ganjavi, Hoja Ahmet Yassawi, Makhmut Kashgari, Genghis Khan, sultan Baybars, Emir Timur, Ulugbek, Alisher Navoi, Mohammed-Khaidar Dulati, Korkyt, Abai Kunanbaev, Ataturk, Bektash Veli, Chokan Valikhanov, Gabdolla Tuqay, Turar Ryskulov, Dinmukhamed Konaev, Mukhtar Auezov, Berdy Kerbabaev, Rassul Gamzatov, Chingiz Aitmatov and others.**

The author represented all these great persons from Queen Tomyris to Chingiz Aitmatov and recommended us to study their works, creations and devoted to them pantheons, monu-ments in Turkistan what would discover the huge information about the depth of our history.

Being a great don at science O.Sabden could discover the in-visible actual for today's life thoughts in Abai's edifications and create very valuable work.

Khairolla Gabjalilov - *President of the center of historic researches Alash One of the authors of the first tenge*

IV SECTION

TURKISH WORLD HISTORY MUSEUM

TURKISH WORLD HISTORY MUSEUM

An imaginative panorama presents a round hall with spheri-cal dome and amounts to a total of 306 square meters with height of 6 meters and length of 51 meters. The exposition allows trac-ing the history of Turkic nations through the ages.

The circle bordering the museum dome and the hall itself rep-re-sents a margent between sky and earth. The upper edge of the circle bears the cited lines from the Kultegin memorial text (VIII century).

…When the sky (Koktengry) and the earth were created the hu-man kind was created between them. It was ruled by my great grand-fathers Bumyn Kagan and Istemi Kagan who founded and preserved the Turkish nation and its culture…

The museum consists of four component parts:

-    The imaginative panorama "The History of Turkic Na-tions".

-    The globe representing the Turkic world.

-    The great thinkers and representatives of Turkic nations. -
The national costumes of Turkic nations.

The imaginative panorama begins from the hall entrance with an image of the Earth and the sacred taikazan (bowl) covering the whole complex of drawings circumferentially and finishes in the point of its beginning. It symbolizes the history and culture integrity of the Turkic nations, "which were born of common predecessor and shared meal between each other".

An image of space in the end of panorama symbolizes a great striving to the scientific world cognition and bright future and the taikazan is a symbol of unity and integrity of the Turkic na-tions.

The imaginative panorama covers seven different subject mat-ters the quantity of which corresponds to the quantity of all Turkic nations.

The first subject:
THE NEOLITHIC ERA AND THE BRONZE AGE

The wall painting, The Sun God

The territories of ancient Turkic tribes' settlement (Altai, Cen-tral Asia and south Siberia) are rich of archeological dis-coveries referring to the Stone and Bronze Ages. Basically they are different household, labor and cultic items. A special place in ancient tribes' life was taken by the Sun god and numerous mythological animals drawn on stones.

The second subject:
THE SUMERIAN CIVILIZATION

The clay tables inscriptions, The fate fighting Gilgamesh, The Sumerian culture

Nowadays a lot of historic and linguistic sources give a great amount of evidences of ancient Turkic and Sumerian civilizations commonness. The scientists have found a great number of com-mon words and expressions belonging to Sumers' and ancient Turks' beliefs and ways of life. The brave feat of the Sumerian epos hero – firm gilgamesh who searched for the source of eter-nal life was repeated through milleniums by Turk – Korkyt ata who strived to cognize the truth of life either.

The third subject:
THE SCYTHIANS, SAKA, HUNS

Queen Tomyris (570-520 years B.C.), The Gold Man (V-IV cent. B.C.), The Saka warriors, The Huns' King Attila (Yedil) (410-453 years), The Scythian and Saka jewelries

The Scythians, Saka and Huns, who were the precursors of ancient Turks and were settled on vast territories of Eurasia, were the representatives of the earliest human civilizations. The spe-cific for them "animal style" in jewelry production and sur-vived to this day burial mounds of tribal chieftains still impress the minds of scientists, historians, archeologists, etc. The Saka Queen Tomyris (570-520 years B.C.) defending her nation and country filled a bag with blood and sank there the head of Per-sian King Cyrus with the following words: "you was thirty of blood thus drink it to satiety!"

One more archaeological evidence relating to Saka period is the gold Man (V-IV cent. B.C.) According to scientists' belief he be-longed to royal lineage, died in early age and was buried with a lot of gold jewelry.

The King of Huns Attila (410-453 years) who thrilled the great Roman Empire with his smashing invasions was also a unique personality of that time.

The fourth subject:
THE TURKIC KAGANATE

The Kultegin Monument (VIII cent.), The Runic alpha-bet, The Sacred Animals (totems) of the Turks: golden eagle, wolf, snow leopard, tortoise,

The Tengriism. The belief elements representation in Ten-gri of ancient Turks and Turks of modern Siberia (Shaman-ism), The Mother land Goddess Umai, The bogatyr Yer Ton-ga (IV-V cent.),

The Turkic Kagans: Bumyn (died in 552), Istemi (died in 576), Kultegin (684-731) and Bilge (685-734)

The Turkic Kaganate (552-745 years) is the state of united Turkic tribes in the Middle Asia. The founding father and the first leader of Turks was Ashina who according to a legend was saved and brought up by a sacred Wolf Before the Turkic Kaganate was founded the state of Turks was known as Turan. It occupied a huge territory from yenisei to Amu-Darya. The most well known governor of Turan was com-mander and bogatyr yer-Tonga (IV-V cent.) known as Afrasiab in Persian sources.

The ancient Turks adored to Kok-Tengri, idolized environ-ment and power of nature. They honored Umai as fertility god-dess, domestic goddess and bearer of humankind.

A lot of survivals of the Tengriism and the whole raw of Ten-gri ceremonies are survived till nowadays by the Turkic nations of Siberia.

The evidence of high culture and high level of spiritual devel-opment of ancient Turks is an existence of their own script. The ancient Turkic written artifacts are called the Orkhon-yenisei Runic alphabet in the language of science.

The fifth subject:
THE NOMAD TURKIC TRIBES

The great nomad camp. The nomadic culture counting more than three thousand years. An image of nomad camp symbolizes also the migration of nomads to the West Europe and Anatolia in different periods of history

The Golden Horde (1243-1503 years), The Manas teller, The ceremonial stone for sacrifice, The stone woman, The sign of eternity, The Mausoleum of Kozi Korpesh-Bayan Sulu (V-VI centuries)

The history of nomadic culture of Turkic tribes begins from the first periods of human civilization. The nomads founded their own specific culture corresponding to their way of life and kind of hus-bandry. They developed their literature and folklore enriching them with beautiful kyuies, songs, poems. They be-queathed to their de-scendants such eposes as "Alpamys", "Kozi Korpesh-Bayan Sulu", "Koroglu" and many hundreds of others. One of the most signifi-cant among the eposes is the longest in the world Kyrgyz epos, the symbol of heroism and glory – "Manas". Already in the early Mid-dle Ages after the West inva-sion of Attila's troops the nomad Turks migrated to the Anatolia, thereby widening the sphere of influence of Turkic culture by its spreading to the West Europe. In its turn the golden Horde (1243-1503 years) contributed the nomad culture development and let it to be kept to the beginning of the 20th century.

The sixth subject:
THE MIDDLE AGES AND MODERN ERA

Emir Timur (1336-1405 y.y.), The Seljuks Empire (1038-1194 y.y.), The Ottoman Empire. The capture of Constan-tinople by Sultan Fatih Mehmed (1453 y.), The Aya Sophia mosque (532-537 y.y.), The Selime mosque in Edirne (1609 y.), The Ottoman Empire symbols, The examples of minia-tures and calligraphy, the arms, the tiles of Iznik, Levni art-ist signature, the caravel is the symbol of Ottoman Empire's sea power.

The great doers of Turkic nations:
Korkyt-ata (VII-VIII c.c.) – the philosopher and musician Ulugh Beg (1394-1449 y.y.) – the astronomer and public
statesman
Abai Kunanbaev (1845-1904 y.y.) – the philosopher and poet
Nizami Ganjavi (1141-1209 y.y.) – the poet and thinker Aby-lay-khan (1711-1781 y.y.) – the last independent Kazakh khan (41)

Alisher Navoi (1441-1501 y.y.) – the writer and public statesman

Yusuf Balassaguni (1020-?) – the scientist and writer Mohammed Haydar Dulati (1499-1551 y.y.) – the historic and writer Al-Farabi (870-950 y.y.) – the scientist encyclopedist Yunus Emre (the end of XIII c. -1321 y.) – the poet Hadji Bektash Vele (1208-1270 y.y.) – the thinker Makhtumkuli (XVIII c.) – the poet

The mausoleum which was built by Emir Timur in honor of the great thinker- sophist, founder of the Turkism ideas, poet Hoja Ahmet Yassawi (XIV cent.)

Arystan-bab (XII cent.)

The mausoleum of Aisha Bibi (XII cent.)

The observatory and celestial chart of Ulugh Beg (XV cent.)

Samarkand and Registan (XV-XVI c.c.) The Taj Mahal (1630-1652 years)

The Middle aged period of the Turkic nation's history as in Middle and in Minor Asia was full of important events and cul-tural shocks which influenced the history of all humanity. Thus, in Middle Asia the Empire established by Emir Timur made supremacy on the whole territory lying from the great Wall of China to Western Europe, and on the territory of Minor Asia such great states existed as the Seljuks' Empire (1038-1194 years) and the Ottoman Empire (XIV-XX cent.). The Ottoman Empire supremacy was spread from Arabian Peninsula till the internal regions of Western Europe. An event of such impor-tance was reflected not only on geographical area, but showed a great influence on developing and spreading Turkic culture. Science, literature and art began to play a paramount role in so-ciety. Mosques, magnificent palaces and complex facilities built in that period became unique creations of that time. Taking into account all said above we can confirm that Middle Ages became some kind of Renaissance Era for Turkic culture.

The seventh subject:
THE XXTH CENTURY AND INDEPENDENCE

Ataturk (1881-1938 years) – the founder of Turkish Re-public, an outstanding statesman

The first campaign of young Turks (the end of XIX – be-ginning of XX)

The map of modern independent Turkish states, Autono-mies and nations location presented in the form of poplar – the symbol of life. Their state flags.

N. Nazarbayev– the first president of the Republic of Ka-zakhstan

Astana, Bayterek (poplar) – the symbol of the Tree of life, which combines past, present and future of our people

The image of space – the symbol of striving for knowledge, science, development of the whole human society

The Sacred Taikazan – the symbol of all Turkic nations unity

The globe with an image of Turkic world is set on sacred turtle and placed in the center of the hall under the dome. It dis-plays modern independent Turkic states, autonomies, nations, separate groups and their state symbols. The 17 portraits with potted biography are hung on the periphery of podium. These are the personalities who are apart from art panorama "The great figures and thinkers of Turkic nations".

Ismail Gasparaly (1851-1914 y.y.) – the Crimean Tatar by birth, enlightener and scientist, public man.

Mustafa Shokai (1886-1941 y.y.) – the state and public man of Kazakh nation.

Chokan Valikhanov (1835-1865 y.y.) – the first scientist-enlightener of Kazakh nation.

Mukhtar Auezov (1897-1967 y.y.) – the writer. **Makhmud Kashgari** (XI c.) – the great scientist of Turkic nation, founder of linguistics.

Zahir ad-din Muhammed Babur (1483-1530 y.y.) – the founder of the state of Moguls and India.

Sultan Baybars (1223-1277 y.y.) – the Turk by origin, founder of Turkic state in Egypt.

Chingiz Aitmatov (born 1928) – the Kyrgyz writer. **Tonykok** (646-741 y.y.) – the great thinker, bright states-

man of Turkic Kaganate.

Zeki Velidi Togan (1890-1970 y.y.) – the state and public man.

Sholpan Abdulhamit (1897-1938 y.y.) – the Uzbek poet, pub lic man.

Berdack Kargabaiuly (1827-1900 y.y.) – the founder of Karakalpak literature.

Gabdulla Tuqay (1886-1913 y.y.) – the founder of new re-al-istic trend in Tatar literature and founder of contemporary Tatar language.

Ziyah Gokalp (1876-1924 y.y.) – the writer, public woman, founder of the Turkic unity idea.

Hoja Nasreddin (XIII-XIV c.c.) – the hero of satirical sto-ries of Turkic people.

Mamed Emin Rasulzade (1884-1955 y.y.) – the state and pub-lic man of Azerbaijan nation.

Berdy Kerbabaev (1894-1974 y.y.) – the popular writer of Turkmenistan.

Along the hall walls the podium is surrounded by an ex-posi-tion of "The national costumes of the Turkic peoples" consist-ing of models of national clothing of Kazakhs, Azerbai-jani, Kyrgyz people, Uzbeks, Turks, Turkmens, Karakalpaks, Sakha, Tuvinians, Tatars, Bashkirs, Altaians, gagauzes, Uig-urs, Chuvashes and Dagestan nations.

V SECTION

STRATEGY OF SURVIVAL FOR MANKIND IN XXI AND FURTHER CENTURIES

FROM THE AUTHOR

Abstract. At a turn of third millennium, the world storms and quickly changes. It became difficult to expect what is to be expected tomorrow. Questions of recovery from crisis and rescue of mankind from forthcoming global changes become the most important: warming of climate, watering and food problems shaking the world of social and economic, political conflicts and other various cataclysms, accidents, negative processes. It puts mankind facing the problems not solved before. All this is caused by ignoring of objective economic laws, wildlife laws, and by violation of laws of management by cyclic development. Time of changes became, first of all, in consciousness of people, changes of world psychology, revival of spiritual and moral values. It is time for mankind to bring order into own house! The present megaproject is scientific hypothesis for the better future. There is neither futurology, nor predictions, imaginations, but there is a development of real **concept for strategy of mankind's survival in XXI and further centuries,** the principles of creation of planetary house for universal civilization of postindustrial world, based on spirituality, scientific and technological revolution, ecology, space exploration, economy and world safety. Only systematic and coordinated measures for these six basic components can provide the world and steady life in this house. It is vital that this fatal, breakthrough new system idea in the science, given rise in the center of Eurasia, was real-ized in XXI century as alternative option, that is able to give to mankind the chance to survive in conditions of globalization.

For laymen, members of the UN, members of international public organizations, scientific centers, corporations, massmedia for everyone who is not indifferent to future human civilization.

Empires of future will be reasonable ones
W. Churchill

CHAPTER I

ROD IDEA OF SCIENTIFIC MEGAPROJECT

Evolution of a terrestrial form of life which has arisen billions years ago, was accompanied by logic of development of world history: **flora** → **fauna** → **mind, human society** → **bio-sphere** → **nanosphere** – these are main stages of development of life on our planet.

In long process of fight for life of people, human beings start-ed studying itself and the world around, learned its laws and to tried correctly to apply them to increase opportunities and satisfaction of requirements. During seven thousand years of development the mankind saved up experience and knowledge to realize responsibility for its future destiny.

In the history there were many crises, the conflicts and wars. But never there was no such critical situation when possibility of exis-tence of civilization as a whole would be threatened, and the problem of limitation of earth and resources would demand the scientific de-cision. Preservation of human civilization, prob-ability of its subse-quent successful development are impossible without studying the general regularities and proportions in sys-tem production consump-tion, developments of bases of reproduction cycles and management of global processes.

Need of development of **integrated concept of transition to post-industrial civilization** is proved by prerequisites and conditions of world historical development's formation of logic that all scientists of the world and world community are trying to ex-plain, considering problem from various points of view [1,2,3].

It can be argued that the objective logic of the world's historical development may serve as a reference (standard) and provide the only accurate evaluation criterion to understand the Past, Present and Future of the development of Mankind. Humanity now enters into a period of global transition from an industrial to a post-industrial civilization.

Conventional efforts to overcome global challenges become less and less efficient while a failure to act promptly may lead to unpredictable and irreversible consequences which are potentially devastating for all of humanity. Therefore today, as never before, we must not only have a clear understanding of the causes of the unprecedented imbalance in the global social-and-public development of the present times, but also have a vision to solve the problem of global synthesis, in other words, we must exercise a truly science-based foresight. From these positions, the consideration of problem has to be based on contours of constructed **planetary house of universal civilization** (figure 1).

For the first time within conditions of globalization and crises there is an understanding of historical need of coordination of all aspects of scientific and technical, ecological, space, spiritu-al, economic security as uniform system of providing universal civilization and transition from biosphere into noosphere with preservation of development of the world not only on Earth, but also in space.

The planetary house of universal civilization and the future new waves in scientific and spiritual revolution, will be founded on **combination of six key Basic Elements of transition** to post-industrial civilization, such, as:

1.   Humanization of world community taking into account logic of world history's development.

2.   New scientific and technological revolution, techno-log-

ical ways (VI-VII-TU).

3.Ecology and stabilization of world power consumption.

4.   Space exploration, space energy and resources of So-lar system.

5.   World safety.

6.   Transition from market economy to innovative economy for post-industrial civilization.

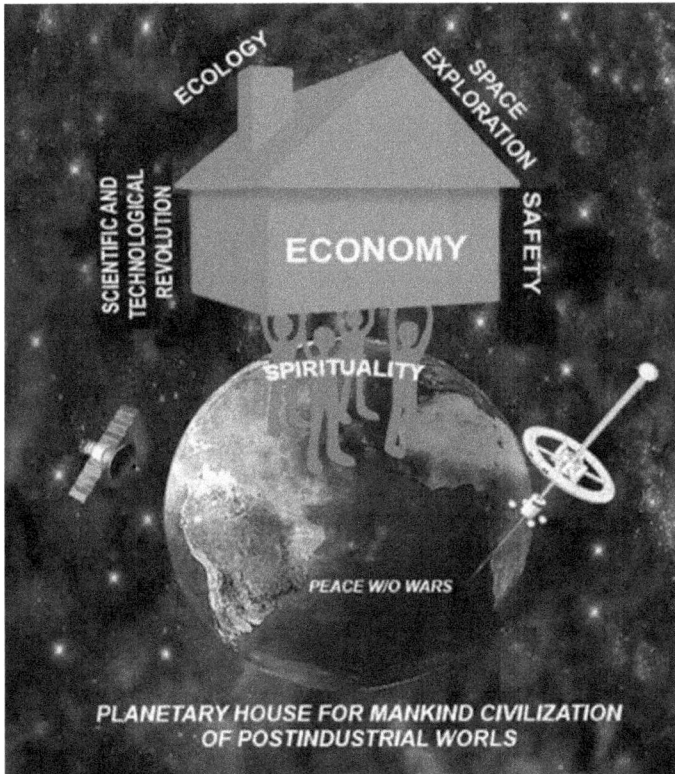

Drawing-1 - **Planetary house of universal civilization for post-industrial world**.

The main objective of presented megaproject is development of conceptual provisions on formation of new transitional model **to post-industrial civilization basing on components of transition offered by us to post-industrial world**: spirituality, society's humanization (defining logic of world history's development), scientific and technical progress (new scientific revolution), greening of society and a material world (ecological revolution), space exploration, world safety, and also world economic power with all its parameters that are to be provided by steady life in planetary house of universal civilization. Conceptual idea is that more than 200 states on a planet turned to members of one family and peacefully lived under a roof of uniform planetary house of universal civilization (see figure 1). All six Basic Elements of civilization genotype are in first quarter of XXI century endured deep transformation in course of changing industrial world civilization into post-industrial one.

Radical difference of this megaproject is that if before re-search and results of scientists, geniuses of science, **Nobel Prize laureates** were based on achievements of stunning opening and achievements in certain important spheres, for example **physics, chemistry, medicine and physiology, literature, peacemaking and economy**, in this monograph author for the first time in the world tried to consider on the basis of system approach **all six basic components of transition to post-industrial civilization as unit of interconnected spiritual and scientific process (fig-ure 1)**. Creation and synthesis of fundamental scientific theories in various subject domains of knowledge and **organization of management** of these Basic Elements are only different parties of uniform creative design process of future civilization. Only these theories on basis of uniform development, uniting philosophy, on a joint of sciences and phenomena can give the overall, complete picture of the new civilization world. Thus each making (party) of general house of civilization is considered as a unit and is based on fundamental factors of sustainable development demanding interdisciplinary scientific development with definition of their criteria and indicators. Creation of such house for civilization on basis of causal communication with offered six blocks allows to reveal stability and logic of world historical development in new conditions of post-industrial civilization. And if as a result of any violation any of six components of the planetary civilization house fails, all the design in what highlight of this idea consists will fail also. Today it is **new system idea,** which can specify the exit direction from global crisis and sustainable development.

In figure 1 peculiar "parental" house for all mankind in XXI century where love reigns, care not only on ourselves, but also of general welfare, of happiness of all people on Earth, about life system on planet, based on new knowledge, spirituality, science, creation and formation and reason is presented. Here merge of material and spiritual in human consciousness is traced.

The most important is that the house of civilization is basing on hands of people, on so-called spirituality of human development, and, naturally, everything that of performing – performs for people, for reaching satisfaction and ensuring quality and level of their life. For the first time the thesis that from economical point of view production should be focused not on satisfaction of material and spiritual needs of the abstract consumer, but **on consumption of the specific person**. Therefore inside on power of economic base spirituality, wellbeing, friendship of the people, harmonious developments of humanity are reigning. And at last, service for reaching future peaks, instead of a mammon, i.e. to wealth is carried out.

If attentively to look at book cover, you can notice that our planet is considered as though from outside – from space. Having rejected local continental conditions, national and social conditions, it is necessary to look at our past, the present and the future from space and at all from neighbour planet of Solar system, and from the galaxy. Perhaps, such vision will give large break of an exit from the deadlock. Perhaps, someone from opponents will consider that it is only creative imagination of the author.

But, probably, it also doesn't suffice today to us. Here it is necessary to quote A. Einstein: "no one of problems can be solved at the same level on what it arose". In the future new knowledge, technological novelties will provide us prosperity.

It is necessary to emphasize that within conditions of globalization and crises only **integration ideas**, joint consideration and solution of problems it is quicker achieved success, than the solution of certain states. For assessment of decisions' efficiency the scientific outlook and scientific instrument of coordination of proposed solutions with fundamental laws of nature which aren't depending on the points of view of heads of the states, multinational companies, Masonic, pan-Islamic and other associations are required especially. If world on basis of **planetary cooperation of nations and ethnos** adopts everything achievement which are made still and scientific instrument of coordination of the purposes and solutions of problems with objective laws of nature, it will rescue a human civilization and big assistance to creation of I type of the Planetary civilization will be rendered.

From there is one more macro idea. We want it or we don't want, burning issues of globalization accrue in world as an avalanche, and all can break, demolish that collected mankind for eyelids. As a whole, in expected plan, it is strategic problem therefore it is necessary to solve it step by step and in process of emergence. Today consideration of acute world issues, such, as climate warming, restraint of armament, danger of nuclear war and other military operations, a demography, hunger and food security is on the agenda. There are also new problems - *joint space exploration, forming VI and preparation for VII techno-logical way, power consumption, new financial architecture, world currency regulation, unification of confessional systems etc.* To solve these global macro tasks is not in power with exist-ing international structures and institutes which work long ago. It is necessary to be in time, react to quickly changing changes in the world.

Time came to raise question **of global control system for civilization and regulation by world processes,** which in end of XX and at the beginning of the XXI century declared itself before the world community. It to mean it is question of global world system of acceptance political and economic decision. At first stage of global management of world for solution of mentioned address problems it is time to have reasonable conversations on creation of world legislature (world parliament), executive body (the world government), judicial authority (world court), security council, world religious union only with certain powers. Thus it is necessary to make use of all world historical experience of development of humanity, including the UN, EU,g-8, g-20, and also international organizations, institutes, etc. Considering that it is most serious question and there will be many opponents, it is necessary to begin with brainstorming, i.e. carrying out various international conferences, forums, it is similar to world Davos, etc. Statement of such macropurpose to mankind deserved as in course of historical development it reached such line of global knowledge of world and civilization that can quite put and solve such global problems which face it. For history I want to notice that since when the mankind for the first time left Africa it is passed about 100 thousand years, existed about 5000 generation, but to us to inhabitants of XXI century, to our generation probably destiny prepared to participate in definition of destiny of whole world, i.e. transition to I to type of planetary civilization which can be reached allegedly in 100-150 years. But the main thing is not to be late.

CHAPTER II

GLOBAL CHALLENGES AND SOLUTION TO CRISES

The world of today is undergoing a tremendous change: eco-nomic crises, global warming, food shortages, famine and other calamities that lead to complex socio-political changes. Changes of that nature have engulfed the whole world and compel the elites and national authorities to take steps ahead of time to try to avoid losing credibility with the public and to search for new solutions to crises.

The rapidly developing mortgage crisis of 2008 which very soon transformed into a general economic crisis affecting most of the developed economies proved to be so profound that it is now compared to the great Depression of the 1930s. The un-employment rates soared worldwide; the crisis penetrated the social sphere which produced a negative impact on the living conditions of the general public due to lower incomes and a sig-nificant increase in the food prices. All that triggered massive so-cial problems in a number of developed nations, while in many developing economies of the Middle East and North Africa the same problems were so colossal that they resulted in social revo-lutions to have overthrown a number of national governments. Experts in the field, however, predict a second wave of the cri-sis which will affect most of the world's countries and is likely to force 'the world government' represented by the g8 and the g20 to initiate a revolutionary monetary reform to replace the crashed US dollar with a world's reserve currency in order to support and improve the regulatory mechanisms of financial markets, establish a fairer international trade environment and stabilize food prices [4, 5].

Furthermore, natural impacts, **such as the global warming** which is known to cause floods, droughts and the spread of epi-dem-ic diseases across the world, raise concern among the world public. It is now a proven fact that by the midtwenty-first century the fos-sil-based economy will have eventually resulted in a global warming. Today people can no longer deny that the earth is gradually heating. Over the last one hundred years the mean temperature on our planet has already risen by 0.7 °C, and this growth now continues at an ever increasing rate. If this scenario persists, the scientists predict that be-fore the end of the century the total growth in temperature will have exceed 2 °C which might be of catastrophic consequences.

Not surprisingly, persistent **social problems and moral deg-ra-dation**, as well as widespread corruption coupled with inef-ficiency of local authorities and their indifference to the needs of ordinary people now plague many regions of the world and *represent one of the most important factors* in catalyzing the atrocities that took place in such regions.

Large-scale corruption with a large diversity of forms and high level of organization, which is especially destructive in de-veloping economies, represents another big hurdle on the way to further de-velopment of the international community. This far truly effective means to combat corruption are yet to be discov-ered.

New global challenges that humanity will soon have to face may be identified by **analyzing the processes** that are presently occurring in the international economic arena, in geopolitics and international relations. The second wave of the global crisis is expected to cause a new economic depression in 2013-2015. Taking into account the cyclical nature of the economic devel-opment, a third wave of crisis should be expected in 2017-2019. Then, beginning in 2020, after all the essential innovations for the sixth technological cycle have been developed, the global economy will go into a long upturn. Experts predict that a rapid economic growth leveraged by the new technologies of the sixth techno-cycle will begin in 2025, provided the mankind avoids going into a global nuclear conflict [7]. Such conflict may po-tentially be ignited between nuclear powers in one of the now existing conflict areas. The countries with nuclear arse-nals in-clude the USA, Russia, Britain, France, China, India, Paki-stan, North Korea and Israel. The toll of a war between any of them may reach as high as 2.5 billion lives taken in the combat zone as a result of military operations, nuclear attacks and radiation sickness. Another 1.5–2 billion people worldwide would have a severe to medium radiation exposure from contaminated air, water and food. Considering the global conveyor of prevailing winds and water cur-rents, only a few hundred million people will be lucky enough to find themselves in low-exposure areas. Uncontaminated water and clean food will be a rare and highly valued resource. This may be our possible future.

Even today millions of people worldwide live in poverty, suf-fer from hunger and hardship. The industrialized countries of the world (we collectively refer to them as the g20 / g8) de-spite existing plans for long-term national strategic development which all revolve around the idea of earning excessive profits and securing the leader-ship in the race for economic supremacy are unable to formulate *any concrete solution to the protracted crisis persistent in the world's economy*. The excessive emis-sions of the US dollar of the recent years have resulted in the volume of money available worldwide outgrowing the globally produced goods by 10–12 times. The laws of economics dictate that such a huge imbalance will inevitably cause a crisis. Many rich countries of the world have been using the re-cent advances in science and technology in order to maximize their growth of capital in the name of the only goal – continued enrichment. It is now the ripe time for the world's elites including billionaires and powerful politicians (political clans) to change their attitude and turn their face toward the global community of nations governed by the UN and other international organizations.

In these challenging circumstances, the UN, the Interna-tional Monetary Fund, the European Bank for Reconstruction and Development and the International Bank for Reconstruction and Development, the European Union and other international financial and public institutions have failed to be efficient. At the same time, the industrial technological development of the III-IV-V-techno-cycles has come to a standstill. Our civilization must now enter the new VI technological cycle to carry on global economic development through the next several decades (2020-2050).

The stated suggests idea to think of formation of **new global control system** structure by world not to allow global crises, accidents, climate warming, and other negative processes and threats which can lead a human civilization to the end. The following head is devoted to these problems, searches of new ways of development.

| | | Scientific center at UN on sustainable development of the _____ | | | Third way of universal civilization. New paradigm of reforming of world community in XXI century | |

| | | **Conceptual model of transition to post-industrial civilization** (system approach) | | | | |

Humanization of world community taking into account logic of world history's development	**Scientific and technical revolution. Technological Ways (TW)**	**Ecology and stabilization of world power consumption**	**World development of space, space energy and resources of Solar system**	**Safety of world**	**Transition from market economy to innovative economy of post-industrial civilization**
Objective knowledge of world history of the past, present and future. Transformation of world psychology, thinking of person. Revival of cultural and moral values (Islam, Christianity, Buddhism, Catholicism, Confucianism, other religions). Harmonious development of society, planetary cooperation of ethnoses, people. Creative development of the human capital. Realization of idea "Specific person, satisfaction of needs and ensuring, quality, level of his life. The concept new spiritual and ideological doctrine. Society democratization, political stability. Creation of artificial intelligence. Spiritual revolution in XXI century. Establishing of social and culture formation	I.-TU 1776-1830 yrs. Steam engines, beginning of industrial revolution. II.-TU 1830-1880 yrs. Electricity, cars, car and steamship building, transport III – TU 1880-1930 yrs. Mechanical engineering, petrochemistry, metallurgy, electrical equipment IV.-TU 1930-1970 yrs. Aircraft, construction, radar, gas processing V.-TU 1970-2010 yrs. Electronics, nanotechnology, molecular biology VI – TU 2010-2050 yrs. Nano, Bio, ICT, robotics, space technologies. Realization of new VI- TU and preparation for following VII-TU Formation of intellectual economy on basis of technological revolution in XXI century	Preservation of planet's global ecosystem with use of natural and resource capacity of Earth. Observance of ecological imperative's conditions. Level restriction of global warming to 20C. Observance of Kyoto Protocol on CO2 till 2020. Balance between economic growth, social requirements and limitation of natural resources. Development of per capita power consumption standards. Coordination of human activity with opportunities of nature. Transition to hydrogen fuel, power ecological revolution. Balance between power consumption and growth of population of Earth Harmonious development of society and nature.	Space problems, space ecology. Technology development, installation of space stations, their safety. Development, biosphere and noosphere protection, transition to noosphere. Nuclear-free world. Prevention of wars, including in financial, economic and information spheres. Intercontinental balance. Regulations of space's commercialization. Creation of public and noosphere civilization. Development of solar energy and satisfaction of power consumption. Entry into era of solar, hydrogen energy; teleportation of atoms and magnetism. Transition to humanistic noosphere and to the I type of planetary civilization.	Safety types: Economical Social Ecological Food Demographic and migration Technological Informational Energetical Innovative Space All types of safety are to be provided with admissible threshold values. Cutting of arms. Prevention of nuclear war treaties.	Strategic planning and global forecast of world economy development Creation of real mechanisms of sustainable development Elaboration of new global strategy of world order, transition to limited reproduction New financial architecture Transition to uniform regulator of world currency Defining of basic mechanisms of reproduction and capital regulation Anti-recessionary measures
Acceptance by UN the concept of new spiritual and ideological doctrine of universal civilization transition to post-industrial development of mankind. Creation of supreme council under UN (wise men of the world).	Acceptance of "Strategy of innovative break till 2050" by UN.	Acceptance of "Power-ecological restrictive pre-crisis declaration" by UN 5	Acceptance of world's rigid regulations of space by UN	Acceptance by UN the system of prevention and overcoming of consequences of global threats, crisis phenomena, accidents, sharp geopolitical risks and conflicts	Five-year message by UN to people of world taking into account priorities of development and world safety. Adoption of World peace declaration and its observance within 5 years

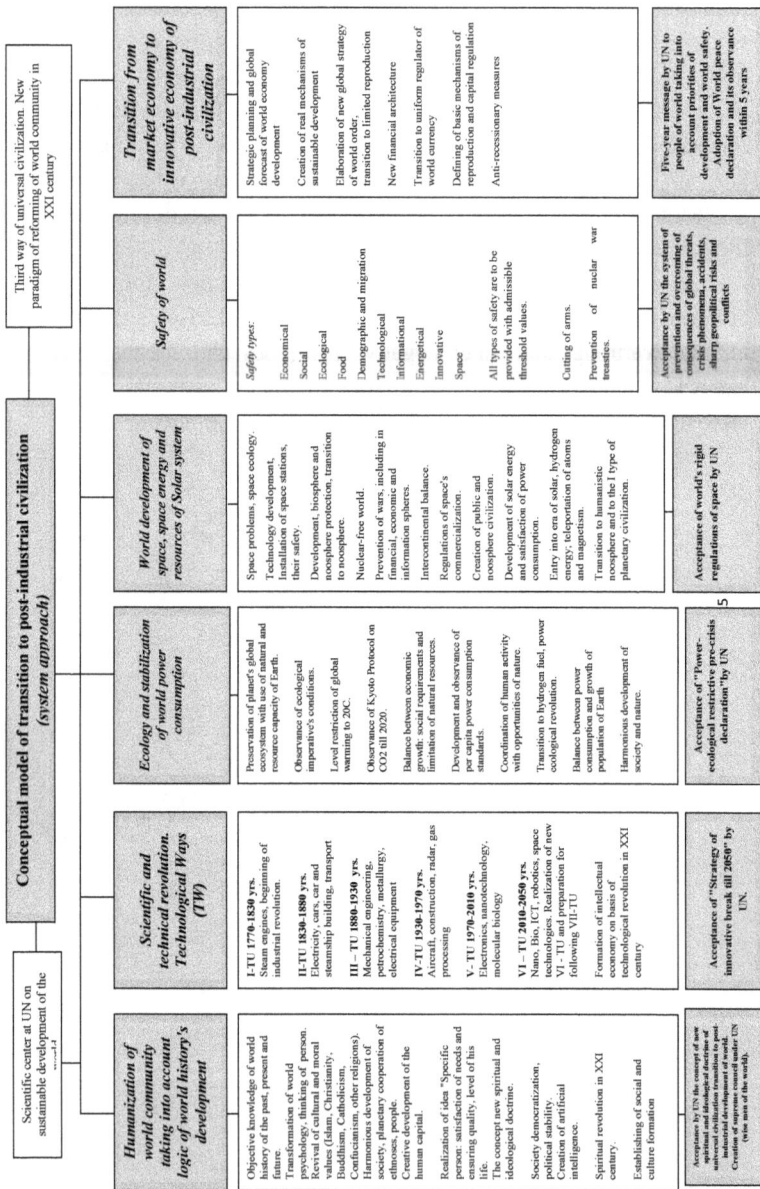

Figure 2   Construction of survival strategy of mankind in XXI and further centuries

CHAPTER III

CONCEPTUAL MODEL OF TRANSITION TO POST-IN-
DUSTRIAL CIVILIZATION (SYSTEM APPROACH)

World crisis proceeds. The reasons of it are system ones, and are
well-known. Best minds of the world are now researching ways
out from current situation. Situation is difficult: certain part of
mankind parasitizes, there are earthquakes, warming of climate and
other cataclysms, there are water problems, on the one hand, and on
another one - billions starve, water and the food are in deficiency,
the world is shaken by social and economic, political changes. All
of these things are caused by ignoring of objective economic laws,
laws of nature of the live environment [8,9].

Now the world is over an abyss, further way of development is in
danger... Time of changes in consciousness of people, changes of
world psychology, revival of spirituality, moral val-ues has came. It
is time to mankind to bring an order in its own house. The challenge
is thrown down first of all to developed states (g8, g20), all world
community, especially scientific as the science has to give an objective assessment to occurring events and develop the mechanism
of preservation and development of life and a sustainable development of the world. In this regard here pertinently to quote UN's general Secretary Ban Ki-moon to «Rio +20» in 2012: «The planet is in
condition of unprecedented crisis. We need to recognize that present
model of global development is irrational. We risk dooming billion
people to life in conditions of endemic poverty. It is necessary to find
a new way for advance forward ...».

In the world scientists create and take root into life most various
scientific and technical openings. But even to Nobel Prize laureates

it isn't allowed to see how these introductions will affect various spheres, first of all natural processes, ecological disasters, accidents, etc. Despite distinctions in existing opin-ions, this crisis as it was already mentioned is system one [6,10]. Therefore answers should be looked for proceeding from system approaches, integrity, and adequacy of the solution of problems. Humanistic world outlook approach is key approach. In this re-gard we consider as most priority solution for problems of humanization of society and safety as bases of world order.

In our opinion, it is necessary to change views on market econ-omy, **the innovative economy of post-industrial civilization** *comes af-ter that. It is based on new knowledge, science and high technologies, competitiveness of human capital with all ranges of spirituality up-grading and updating of values' system.*

If to consider problem in other global plane, it is possible to no-tice following. One world schools of sciences, thinkers stood up for control over population growth, others - for observance of doctrines (strategy of eternal life), and the third suggested to consider strategy of noosphere development. All of them are in own way right. But the world moves on unpredictable way, giving mankind various surprises, and only in these new conditions, entirely considering scientific solu-tions of all fundamental results and all existing progressive schools, it is possible to come nearer to solution of raised problem. In other words, systemically eliminating world crises, global threats, it is possible to pass to sustainable development.

Modern capitalism, and socialism as well are on threshold of Renaissance's changes. Time of post-industrial civilization came, and space exploration, a noosphere era, an entry into other system of coordinates and values become one of very important factors of de-velopment. In this regard agenda of history is **the third way of development of humanity**. It is born on a joint between capitalism and socialism. Conditionally the third way of development can be presented as **transition to innovative economy of post-industrial**

civilization (innovationist). In XXI century, the century of noo-sphere, break of development of humanity, noosphere civilization of all systems of activity of society on Earth and in space has to be created, there will be innovative and technological breakthrough. For this reason now we make attempt to carry out integration process of all separate scientific and technical, ecological, economic, space and spiritual and humanistic directions and to ensure their safety in the world. Such system approach with use of key elements of devel-opment of the world to solution of problems at macro level deserves public attention and can be serve as potential idea of sustainable development. It is some kind of complete adequate method, which gives opportunity to solve objectives.

On basis mentioned above, the author made an attempt to develop transition concept to post-industrial civilization where all six Basic Elements of transition, i.e., the spirituality, new scientific and tech-nological revolution, greening of society and material world, space exploration, world safety and economy as a whole are systemically considered that as a whole can be provide large break.

Scientific novelty of megaproject consists in complex consider-ation of all components (i.e. basic components) as uniform world out-look development of global world and on basis of it to development of network model for global control system and regulation by world processes and possibility of preservation of sustainable development of world upon transition to post-industrial civilization (figure 4).

To be fair it is necessary to notice that earlier though very im-portant scientific researches and opening were made, they couldn't provide sustainable development in world because of separation, unsystematic character of world problems' solutions. Thanks to sci-entific achievements we far promoted in some directions, while in others lagged behind therefore there was no balanced development. For example, development of the g-8 and g-20countries in pur-suit of excess profits to please to multinational companies happened without spiritual component of development of the world. It is rec-

PROJECT «NEW TURKESTAN»

Creation of spiritual and technological cluster

CITY OF SPIRIT CAPITAL
- TIMURS, UZBEK, KYRGYZ, AZERBAIJAN, TURKMEN, TATAR PEOPLE SETTLEMENT (TIYZ, KYRGYZ, AZERBAIJAN, TURKMEN, NEAR PROJECTS OF THE ISLAMIC WORLD OF 9TH-XIX CENTURIES)
- KAZAKH PROJECT. HISTORY AND CULTURE APPLICATION (BUILDINGS, PAVILIONS, PANORAMAS SINCE ANCIENT TIMES AND DIFFERENCING FINDING)
- PANORAMA OF WORLD-WIDE AND HISTORICAL DEVELOPMENT
- INTERNATIONAL ACADEMY OF RELIGION LYCEUMS. MADRASAH RELIGIOUS STUDIES CENTER
- THE ACADEMY CULTURAL CENTER OF TEAMS, CENTRAL MUSEUM, HIGH ELECTRONIC LIBRARIES, ETC. CULTURAL SECTION TREASURY
- SCIENTIFIC CENTER OF A RUSSIALIZATION OF SOCIETY. NEW CODE OF MORALS
- PROJECTS OF HOUSING CONSTRUCTION. PARTICIPATION OF REGIONS

KENTAU'S TECHNOLOGICAL CLUSTER
- PLANTS OF THE 6TH TECHNOLOGICAL WAY
- MODERNIZATION OF PRODUCTION. REPRODUCTION
- TECHNO POLICIES
- SCIENTIFIC, TRAINING, PRODUCTION CENTERS. TRAINING OF STAFF ON NEW DIRECTION
- CENTRAL TEAR STAGE AVENGERMEDIA
- YOUTH TOWN, HIGH TECHNOLOGIES

CLUSTER NEW AUL, 2000 WORK PLACES
- CONSTRUCTION PROJECT OF NEW INDUSTRIAL COMPLEX. CONSTRUCTION OF 150 NEW HOUSES
- MINI PLANTS. 140 INNOVATIVE MINI-FARMS, GREENHOUSES, ETC.
- SOCIAL INFRASTRUCTURE: SCHOOL, CULTURAL MALLS, SCHOOLS, FIRST-AID POSTS, KINDER GARDENS
- PROVIDING WITH THE DISTRICT FOOD. RESEARCH AND PRODUCTION BASES
- THE PROGRAM OF EXTRACTION OF 1—TH THE AUL TRAINING CENTER

TOURISM CLUSTER
- COMPLEXES OF CULTURAL AND HISTORICAL HERITAGE. ARYSTANBAB, OTYRAR, TARAZ, SAMARKAND, ETC.
- INVESTMENTS TO SILK WAY PROJECTS
- NATURAL AND ECOLOGICAL TOURISM
- BUSINESS TOURISM. PROMOTION AND TOURISM ADVERTIZING
- TOURISM INFRASTRUCTURE. HOTEL, SERVICE REST. WORLD PLACES, ETC.

INFRA-STRUCTURE
- TRANSPORT AND LOGISTIC CENTER "SILK WAY"
- NEW WAYS, HIGH-SPEED TRAINS
- AIRPORT
- SATELLITE COMMUNICATION. TELECOMMUNICATIONS. ELECTRONIC MEDIA, ETC.
- INTERNATIONAL TELEVISION CENTER "TURAN"

ognised even by billionaires (B. gates and others). The author tried to meet this lack, in com-plex using of all components of transition to new stage of civilization development.

As new knowledge methodology of civilization's development connection of achievements of natural sciences (STP) with pub-lic, society humanization, spirituality, religions in uniform design of planetary house is for the first time shown. Further briefly we will stop on each of six blocks (figure 2).

BLOCK 1
Humanization of world community considering logic of world history development

Global changes, world crisis lead to difficult socially and po-litical changes[11]. These changes are like tremors, - occur first in one place, then in other ones. Changes can't be predicted because it can arise worldwide. World crisis forces influential forces of society and those that are in power, to take measures beforehand in order to prevent mistrust of people and to look for new ways of recovery from crisis.

The most essential factor in development of world community are collected for many years social problems, spiritual degradation, corruption, idleness of local authorities, their indifferent relation to needs of people in various regions of world [7]. Many countries, with-out having accurate state ideology, had lost social orientation and fol-lowed a way of thoughtless consumption. The national idea, focused on consciousness of people, is necessary for states,. It has to be based on the principles of nation's unity, development of its language, cul-ture and customs. But the na-tional idea is a not only spiritual phenomenon, it is integrally connected with interests of nation and its' realization. Thus any nation isn't capable to exist separately, in separation from other nations, its interests and separated contradic-tive interests form other nations. Therefore understanding of national idea, national interests and mutual trust is indispensable condition of its realization [2].

World religions very poorly protect the population from moral decomposition and crime, don't bear original spiritual re-vival and a national unification, create only imitation of it. All this influences national security of the world. Though as a whole the religion always played and plays a rod role in attempts to find support by means of which it is possible to move heaven and earth and not to drop out of it. Who will deny that religious-ness doesn't do believers happy?

It is probably correct that spiritual representatives of world always first of all put forward ideas promoting **awakening of consciousness**, to its release from stereotypes, and only then recommended to apply technologies improving physical body without which the consciousness can't realize completely itself and exist in a material world. Unfortunately, representatives of developed countries understood it just the opposite. If society's development during number of centuries submitted not so much to reason, but to market relations and private capital. It is time now to trust in power of human reason and spirit, differently – deadly threat.

In an unstable century of globalization the idea about **hu-man-ization of society** can become a factor of unification of peo-ple and states. After implementation of listed actions by revival and use of centuries-old historical values there will be opportu-nities of global changes in spiritual and cultural development of mankind. It will be a big step maintaining honor of society not to become stagnation sources. **The main task of humaniza-tion ideas is to change thinking of person, his consciousness according to requirements of new civilized society of XXI century. A lot of things should be done on settling of disa-greements in the world.**

Restoration of harmonious development of society and na-ture in XXI century is possible by elimination of large shortcom-ings – instead of production and development of not infinite raw material resources and minerals it is necessary to develop the new vision, the new ideas, new projects of development. Proj-ects have to become measures, being urgent. Is vital **to follow laws of historical development** therefore problem of spiritual and cultural development of society has to become a problem of paramount importance.

In answer to question what has to be a new form of society in the XXI century, it is expedient to consider two factors.

First, use of logic (experience) of world-wide and histori-cal development, and also primordial national history, spiritual cultural values of each country and region.

Secondly, new requirements of the XXI century and **transi-tion to a post-industrial humanistic and noosphere civiliza-tion**. As its first stage, acts the development of new technological way. It is necessary to invest capital to innovative technology, to research and development, and to human capital.

All stated above testifies that in world development there comes such moment, the truth moment, when there will be
need of elaboration new global strategy of world order. Seems that it is necessary to begin with development **the correct state ideology directed on preservation of moral, spiritual cultural values and traditions.**

Key components of society's humanization and spirituality revival taking into account development of world history are following **(see Fig.1)**:

-        *history of past, present and future; -change of world psychology;*

-        *revival of   spiritual and   moral   v a l u e s , world religions,including Islam, Christianity, Buddism, Confucianism, etc.;*

-        *harmonious development of society;*

-        *creative development of human capital in a sharp decrease in the number of people in the world;*

-        *spiritual revolution in XXI century.*

The global crisis made us open our eyes. There are many reasons to try to **revive high moral and spiritual** values acquired by the mankind over the centuries which today so sadly seem to be readily rejected by many. The world once again seeks the ideals of humanism and justice. That being said, fundamental moral standards and spiritual values are the product of the development of human civilization. In the world today we are witnessing public unrest, natural calamities, dictatorships which all contribute to moral decline and the rupture of social ties result-ing in a moral crisis.

It is sad that **we forget about society humanization** taking into account logic of world history, we forgot about need of co-existence under nature laws. But law has chance to work only if it meets ethical standard. Society always has to remember natu-ral basis of the development – the nature. However natural and human capital are not having paramount significance and cultural wealth is forgotten

Therefore laws of harmonious development of society are broken, "the invisible market's hand" played role, and **rich states became hostages of world crisis**.

To answer how global problems are to be solved, time came under the auspices of the UN to accept **Concept of new spir-itual and ideological doctrine of universal development of the world**. It will provide lifting of spiritual forces of nations and nationalities of the world and their social and economic pro-gress. Finally there will be a transition to a post-industrial para-digm of spiritual development (**see fig. 2**).

As an example briefly we will state idea of revival spiritual be-ginning in one of the Euroasian regions. We are speaking **about creation of the NEW SPIRITUAL and TECHNOLOGICAL CLUSTER "Turkestan Valley"** *(it is represented in form of uniting West and East on Great Silk Way of regional model of the world order, new spiritual, technological development and international security)*. From history it is known that ancient Turkestan which was the spiritual center, took a special place on the great Silk way.

The main **objective** of it which doesn't have analogs in the world of the international national megaproject - to turn Turkestan into the international level spiritual center (megalopolis), to take new step to ensuring the international security. For the first time in history on the example of one region, having coordinated two especially large cardinal problems: on the one hand, spirit-ual and cultural development of society, from the other hand the new, sixth, technological way – to present to the world new Re-naissance model of opportunity spiritually - innovative develop-ment [12]. Around large Turkestan settled many countries (over approximately 400 million people may be involed in this idea).

Difference of this project from the **Silicon Valley** in USA is that close coordination of spiritual and cultural development and aul revival according to requirements of new time, with innova-tive sixth technological way will force it to work for the man-kind benefit. at international level "New Turkestan" will unite West and East and will attract potential opportunities of **Great Silk Way**. With the centuries-old history and culture the project will make changes to spiritual consciousness of people. The unity of society and people will increase, the scheme of sustainable develop-ment of the region will be created.

In XXI century new moral will be created, spiritual and cultural institutes as social problems come to forefront. One of them is project of revival of Turkestan in new way. The purpose is not creation of state territory Turkestan, but solution of mankind problems by trans-formation of it into Euroasian integration cent-er – some kind of new step to ensuring the international security in the XXI century. **Ka-zakhstan** declares itself as nuclear-free country, though we have richest in the world uranium stocks, Baikonur spaceport and other opportunities to be the nuclear power state.

The most important is that as a result of managing uniform process of coordination of spiritual-cultural development and new innovative and technological way will be provided effective use of most expensive capital human. Such know how becomes new push for the whole world. **Differently, in XXI century this project will be courageous step to spiritual revolution in new thought, consciousness of mankind.**

Within project for the first time in center of Eurasia on great Silk Way the new Turkestani spiritual and technological valley will be formed, i.e. there will be a new megalopolis for development (**Fig. 3**).

Today in the world still there is no such spiritual and technological center focused on civilized development. It is some kind of fearless step to spiritual revolution in consciousness of mankind. **The offered megaproject becomes regional model of new spiritual and technological development of world order and international security.**

New Turkestan will turn into Euroasian integration center – a place for cultural wealth of many countries

- As a result, unity of As soon as this regional project will yield the results, its universal use as the Turkestani spiritual range becomes agenda for ideal development of the world progress in science and technology. Most of the developed nations of the world, guided in their endeavor by the Theory of long Waves, are now completing the fifth technological cycle and are actively engaged in building the foundation for the sixth techno-cycle. The core factors of the next technological cycle will be biotechnologies, nanotechnologies, genetic engineering, information and communication networks, artificial intelligence and space technologies. **Innovation seems to be the only appropriate solution to the global crisis, which means developing strategies for innovative breakthroughs through large-scale international development programs tailored for specific clusters.** In the conditions of transition to an innovative economy, it is advisable to modernize science, education and public health to boost the advent of the new techno-cycle. The above core areas each therefore require a comprehensive cluster program to put all the accumulated knowledge to practical applications.

Later on, after the VI techno-cycle has been fully expressed (possibly by 2050), the global economy will go into the next long-wave technological cycle at a new level of the post-industrial civilization.

Before full development of results of VI technological way this period becomes time of deep geopolitical and geo-economic transformations. There will be essential changes in structure of our planet population. Considering these circumstances, together with states g8, g20 it is desirable for structural divisions of the United Nations to develop joint structure on accumulation of all knowledge of world history's development, to create intellectual product from mankind origin about one today, i.e. to have strongest base of scientific and technical information which will be necessary for development of any megaproject, assistance on development and transfer of new knowledge. It might be correct to consider correct structural divisions of United Nations together with the states g8, g20 **expected scenarios of development of international problems in XXI century** for receiving corresponding decision and anticipatory measures.

The future is in behind intellectual economy, creative opportunities of society, accumulation of value system for post-industrial civilization. On this way superiority will be taken by countries with high intellectual potential developing on basis of high technologies and information base (Internet resources). But also this power won't solve safety of planetary house for universal civilization.

Globalization and world crisis showed that for transition from market economy to innovative economy post-industrial civilization, absolutely new approach needed and **new paradigm of world community's reforming** as well. Even developed states understand it. It seems that reference point has to be on system approach to reproduction process taking into account spiritual, historical, investment, innovative and safe components of new universal civilization. At final formation of VI technological way for scientific and technical progress this situation has to be considered. Balance of world development consists in it.

Innovative break in development of human capital on basis of increasing its competitiveness. The post-industrial civilization puts in forefront human factor and spiritual sphere. The science, culture, education, health, religion, moral and other universal civilization values define social economic progress for more and more. Development of these spheres can't be let ride and furthermore to save at their expense budgetary funds. Favourites are capable of it, but not far-sighted authorities.

Innovative break will be carried out by investments, increasing expenses on health care, science and education, which will give new impulse to development of new technological way. In this regard in first quarter of the XXI century it is possible to create new institutes, to revive moral systems and moral values. International organizations and public forces have to favor these changes, differently world by first half of XXI century can choke in fierce social conflicts, as occurs in number of east countries. Only such positive actions of the international organizations will possibly preserve the peace.

Globalization will be shown more strongly in spiritual sphere. It will lead to statement of law, **consent** and peace in international relations. **Sharp reorganizations of spiritual consciousness of people and change of world psychology are necessary.**

Transition begins with reconsideration of former ideological postulates. For example, from economic point of view, production is to focus not on satisfaction of needs of abstract consumer, but on consumption of **specific person**. Possibly, one of factors bringing to crises is «excessive» consumption.

Development of world history shows that mankind reached good results and progress in its civilization development. It is time to live comfortably though it is known that in the world there are more than 1,2 billion population starve. In this regard it is **expedient to establish the minimum barriers to normal life** and transition to increase of competitiveness of economy in such spheres of human capital, as (**see fig. 1**):

-       *health care (health care financing according to recom-mendation of World Health Organization has to be not less than 6% of GDP);*

- *science (for normal development of the state, science funding has to be not less than 1,5% of GDP);*
- *education (not less than 6% of GDP);* -   *culture   (not less than 5% of GDP);*
- *formation of intellectual economy, creation of artificial intelligence;*
- *realization of consumption ideology of competitive per-son and his standard of living.*

Only by establishment of such **minimum social and economic standards** (certain standards of life) in the field of the human capital it is possible to provide comfortable life really. Having coordinated minimum standards to growth rates of economy, it is possible to define norms of level and quality of life for developing countries and Third World countries. If these norms provide high rates of economic growth, automatically the standard of living of the population depending on abilities of the personality and competitiveness of each person, the nation, the people and the country as a whole in proportion will raise.

At such approach people will know in advance that without increase of competitiveness of human capital it is impossible to reach a high standard of living. Everyone, at first, will aspire to it, secondly, he will know, on what to it to count. People won't be submitted influence of various ideologies, religious trends.

As a result of fair approach, to all and each person on planet identical conditions for providing peace and harmony, and also increase of competitiveness of countries will be created. In my opinion, to be very developed and rich country, it is possible to use various methods, effectively to apply both capitalist, and socialist ways of production. Rising of living standard on planet, an achievement of peace and consent on the basis of acceptable ways has to become the main task. At such approach there is an aspiration to alignment of operating conditions of citizens, identical opportunities of abilities manifestation, and also to rapprochement of living standards for various segments of the population of our planet.

World crisis bared negative consequences in sphere of spiri-tu-al reproduction, sociocultural civilization, particularly in sci-ence and education, culture and moral, moral values. The question is in threat of moral degradation of society. One of the main signs of it is obviously expressed **professional incompetence** in all spheres of human capital, from lowest level to highest one in public admin-istration. Especially it is visible in devel-oping countries. Even developed countries during crisis felt acute shortage of shots on risk management in system of crisis management at international level. Therefore EU during crisis urgently allocated big allocations and began to train qualified personnel in this direction. To it compel proceeding growth rates of unemployment in these countries.

From here **new paradigm about educated society, the per-son** is born. In conditions of global crisis science and education come to forefront and become **basis of all system of reproduc-tion cycle**, since birth of ideas and finishing receiving profit for satisfaction of person's needs, and also start of investments for new civilization development. Quality of education, sciences and revival of spiritual cultural values has to be basis of reproduc-tion of modern world community in XXI century. If we want to preserve the peace, then education is to be public benefit instead of as to the market relations that still, unfortunately, proceeds. In XXI century formation total in-tellectual capital becomes basic task. In this regard it is necessary to reconstruct cardinally all education system, especially in receiving new knowledge that university graduates got at once to sphere of process of repro-duction, instead of being unemployed.

All social spheres have to work for spiritual reproduction, re-production of the human capital that will significantly affect innova-tive break. Such large divisions of the UN, as UNESCO which have to develop **Universal declaration on spiritual re-production of sociocultural sphere, including education, culture, science and health care where it would be possible to establish admissible threshold values to increase competi-tiveness of economy of the**

countries have to become chief coordinators in this area. It will be real steps to a new post-industrial social civilization.

Thus, key factors in development of human capital are **in-vestments into people, establishment of social and economic standards, increase in innovation and optimization of people consumption.** UN as the international organization could ex-ercise supervision of performance of these indicators in world countries as regulating and coordinating body for providing sustainable development in the world. For definition of these minimum social and economic standards and further monitoring at UN, it is necessary to create **World advisory council**. The United Nations expedient to carry out the **5-year Message to people of the world** in which all stated could be reflected. The future of the world depends on development of new paradigm focusing the states of the world and world community on revival and enhancement of spiritual and cultural potential of the world community.

The problem of a world civilization is that **it has to en-ter again to condition of innovative break on basis of new paradigm for basic development of education, sciences and cultures by powerful investing the sphere. It will be main demand to transition, that is, to the first type of planetary civilization. (Figure 4)**

BLOCK 3
Ecology and stabilization of world power consumption

According to some scientists, mankind now is in the first phase of global ecological disaster. But opportunities to avoid ecological deadlock still are, "the non-return point" isn't held yet.

The biosphere of Earth has huge resources which are used by mankind, but are limited and can be exhausted by the end of current century. Mankind closely came nearer "to a non-return point", especially in development of processes of global eco-logical disaster. In this regard preservation of our planet global ecosystem with rational use of natural and resource capacity of Earth is especially actual in XXI century. By estimates of some scientists-experts if mankind doesn't take urgent measures for preservation of planet ecosystem, then ecological death of man-kind can already come in XXI century, i.e. on first phase – a phase of global ecological disaster [9]. As known scientist in the field of the biosphere N. Moiseyev claims, there comes prob-ability of stability loss for biosphere of complete system and, probably, parameters of biosphere will be improper for human life [13].

In our opinion, still in basic and successful states of world and underdeveloped countries local problems were solved one by one, except for some attempts of USA and the former USSR to create balance of forces between them. The powerful USA and USSR provided stability in the world due to equality of forces between superstates. After collapse of USSR, the responsibility for destiny of mankind passes to USA. But, unfortunately, they don't hurry.

Problems of planetary scale, Earth biosphere and noosphere co-operation of mankind were put seldom. Now, irrespective of states' status, it is necessary to go on compromise solutions, fruitfully to develop international cooperation to prevent possi-ble catastrophic ecological consequences for human civilization. Despite rapid growth of NTP, priority role of power will be for long time, until the end of this century. High technologies of future will need enormous quantity of energy. Problems of stabilization of world power consumption, which exceeded 10 bln.n.e. become a mansion. [14]. How to find balance between effective power consumption and growth of Earth population, on the one hand, and with nature opportunities – from another hand? It is necessary to come to certain standards of **per capita power consumption** by its decrease and restrictive consumption. Certainly, here it is necessary to apply differentiated ap-proach, to classify developed, developing and lagging behind countries by energy consumption level, and also step by step to resolve issue of world stabilization of power consumption. All these questions have to be considered in 2015 in Paris and widely be discussed at level of experts, UN working groups with further removal of question at UN sessions.As for observance of the Kyoto Protocol on CO_2 till 2020, leading countries of the world –USA, People's Republic of Chi-na, EU, India and Russia don't carry out it. Therefore time came to take radical measures for reduction of emissions and greenhouse gases to safe level. In this plan neither Copenhagen conference (2009), nor conference of UN on sustainable development "Rio +20" didn't help to solve matter considerably (2012). Probably, first, it is necessary to enter rigid sanctions and tax regulations on CO_2 emissions, secondly, to create **global power ecological fund** and as a whole to stimulate this process.

It is necessary to consider this problem at session of UN and on next meeting and g-20 with connection of world community, politicians, ecologists, climatologists, etc. It is necessary to adopt new convention, obliging to solve two-uniform problems: on one hand, transition to **energy saving technologies** (applica-tion of light-emitting diodes, electric car), and from another hand – transition to power based on energy of **renewable sources** (a wind, sunshine, hydrogen and thermonuclear energy, magnetism etc.). Thus consumption of energy will cardinally decrease be-cause lion's share of energy at movement of car and other means of transport leaves on friction force overcoming. Though share of solar energy while is scanty - 0,5%, but its annual production grows for 45%, i.e. in two years almost doubles.

It is planning to implement many solar power stations in world. In this aspect, USA, People's Republic of China and some other countries actively work.

Restriction of global warming to 20C was confirmed with UN in declaration adopted by Copenhagen international conference on climate change in 2009. But, unfortunately, even UN – the most authoritative organization, can't actively interfere and is powerless before such world authorities, as USA, People's Re-public of China, etc. It testifies that status of UN is insufficient for solution of global problems, and also there is no political will of heads. And when there will come ecological crisis, it will be late to undertake something.

So, conclusion is that considering new conditions of globalization, crises, global cataclysms, geophysical accidents, climate warming, food crisis, transition to new technological ways, and also approach of period of space development and safety in space and on Earth etc., it is **necessary to reform radically in shortest time all UN system, having moved its headquarters on other continent**. For implementation of it, it is necessary to create working group of experts, analysts, independent scientific organizations, strong minds of world for preparation of offers on UN reforming.

Perhaps, it is time to create under the UN new body – **Supreme council of wise men of world**.

Summing up result, we will note that if we really go to society humanization, need of **harmonious development of society and the nature** for XXI century paramount task in creation of general planetary house of universal civilization **(see figure` 1)**. As quintessence of all this we recommend to admit to UN the power ecological global strategy reflected in restrictive pre-crisis declaration **(see figure 2)**. The era of power economy, i.e. economy of energy for normal, comfortable, safe use by its man-kind excluding various accidents and ecological crisis begins.

In conditions of becoming aggravated global crises of UN has to join actively in control process over sources of power ecological resources and their effective use for benefit of all mankind. It is necessary to go for **change of existing model of economic growth**, especially in developed countries, i.e. for decrease in annual world economic growth, investing introduc-tion of high energy saving technology to reduce risk of power ecological crisis.

Very fatal there is exit search from impasse of "Death Valley" by means using noosphere power ecological way of production and consumption of solar energy, hydrogen fuel and energy of magnetism. It will be new paradigm of power consumption, new power ecological revolution of second quarter of XXI century which is based on development of VI technological way. To carry out this revolutionary jump, huge efforts of partnership of world civilization are necessary.

BLOCK 4
World development of space, space energy and resources of Solar system

Ever since the beginning of the space exploration era, the military circles of every superpower have contemplated military applications for space technologies. **Prof. Vladimir Vernadsky** puts moral values way above material ones, whereas in the real-ity of the 'technological man' of the present day this value scale is reversed [15].

Humanity will always keep demanding more and more en-ergy, whether of cosmic nature or otherwise, to continue the pro-gress of the human race going, although our science and technol-ogy will not always be ready to provide power in ever increasing proportions. yet, as we know from history we should expect new discoveries and inventions, such as teleportation of atoms, for instance, that will enable the mankind to make another techno-logical leap forward in pursuit of new horizons and continue its development at a faster pace still. Not surprisingly the fantastic predictions made many years ago by **Leonardo da Vinci, jules Verne, Benjamin Franklin and the Marquis de Condorcet** now have become an everyday reality. In the nearest future solar power and hydrogen power will dominate the energy balance, while their market share today is only 0.5% of the total human consumption).

V. Vernadsky [15] wrote: "We endure not crisis exciting weak souls, but greatest change of Mankind's thought, time coming true only once during millennium. Standing on this change, cov-ering look the revealing future, we have to be happy that we are fated to endure it and to participate in creation of such future". The huge contribution to development of noosphere civiliza-tion was made by following scientists: **I.Kant, Zh.Lagrange, A.Einstein, V.Vernadsky, N.Moiseyev, K.Tsiolkovsky, P.Kuznetsov, R.Bartini, A.Chizhevsky.** In XXI century noosphere break of universal civilization is fated to be carried out.

In post-industrial civilization land-based sources of energy are exhausted and will be insufficient, and also for ecological reasons will be limited [3]. In these conditions to forefront there is space development, use of space energy and resources of So-lar system for deduction of international stability [9].

Earth-based energy sources will have become depleted and will not be sufficient to satisfy the needs of the post-industrial civilization [15]. Environmental concerns will also put further restrictions on the use of such sources of power. Space explora-tion with the view of harnessing cosmic energies and tapping into the resources of the solar system will therefore play a vital role in maintaining international stability.

We don't know, whether is and what civilization in space or on other planets. Therefore having get exit to space, mankind as sample of land civilization has to bear with itself intellectual, spiritual and moral, humanistic values adequately to meet pos-sible civilizations of other planets. It is unreasonable to connect sustainable development with continuous use of non-renewable natural resources, but with use of renewables, resources of noo-sphere it is possible to approach solution of main problem of sustainable development of mankind reasonably.

The time period up to the complete expression of the VI tech-nological cycle will be a period marked by a deep geo-politi-cal and geo-economic transformation. The world's population structure will undergo a significant change. Taking the above into consideration, it is advisable that the United Nations to-gether with the g8/g20 members form a joint institution with the purpose of accumulating all of the historical knowledge on the development of the mankind spanning the time period from the origin of the human race until the present moment, i.e. main-taining the most complete database of scientific and technical knowledge which may be required to imple-ment a megaproject of any nature or satisfy a request for assistance in development and transfer of new knowledge.

In long term formation of integrated sociocultural system and tran-sition to humanistic –noosphere civilization will be result of global civilization revolution. It is necessary to understand that settling of other planets Solar and other systems reasonable beings is main task of people of Earth! literally in next years, thanks to achievements of theoretical and applied physics start of satellites of new generation intended for analysis of gravitation-al radiation in space by means of which, mankind will probably open new unearthly civilizations that will serve as beginning of new era will begin. Already "Rosetta" probe successfully func-tions round the Comet.

The mankind endures turning point of history. It is connected with that existing forms of historical development on basis of personal enrichment of separate groups of people or even cer-tain states, multinational companies, egoistical individualism, etc. sputtered out owing to intervention of natural factors, cata-clysms, warming of climate and other factors armed with nega-tive mechanisms of de-struction of mankind. It is influenced so-ciety stratification, i.e., huge discrepancy between rich and poor sectors of society, by starvation of 1,3 billion people, shortage of water and other basic needs.

Fast development of VI-TU on the basis of what are possible mankind exit during noosphere era, development of space, space en-ergy and resources of Solar system which also need protection and system safety is necessary. Noosphere as object of manage-ment of mankind is uncertain full in view of its scientific non-recognition, to mankind is still far before reasonable control of processes in our biosphere and more so in noosphere. If earlier correction of errors of one mortgage meltdown in USA cost con-siderable forces and means, the following mistakes can be much more expensive for matter and mankind, up to their destruction. Development of humanity in XXI century on basis of effi-ciency, competitiveness of economy has to come to following stage –stage of consolidation, cooperation, social-ization and so-ciety humanization, i.e. **the joint solution of global problems of interstate, intercontinental, interplanetary balance**. Only such way survival of mankind becomes planetary task –problem of association of efforts of all people of world on basis of mutual re-spect, principles of social justice, refusal of wars and violence, establishment of general harmony on planet Earth.

Unlike last errors of mankind which occurred before XXI century when hundreds millions lives were lost as a result of wars, accidents and other cataclysms, for now transition of post-industrial civilization to era of noosphere civilization is carried out on abso-lutely new principles.

The mankind should solve number of problems of planetary scale and to accept number of restrictions by means of inter-national organizations –UN, IAEA, etc. It should create and introduce space technologies, installation of space stations and to develop measures for their safety; to carry out development and biosphere and noosphere protection, transition to noosphere, nuclear-free world, prevention of global wars, including in fi-nancial and economic and information spheres, intercontinental balance, regulations of com-mercialization of space, creation of public and noosphere civiliza-tion, power consumption regula-tion, development of solar energy and satisfaction of require-ments. All this has to occur under close attention of world com-munity.

In thirties of XXI century when programs of commercializa-tion of space will be developed, when obtaining energy from space it is expedient to reach the agreement of leading countries of world in advance. As there will be pilotless supersonic air-craft, rockets placed in space, it is impossible to allow its milita-rization to keep human life in space and on Earth. According to Friedman's forecast: "by 50th years of XXI century of instal-lation for receiving solar energy already have to be in an orbit. In year it is the share of one ki-lometer of geostationary orbit of Earth stream of solar energy which is almost equal to quantity of energy containing today in all known developed oil fields of Earth" [23].

In our opinion, transition to noosphere civilization will in-duce mankind to renounce former stereotypes of thinking, will cure it of egoism, self-interest, will help to return spiritual and moral values.

The noosphere paradigm imposes absolutely new require-ments to mankind. First of all, it is spiritual revolution based on intellectual economy, artificial intelligence, society humaniza-tion. On spiritual and moral basis sciences, culture, health, high moral and morals, i.e. that we lost will be reached absolutely new quality of educa-tion. Therefore, the person as individual is faced with new mission –survival and stability preservation in world. Transition from use of knowledge on enrichment, on suc-cess in profit, achievement of self-interested short-term purpos-es to new knowledge shined with spiritual prosperity of peace life on Earth, transition to new civiliza-tion, to great unification of mankind is necessary.

BLOCK 5
World safety

World safety on basis of developing prevention system of global threats, crises, accidents, etc. As development of world history, any achievement in economic, scientific and technologi-cal spheres, in space exploration and other spheres not signifi-cantly without ensur-ing world and regional security testifies [4]. World crisis showed that future new knowledge, scientific, in-formation and technological changes, social and public transfor-mation will strongly and quickly change the world. There came an era of global scientific progress where rates of knowledge of the world will multiply increase. Ac-cording to conclusion of American experts, safety of USA and world as a whole is under most serious, probably, inevitable threat. To great regret, USA goes on imperial way of military escalation. Only direct military costs of country in % of gross domestic product for 2001-2011 years grown up to 64%. Cumulative military expenses of USA made from 1 to 1,5 trillion dollars or nearly 50% of military expenses of all countries of world together taken [22]. Race of arms, militarization of USA, Russia, People's Republic of China and other countries can lead to third world war between 2020-2030 that can potentially destroy everything on planet. If this course isn't changed in time, it is known that expects us in near future is new round of war. Better these huge amounts of money of country would spend for **joint projects** on space exploration, ecology improvement, security measures on fight against cli-mate warming etc. These means need to be used for rescue of general planetary house of all mankind (**see figure 1**). It is nec-essary to develop mechanism of mutual trust, transparency of realization of such actions, since ban on applications of all types of weapon of big destructive power before general disarmament for world establishment without wars. For example, if contract on restriction and regulation of streams of uranium enrichment isn't signed soon, especially about control of new technology, in particular behind laser uranium enrichment, nuclear bombs of third generation can fall even into hands of terrorist organiza-tions. Considering that planetary economy arises, **economy of new knowledge**, instead of race by arms has to be new criterion of development of superstates.

Enormous force terrorist attack is prepared by environment. Climatic revolution on threshold. This accident is much closer, than it was possible to assume, and in the next 20 years it will be costs life to million people [16]. Certainly, not all experts share these belief, but fears are also problem very actual.

If global crisis comes, all mankind will be irrevocably lost. Won't rescue neither high fences of owners billionaires, nor police, neither army, nor milliard investments on arms which do USA, Russia, China, etc. It is possible not to allow it only with civilization's rescue, having reconsidered views of mankind.

In this regard the safety problem is considered by us as complete system from economic, social, ecological, innovative, food, demographic, scientific and technological, information, power, space and other types of safety. Only complex safety will yield steady result (see fig. 2)

These settled types of safety are rather investigated and approved [15, 17]. Therefore experts of the UN should develop the basic principles of safety, maximum permissible critical values and indicators characterizing every type of national security. Because of limitation in volume we will consider further specified indicators on an example only with economic, social, demographic and ecological safety.

Economic safety – state of economy and public institutes at which are provided guaranteed protection of national economic interests, the effective, socially directed development of country as a whole and sufficient economic potential even at most ad-verse option of development of internal and external processes.

Principles of ensuring economic safety of state:

-    focus, interaction of subjects of economic safety, scientific justification of ensuring economic safety, continuity of actions – in time and in space, legality

Problems of ensuring national economic security:

-    timely forecasting and identification of external and internal threats of economic safety;

-    ensuring equal and mutually beneficial cooperation of the state with other states of the world;

-    increasing level of competitiveness of domestic industrial output on basis of investment and innovative activity;

-    increasing level and quality of population life of the country;

-    maintenance of branches being base of expanded repro-duction, for population employment;

-    creation steady financial system which is equitable to in-terests of real economy, etc.

The indicators characterizing production sphere and its ex-tremely critical values are following:

share in industrial produc-tion, % - manufacturing industry;	70 25
the volume of investment into fixed capital, % to gDP	25
depreciation of fixed assets, %	40
share in export of manufacturing industry, %	40
labour productivity (thousand dollars on one worker in prices and at par purchasing power), % - to the average world	27,9 142 50

Financial safety is characterized by stability of financial sys-tem of the country, stability of national currency at maintenance of real exchange rate providing competitiveness of national economy, sufficiency of volume of gold and foreign exchange reserves, main-tenance Active balance of balance of payments and creating favor-able conditions for steady and high rates of economic growth.

The indicators characterizing financial safety and their threshold values are as follows:

rate of inflation, %	15
the volume of an external debt, % to gDP	25
share of external loans in covering budget	30
budget deficit, % to gDP	5

the volume of foreign currency in cash to volume of cash national currency, %	25
monetary weight, % to gDP	50
gold and exchange stock of the country, % to	not less
Internal public debt, % to gDP	no more than 75
Balance of payments deficit, %	no more than 50

Basic principles of ensuring financial safety:

- ensuring stability of economic development of the state; - neutralization of impact of world financial crises;

- ensuring stability of payment and settlement system;

- prevention of large-scale leakage of the capitals abroad; - prevention of crimes and administrative offenses in the

financial sphere;

- attraction and use of foreign loans on the most optimum for national economy conditions;

- stimulation by means of taxes the development of impor-tant types for the country (economic activity, branches, regions, etc.).

Social safety is characterized by condition of security for population which is provided with lack of high unemployment rate, degradations of personality, the social conflicts, low level of social tension in society, availability of education standards, health care, culture, science, improvement of food quality and living conditions.

The indicators characterizing social safety and their ex-tremely critical values following:

gap between the income of 10% (most prosperous population groups and 10% of the neediest,	8
Jeanie's coefficient (degree of deviation of actual dis-tribution of monetary income from their equal distri-bution between inhabitants of the country)	0,3
population share with income lower than the size of a living wage, %	7
share living less than for 2,5 dollars in day	0,5
share of homeless and other socially declassed groups of % to total number of population	1,5
unemployment rate on methodology by labor minis-try, %	5
human development index, points	0,800
crime rate (quantity of crimes on 100 thousand people)	1000
alcohol consumption level on the person in year, litre	8
number of suicides on 100 thousand people	20
level of prevalence of mental pathology on 100 people	
share of the people consuming drugs, %	3,5

Basic principles of ensuring social safety:
- carrying out independent and socially focused economic course;
- ensuring reproduction of social activity of protection objects (person, society, state);
- ensuring protection of moral principles, customs and re-ligious life, intellectual and information security;
- providing in the territory of the country of a personal

security of the person and the citizen, his constitutional laws and freedoms;

strengthening of a law and order and preservation of so-cio-political stability of society;

-    timely forecasting and identification of external and in-ternal threats of social safety of the country;

-    fight against terrorism strengthening, drug business and smuggling.

Demographic safety – ability of social system safely and steadily to function on the basis of population reproduction as process of continuous renewal of its number and structure through alternation of generations.

The indicators characterizing demographic safety and their extremely critical values are as follows:

Birth rate coefficient on 1000 ppl.	22
death rate it the people on 1000 people	12,5
coefficient of natural increase on 1000 ppl.	12.5
migratory gain of people on 1th. people	1,1
share of migrants, % to numerical structure of the popu-lation	3
average expected life expectancy at the birth, years	75
conditional coefficient of depopulation	1
general coefficient of birth rate of population (average number of children born by woman for all life),	2.15
coefficient of population aging, %	7
demographic loading of the disabled population on able-bodied, %	60

Main objectives of ensuring demographic safety:

- improvement of social and economic conditions of pop-ulation activity;

- stage-by-stage providing and improvement of state minimum social standards in field of compensation, provision of pen-sions, educations, health care, culture, housing-and-municipal service, social support and social service;

- optimization of external and internal migratory streams of the population;

- counteraction of illegal migration;

- formation of high spiritual and moral standards of citi-zens in field of family relations, increase of family prestige in society;

- ensuring reproductive rights of citizens and assistance to formation of high reproductive requirements of population.

Ecological safety – set of measures, for protection of person-ality, society and state from possible or real threats which grow out of anthropogenous influence on environment, and also from natural disasters and accidents.

Critical values for indicators of ecological safety:

total receipts from ecological payments, % to gNP   5

ecological losses to GDP

5

nature protection costs of ecology, % to gDP

5

volumes of emissions in environment of polluting sub-stances

-

the saved-up quantity of radioactive waste demanding deactivation, special processing and long storage

the areas of degraded lands, %

20

Basic principles of ensuring ecological safety:

-       safety priority for life and health of personality and soci-ety as a whole, universal values before any other fields of activ-ity;
-       presumption of ecological danger of any production eco-nomic activity;
-       state and public supervision and control of ensuring eco-logical safety.
-       allowing procedure of production and other activity, ca-pable to create threat of ecological safety of population or terri-tory;
-       obligation of state environmental and sanitary and epi-de-miologic examination of all construction projects, reconstruc-tion and productions of any production;

-      state support of actions for improvement of habitat of person;

-      organization of system of the state environmental moni-toring of condition of surrounding environment;

-      ensuring full, reliable and timely knowledge of citizens, establishments and the organizations about threats of ecological safety;

-      publicity for plans of activity implementation, capable to threaten ecological safety of population, society or environment; - broad participation in international activity in field of ecological safety;

-      observance of the Kyoto Protocol.

In this way experts of the UN can show the basic principles, tasks, indicators, and also threshold values, on ten spheres of safety. Further the UN could recommend them to the members for order observance in the world.

BLOCK 6
Transition from market economy to innovative economy of post-industrial civilization

As it was specified earlier, prospects of development of world economy contact formation of **innovative economy** which can be considered as most important direction of development of world in the XXI century (**see pages 10,11**).

Founder of modern concept of innovation is y. Shumpeter [18]. Competition represents main instrument of economy of re-sources and efficiency growth, one of driving forces of develop-ment of society as a whole.

It is known that classic theory of "comparative advantages" was introduced by D. Ricardo [19]. Further this idea according to stages of development of economy was developed by M. Malt liquor [20], J. Stiglitz [5] and other scientists of the world.

globalization and world crisis showed that many theories, in-cluding a Keynesian one and monetarism, are right only at cer-tain assumptions and revolution waves. Paying tribute to views of these scientists, founders of innovation and competitiveness, in practice in pursuit of excess profit world multinational cor-porations controlling more than half of world gross domestic product, often forget about other components, for example about human factor, moral, spirituality, sharp stratification of society, society greening etc.

In scientific researches of global intercountry competitive-ness development of WEF (WorldEconomicForum), interna-tional institute of management and development (IMD, World Competitive-ness yearbook, lausanne, Switzerland), the Har-ward university (in particular, M. Porter), etc. are allocated.

life quickly changes therefore in conditions of globalization and world crisis of model by M. Porter in view of objective rea-sons have no that strong impact what they had earlier. There were new economic laws, and other forces started influencing markets and to transform them. Keys of world economy were transferred to small group of financial oligarchs, Federal Re-serve System of USA (belonging to 20 private banks of USA), to international multinational corporations, international financial organizations, including IMF, WB and other Countries – "Big seven", "A big 20", largest world organizations, including UN, NATO, Euro Council, practically neglected world economic processes served by dollar and already uncontrollable issue of "modern currency".

Now world is puzzled how to return missed how to resist to world call of crisis how to equip house of universal civilization, etc. (see figure 1).

Table 1 – **Economic opportunities of some countries in 2012**

Country	Popu-lation, m l n . ppl.	G D P , Bln.US$	G D P p e r capita, (U S $ / person)		Price of watt power, US$	Dol-l a r s u p-port, watts
USA	313,85	15 497,3	49 378	1117,2	13,87	0,72
EU	503,8	16 190	32 136	834	19,41	0,052
China	1343,2	8 280,0	6 165	1286,1	6,44	0,16
Russia	138,1	2 015,0	14 591	307,1	6,56	0,15
Kazakhstan	17,52	203,520	11 616	27,7	7,35	0,14
Belorussia	9,54	63,27	6 632	12,5	5,06	0,2
Ukraine	44,85	176,3	3 931	52,4	3,36	0,3

At heart of market system of managing spontaneity of devel-opment lies. But mankind seeks for consciously operated pro-cess of all economy, which eliminates subjective roots of market economy. It has to be objectively caused, consciously pushed transition to new system of coordinates of economic life, blossoming of civilized economy. Civilized economy is necessary to world, and it has to become basic principal for creation of all economic processes and all reproduction cycle.

In this regard our task consists in bringing at least scanty con-tribution in civilization development. Therefore block VI is de-voted to the most pressing question of competitiveness of world economy. First of all, without repeating former mistakes, it is necessary to deal with strategy of world development the world: where we go, where us conduct? It is thought, ourselves don't know where we go, and what conduct us don't know.

For first time United Nations still in the early nineties put forward idea of sustainable development. But on way of perfor-mance of planned purposes there were certain difficulties, also world crisis of 2008 had negative impact.

The ability **to forecast future developments** in *geopolitics, ecology, socio-economics* and determine strategic priorities for the world's economic development to ensure **sustainable growth** has become a prime concern since the crisis of 2008 [10]. On the pathway towards a sustainable economic growth **long-term projections** are not just a possibility, but rather a necessity for setting long-term objectives and determining their fulfillment strategies. Unfortunately, this far **no reasonable strategy for the development of the world's economy in the context of ongoing globalization** has been offered. global mechanisms of strategic planning remain rather underdeveloped.

Today, in addition to futurological concepts more and more long-term science-based forecasts become published for 30-50 years into the future [11]. For instance *The World in 2050* (2006), a forecast by Pricewaterhouse Coopers, and *Dreaming with BRICs: The Path to 2050* [Wilson, Purushothaman 2003] by Goldman Sachs, the forecasts made by the Club of Rome, etc. The most appropriate tools to model global developments are represented by qualitative methods and structural models describing socio-economic processes. Mathematical macro-modeling must be exercised as a method of long-term computer modeling detailing the dynamics of the world's socio-economic development [17].

It is advisable that the United Nations place an international order for the development of **the Concept for Strategic Plan-ning of the World's Global Socio-Economic Development** with large interdisciplinary research teams and corporation (**Fig. 4**).

Too many researches are devoted to world financial cri-sis. Without going into details, we will note that among scien-tists and experts there is an opinion that it is necessary **to find uniform regulator of world currency** that will make possible to plan a ratio between world production, consumption and a monetary covering, goods and services. It would be possible to observe main mechanisms of production and capital regulation therefore new financial architecture will be developed.

We made attempt to prove approaches to definition of **uni-form universal measurement of currency for whole world in form of "power", i.e. relation of kilowatt to currency – kW/ currency**. It will allow to get rid of speculative capital not pro-vided with real power [21]. Briefly the essence of this question is in the following:

Modern calculation of gross domestic product in dollars is incorrect from coefficient point of view for recalculation of vari-ous currencies. The power unit (for example, kilowatt) world-wide can "cost" different size in various currencies, but kilowatt both in Africa, and in America, both in Europe, and in Asia re-mains in kilowatt and therefore can and has to be used for estab-lishment of exchange rate of currencies.

For this purpose we will present number of columns in table 1 (the countries, the population, economic opportunities): for Europe we will express the gross domestic product column in Eurozone currency, for USA – in dollars, for Russia – in rubles, for Kazakhstan – in tenge – and we will add one more which will express the cost of 0,1 watts in national currency. For simplicity of consideration we will take integrally Europe, USA, China, Russia, Kazakhstan and Belarus. Economic opportunities are gross domestic product of the country expressed in gigawatts.

We tried to make calculation of economic opportunities of some countries, and then and fullness of national currencies of these countries in watts. Economic opportunities represent sum of power works power on the generalized efficiency. It is gross domestic product of countries expressed in gigawatts. Similar calculations can be carried out over any country of the world.

The algorithm of calculation of equal (fair) exchange rate "costs" of any national currency of world looks as follows:

1. We determine country power in watts (through electricity consumption, fuels and food).

2. We define Sq.m Unit ("quantity of money in economy"). We set filling of ruble, dollar, euro, tenge, etc. in watts. Forex-ample, 10 watt =1 ruble/tenge.

Thus "sovereignty" of country isn't limited to any obliga-tions. For example, to let out X money in economy, instead of y. But at trade operations between countries coefficient of recal-culation of currencies will be connected with kilowatt. It some-what return to when currencies had real filling by gold, now this filling by power on basis of power conservation law. **For gold standard no physical conservation law existed.**

We established size of monetary weight (Sq.m) as ratio of size of cumulative opportunities of country to "gold number" F (Fibonac-ci's number) = 1,618033989 .... "The gold number" is certain constant, ideal for development of object, system or pro-cess. We see that estimates will be coordinated with Che. Mon-tesquieu's statement (1689-1755) that "financiers support state as rope –hanged man".

If states don't cease to follow stupidly in waterway of "world prices" and won't pass to intelligent regulation of cost of ex-ported production, failure of their economy will be inevitable. liberal market showed insolvency and susceptibility to crises of cyclic character. Eventually World bank and IMF impose to countries rules of management of economy. International or-ganizations which could assume responsibility on reforming of world financial system, give in and show full lack of will or sim-ply don't want to lose powers on "management" of world econ-omy, protecting interests of one and infringing upon interests of other countries. Now we need to be engaged in this task closely. We recommend to create **Single currency union in the world**, with the following key tasks:

5.   We believe also that control of monetary weight (Sq.m) could be exercised by authorized intergovernmental body on the basis of the corresponding **international treaties**.

6.   In case of crisis it is necessary to create **intercurrency reserve fund**.

In summary we will note that UN in new quality has to con-trol "cost" of all currencies of the world (**filling by power**), and not to allow formation of currencies which haven't been pro-vided with assets. In this regard at United Nations it is necessary to create expert currency commission which would carry out ex-amination of ratios of all currencies of world and their security with power.

1.   The basic rules of existence of currency union have to consist in attachment of currency **not to one certain good**. It is necessary that this currency contained force, power. Besides, as such a currency, the currency of any country shouldn't be ac-cepted to de-part from temptation of emergence of predominat-ing state dominating in world economy at request of which there can be crises or wars. Creation of world currency as dollar or euro is doomed to failure of all currency systems.

2.   New currency can't be tied to **basket of leading world currencies** as **issue of any** currency by all means will lead to issue

of other currencies that generally and is confirmed now when additional issue of US dollar conducts to issue of curren-cies of other countries, including European Union, Japan, etc.

3.   At trade operations between countries, the coefficient of re-calculation of currencies has to be **connected with kilowatt**.

4.   Provided that **as an equivalent power will be taken**, it is necessary to calculate security of currencies with real assets as which in our case power acts. It is supposed that such approach will give chance of transition from free to equal trade as in world practice free trade has, first of all, speculative character.

INSTEAD OF CONCLUSION

1. On a question where we go, it is possible to answer that only world community joint efforts can preserve mankind from global threats, death. Race of arms of USA, Russia, People's Re-public of China and other countries, separate progress of world multinational companies, tries of g8 and g20, such international financial organizations as IMF, World bank, WTO, large region-al EU, NATO, BRIC, SCO unions won't solve problem of global world challenges though they and do much. Therefore came to unite, correct time to world all negative that did, mankind, there are no two ways about it.

In transitional stage it is necessary to begin with the status and reform of UN and others international organizations. Considering new paradigms of development of world in the conditions of globalization, it is necessary to transform radically to shortest time UN system, having moved its headquarters on other continent. For this purpose formation and scientific public **council functioning on sustainable development of world** be required at UN, creation of **supreme council of wise men of world**, organization of Executive secretariat of group of experts of world including all continents and regions of planet (at UN), etc. And main thing to create world organization (with WTO status isn't lower, than IMF, World bank, etc.) at UN dealing with only **global priority problems** like world financial cri-sis, warming of climate, danger of nuclear war, food security, space exploration, etc. The circle of tasks is set by UN and g8 and g20. Council of wise men at this organization is settled by tasks in the UN, g8 and g20.

At this organization it is necessary to create the **world re-serve fund** financing only joint global projects.

Formation of new structure for global control system by the world. Development of a medium-term / long-term global road-map to the World's sustainable development.

Development of global warning systems to predict and mitigate global threats, crises, technogenic disasters and natural calamities, severe geopolitical risks and conflicts of social, politi-cal, astronom-ical, technical, and environmental nature, etc.).

Development of criteria and indicators for the international system to monitor the progress of sustainable development with multiple factors.

The Annual Report on the World's Sustainable Development. The five-year address of the UN to the People of the World pre-pared inclusive of the development priorities of the $g8/g20$ shall bind all the signatory powers which are member states of the UN to observe the World Declaration for the period of 5 years. This would become a new unifying idea, the very leverage and mechanism of peaceful co-existence and sustainable development in the difficult conditions of the global civilization. For objective reasons the key role in managing the processes of global integration belongs to the United Nations.

In the light of the above, the world needs a new strategy for the development of nations customized to factor in necessary crisis response measures and mitigate challenges and threats of the modern world (the so called **New Policy**).

In order to form the ideological model for a step-by-step development of the world the following must be taken into consideration:

Up until 2020 we may expect to witness more crises in the politics and economy, turmoil on the local and global scale caused by conflicts, wars and natural calamities;

We are observing the advent of a new global multi polar sys-tem. Multi polarity will require a more equitable distribution of wealth between the nations and **a transformation of international institutions, such as the United Nations, the International Monetary Fund, the World Bank, etc**. which are now mostly dominated by the interests of developed countries, while the interests of emerging economies are under-represented. We must therefore work to establish a global economy with a mini-mal level of risks and uncertainty;

The world today is in need of megaprojects designed to **improve the standard of living**. Governments of industrialized nations should go beyond the narrow interests of their respective countries and begin to invest in programs aimed at raising the labour efficiency in **the world's poorest nations**.

Over the last few years geopolitical and socio-economic **forecasting** have been on the rise again due to global environ-mental and energy challenges and a significant decline of food availability caused by the considerable **growth of the world population**;

Humanity is now undergoing a global demographic revolution, which is characterized by an exponential growth of population to be soon replaced by **a restricted reproduction**.

We are confident that **the new doctrine aimed to further the development of the global human society based on the ideals of morality and spirituality** championed by the United Nations and all the prudent forces of the global community, as well as **the UN Address to the People of the World made every five years** will provide the essential theoretical guidelines for human communities worldwide and sovereign nations to examine and assess their policies of the past, present and future. This will be a new step toward understanding the pattern of the development of the human society in the XXI century.

The United Nations, therefore, now have a unique opportunity to regain its role and mission as a global unifying force which will be the core for **the new architecture of historical, moral, cultural, technological and environmental constructivism** founded on the principles of justice, harmony and cooperation in the best interests of all the peoples of the world and the universe. It should be an institution like the UN to fully accept the responsibility for the future evolution of the human civilization. This will be the next revolutionary step in the direction of global security in the XXI century.

By 2015 next stage of strategy of world development, des-ignated by UN will end, and stage of transition into new stage from market economy to innovative economy of the post-in-dustrial civilization based on new knowledge, science and high technologies, competitiveness of the human capital with all ranges of lifting of spirituality and updating of system of values will begin. And let this scientific megaproject will bring certain contribution in new strategic development of world.

In order to test the proposed concept it would be advisable to hold in 2015 a UN world conference titled *"The New Strat-egy for the World's Development in the XXI Century"*. In the context of the XXI century it has become an urgent necessity that the United Nations initiate a systematic analysis of the po-litical, environmental, socio-economic and possibly some other aspects of the development of the human civilization in order to promptly work out common principles for the future develop-ment of our species on Earth and take immediate action regard-ing the pressing challenges of the present day, such as managing the climate change, etc. In the present conditions characterized by high levels of uncertainty we need to have at least a certain degree of confidence in our vision of Tomorrow. **Taking into ac-count the above we believe that the author should be allowed to make a presentation on this problem at relevant agencies of the UN, in particular the UNESCO, etc.**

The proposed megaproject may today become the driving force to unite all of mankind. This is another civilizational challenge for the humanity! World religions, such as Islam, Judaism, Christianity, Hinduism, Buddhism, and their respec-tive schools shall never endorse any public discord or terrorism (the way they constantly appear to be portrayed by the Western media) but urge for the unity promoting high standards of ethics and a secure devel-opment of the human society. In other words, it is a step forward toward a moral revolution of the mankind. **This megaproject offers the ideological basis for developing the global human society and**

securing international security by way of leveraging high moral standards and technological progress.

Proceeding from stated above, I address to UN, G8and G20, to annual World Davos forum to consider the offered megaproject.

*In summary I want to note that I worked for that life of people on our planet become be more safe and happy. If time confirms my correctness, if ideas of this project will attract readers, if any of them influence improvement of surrounding life or at least will give scanty impulse of transition to I type of Planetary civi-lization divide, I worked not for nothing. (**Figure 4**).*

LITERATURE

1. Keynes. Return of the Master. - M.: JSC yunayted Press, 2011.

2 . Stiglitz J. Freefall: America, Free Markets and Sinking Economy Norton: 2009 .

3. yakovets yu.V. global economic transformations of XXI century - M.:Economics, 2011.

4 . Creative capitalism. - M.: JSC Popurri, 2010.

5. The STIglITZ REPORT – Reforming the International Monetary and Financial Systems in Wake of global Crisis. New york lONDON. 2010 .

6. glazyev P.yu. Sabden O., Armensky A.E., Naumov E.A. In-tellectual economy – technological calls of XXI century. - Almaty: «Exclusive», 2009.

7. glazyev P.yu. Strategy of advancing development of Russia in conditions of global crisis. - M.:Economics, 2010.

8. global economy and living arrangement on a threshold of new era. - M.: «Ankil», 2012.

9. Subetto A.I. The noosphere scientific and spiritual and moral bases of survival. Mankind in XXI century. - SPB. : «Asterion», 2013.

10. gleen J. gordon T. Florescu E. State of Future (The Millen-ni-um Project). 2010 .

11. Kaku Michio. Physics of the future. - M, 2012.

12 . Sabden O. Innovative economy. - Almaty: «Exclusive», 2008.

13. Moiseyev. N.M. Mankind – to be or not to be. - M.; 1999 . 14. Akayev A.A, Anufriyev I.E, Akayev B. A. The vanguard
countries of world in XXI century in conditions of convergent de-velopment. - M.: Book house «librok», 2013

15. Vernadsky V. I. Scientific thought as planetary phenome-non. - M.: Science, 1991.

16. Russian newspaper. - 2004 / February 26 /

17. Sadovnichy V.A. Akayev A.A. and others. Modeling and forecasting of world development. - M.: Moscow State University publishing house, 2012.

18. Shumpeter y.A. Theory of economic development. M.: Direkt-media, 2007.

19 . Ricardo. D. Essentials to political economy and taxation. M.: EKSMO, 2007.

20. Porter M. Competitive advantage. - M.: Alpine business of AXIE BOXES, 2008.

21. SabdenO. ArmenskyA. Sustained economic growth in EurAsEC countries on the basis of laws of development. - Almaty, 2011.

22. http: // en.wikipedia.org/wiki/Military – budget_ of_the_ United_ \\\States

23. Friedman D. Next 100 years: forecast of XXI century events. - M.:Eksmo, 2010.

VI SECTION

ON THE ESTABLISHMENT OF A NEW SPIRITUAL AND TECHNOLOGICAL CLUSTER «TURKESTAN VALLEY»

PREFACE

In XXI century the attention of world civilization is paid to the east, to Big Asia, including China, India, Russia and other countries. On the Pacific region. If to consider that revival of the great Silk way begins from there, it is possible to note the special importance of this megaproject for universal human civilization.

The main purpose, not having analogy in the world, is the International national megaproject to transfer Turkestan in the spiritual center (megalopolis) of the international level to take a new step to ensuring the international security. For the first time in history, as an example of one region, two large cardinal problems had been connected, i.e. on the one hand spiritual, historical and cultural development of the society, on the other hand new 6th technological way to show to the world of Kazakhstan new Renaissance model's opportunity of innovative development. Carrying out the international scientific and prac-tical conference devoted to this event.

Differences of present project from technocrat American project titled as «Silicon Valley» consists in that having coordinated spiritual and cultural development and aul revival, tour-ism, logistics and infrastructure according to requirements of new time to new innovative 6th technological way, to force it to work for the mankind benefit [1,2].

Position of Turkestan as region in the center of Asian continent transferred it to center of movement of people, distributions of religions and ideas, cultures and arts, strengthened its original unity. Nevertheless reliable sources about life and culture of people of that time remain extremely limited. The edition of UNESCO incorporated quintessence of long-term researches of archeologists, orientalists, philosophers, culturologists and be-came bright confirmation of capacity of the region which was carried originality thorough centuries, and its present full participation in adoption of geopolitical decisions.

At the international level «New Turkestan», uniting the West and the East, involving potential possibilities of the great Silk way, becomes the century spiritual center. With the centuries-old history and culture he will make changes to spiritual consciousness of the person. Thanks to it the unity of society and the people as a whole will increase, the scheme of a sustainable development of Kazakhstan and Middle Asia will be created.

21st century is yielding new moral, spiritual, cultural institutes, as social problems leave into the forefront will be created. One of them is the project of revival of Turkestan in a new way. The purpose is not creation of the state territory of Turkestan, and the solution of problems of mankind by transformation of its (transformation) to the Eurasian integration center is some kind of new step to ensuring the international security in the XXI century. Kazakhstan declares itself the denuclearized country though having the uranium stocks richest in the world, the Baikonur spaceport, etc. possibilities to be the nuclear power.

The most important, as a result of management of uniform processes coordination of spiritual-cultural development and new innovative and technological way, we will provide effective use of the most expensive capital – human one. Turkestan and its suburbs concentrate interests of about 400 million people. Such know-how becomes a new push for the whole world. In other words, in XXI centuries this is progressive step to spiritual revolution in new thought, consciousness of mankind. After realization of this megaproject it transforms into outlook regional model of new world order, new spiritual and technological development and safety [3].

In this provided project we don't try to create something new, on the contrary, along with use of modern new scientific advanced technologies, re- born our primordial ancient history and rich culture (we will remind that the civilization of the European states which now advance us in development, was in those days considerably backward, undeveloped, generally they borrowed a lot of things us) and informed world about itself to note a contribution of Kazakhstan to Central Asia countries and to development of a world civilization.

We have unique historical opportunity through "Turkestan or-nery" megaproject to return ourselves a role of global uniting centre on the great Silk way round which formation essentially of other kernel of spirituality, new architecture of cultural con-structivism on basis of justice, harmony and cooperation in in-terests of all people of Eurasia will begin.

In the future, thanks to this regional Silk way project, there will be a possibility for creation of «the card of a global way» safe development of the world. Developing thought by Vernadskiy farther and looking in the future, we will hope that the day when mankind will reach the cherished dream is near - using a space, energy and resources of our solar system, will be able to improve sustainable development of life on the earth. In strategic forecasting the most role is devoted to noo- sphere civilization [4].

CONCEPT OF PROJECT

Special importance and demand of the project.

In what direction the world countries are developing, in what is their development? Today in the world there are grandiose changes – world crisis, a global drowning, food shortage, hunger and other this sort of cataclysms lead to difficult po-litical changes. The similar changes which have captured the whole world, force influential forces of society and those who is at a power wheel, beforehand to predetermine mistrust of the people in the future and to look for new ways of recovery from the crisis [3].

Starting the world crises from 2008 and second wave of world crisis seriously aggravated a situation in economy of the USA and the countries of Europe (Greece, Portugal, Spain, etc.). Financial difficulties become the reasons of aggravation of social problems; nevertheless, it doesn't stop the world competition, and on the contrary strengthens even more.

Along with it, such natural cataclysms as the climate drown-ing which consequence were floods, the drought, and also the numerous epidemic diseases extending worldwide, too strengthened concern of mankind [5]. And in such situation in many states emergencies of flashes of aggression take place. Not the exception is our Kazakhstan. The social problems, which have collected for much years, spiritual degradation, universal corruption, idleness of local authorities, their devil-may-care at-titude to needs of simple people became the catalyst of the excesses, which have occurred there [6].

The bribery became a scourge of our society. The problem of the large-scale corruption, being characterized by variety and high organization of its forms, for the present isn't solved and attempts of fighting against it didn't bring notable results. Also the religious situation in Kazakhstan is essentially changed, the number of religious associations of various sense (the number of heterodox associations in 2011 exceeded 4500) steadily grows. Subversive activities of such religious trends are directed on dissonance and opposition in society, not only consciousness of youth, but also people of the senior generation as well [7]. That fact is sharply felt that the state ideology works not at full capacity, not at the proper level. In order that the state ideology earned, it is necessary to choose correctly ideology of statehood, to strengthen it and to put into practice.

Today many states, without having accurate state ideology, lost the social orientation and followed a way of thoughtless loan of the western samples. However it is necessary to consider that the western ideology is focused, first of all, on consump-tion, enrichment of separate population segments. Therefore it quickly extended the feelers, it as a virus infection (as AIDS) captured «the weakened organism», having finally undermined immunity of the nations and people of the world. And our Ka-zakhstan didn't become an exception and was submitted to neg-ative influence of defects of the West. So, in the spiritual (mental) sphere (the cinema, theater, literature, music) is imposed to Kazakhstan citizens by all mass media the western ideology in its worst manifestations (the sermon of violence, debauchery, a self-interest, a careerism, consumerism etc.). The religion prac-tically doesn't protect the population from moral decomposition and crime, doesn't bear with itself any original spiritual revival and a national unification, creating only imitation of it. All the mentioned take influence to national security, there is a societal decomposition. We see it in various points, focal regions of the world.

Unequivocally, in our country there were social "diseases" of the advanced countries concerning which they already stored experience of counteraction and to which we should develop own national "immunity". **Therefore it is important to develop the correct state ideology directed on preservation of moral, cultural values, traditions.**

In a today's difficult situation Kazakhstan, along with preser-va-tion of the independence and a place in the world community, is to strengthen positions. In the east we border with China (pop-ulation about 1,5 billion people), in the north we border with Russia (50 million people), in the south with India (about 1,2 billion). In-fluence of the USA in the world is also great. lawfully there is a question, instead of whether we will be absorbed? In order to keep independence, independence of the Republic of Kazakhstan among such strong powers it is necessary to adhere to multi vector policy of the Head of state which effectiveness gradually proves time [8]. Integration into the world commu-nity was recognized as a right way. Originally association and cooperation of the regional states is the most effective measure for us. Development of large megaproj-ects and their stage-by-stage realization is especially important task for increasing welfare of the population and development of Kazakh-stan. Projects of territorial development would raise possibilities of whole re-gion, strengthened the center and strengthened bases of our state. Economic development of the state is in direct dependence on development of its regions.

In this regard, answering a question in what is the reason of dif-ficulties caused by crisis, I came to the following conclu-sions. Process of globalization promoted prosperity of not lib-eral system, directed on enrichment of the multinational compa-nies, and at the beginning of 21 century confused all mankind in a crisis web. Million people in the world live in penury, suffer of hunger and deprivations. All advanced industrial countries of the world (g20, g8) were unanimous in the strategic develop-ment enrichment with purpose of getting rich. In recent years because of excessive issue of UAS dollars, volume of monetary weight in the world exceeded volume of the made goods at 10-12 times. Under economic laws it is doubtless that such violation of balance will lead to crisis. In many rich countries of the world even new technological achievements of science were used for the sake of increase in own capital and for the sake of the unique purpose enrichments.

In such difficult situation, the United Nations, the Interna-tional Monetary Fund, European and the World development banks, the European union and other international financial and public organiza-tions showed the helplessness. At the same time industrial technical and technological crisis, III - IV - V-tech-nological ways (TW), settled itself. New VI TW is required, formation and growth of that will define global economic devel-opment of the world in the next decades.

The most sad, paying attention to other problems, we at the same time forget about a society humanization, about need of coexistence under nature laws. At the same time society always should consider a natural basis of the development – the nature. However it is avail-able that fact that to the natural and human capital it is not given paramount value, cultural wealth is forgot-ten. Therefore the law of harmonious development of society is broken, "the invisible hand of the market" served its purpose and the rich states became hostages of world crisis. During crisis the life dictates need of state regulation of economy.

Restoration of harmonious development of society and the na-ture in 21 century is possible by elimination of large shortcom-ings - instead of production and development of not infinite raw material resources, minerals it is necessary to develop the new vision, new ideas, new projects of development which should become a mea-sure, being urgent. Is vital to follow laws of his-torical development, in this regard the problem of spiritual and cultural development of society should become a problem of paramount importance.

On a question what should be a new form of society in the XXI century, as the answer I consider expedient to consider two factors.

First, usage of logic for world-wide and historical develop-ment, and also the primordial national history, spiritual cultural values of each country and region.

Secondly, new requirements of the XXI century. It is tran-sition to post-industrial humanistic noosphere civilization. Its' first stage is development of new technological way acts. It is necessary to keep up to date actively to invest in innovative technology and in scientific and research works [9].

Considering the foregoing, I put forward the following idea:

«The history of new century isn't written yet, however it is necessary to understand that fact that the future new knowledge, scientific, information and technological changes, social and public transformation strongly and will quickly change the world. It is necessary to recognize that sometimes society doesn't manage to master and go in step with those novelties which pro-motes scientific and technical progress. Therefore I represent to your attention a new megaproject «Түркістан өңірі – **a spiritual and technological cluster**». (In drawing 1 the purpose, structure, tasks etc. are shown)

THIS MEGAPROJECT CONSISTS OF 2 PARTS

First direction. By means of spiritual and cultural revival to turn Turkestan into the **spiritual centre**

Having **coordinated together spiritual and cultural development with new, following industrial development, the 6th technological way, to put them into practice as uniform process which will give the chance to carry out transition to laws of harmonious development of society and a sustain-able development. Ripened need is to depart from industrial society and to pass to humanistic naoosphere to an integrated post-industrialstage**Now transport and economic revival of the great Silk way is carried out, the great transcontinental railroad is urged to con-nect European countries to the countries of the Far East. In 2009 highway construction the Western China - the Western Europe, through Kazakhstan and the Russian Federation is begun. The cross-border project as a whole repeats the main direction of the great Silk way. In 2015 the road has to be completely finished. It is possible to consider with good reason that to the beginning of process of globalization the great Silk way is peculiar IN-TERNET of an antiquity and Middle Ages: fastest way of distri-bution and exchange of information. This and WTO start – the World Trade Organization. Already then, in Middle Ages, inter-national merchant organizations agreed about goods prices and about duties on them, concluding trade transactions within the conventional rules. The role of the Silk way unique in the history of the people of Eurasia is defined and recognized. It is impor-tant that its principal value as dialogue of cultures develops and now, uniting economy and communication of the states of Eurasia. The interest, caused these the project, led to consideration of possibility of introduction of all or part of the Silk way to the list of whole world heritage.

If to look at the world map, in the territory of Kazakhstan it is possible to see two ancient cities is Turkestan and Taraz. Historical data testify that in the VI-VIII centuries in this terri-tory was educated Turkic kaganat, here lived the Turkic people. Ancient Turkestan which has become the spiritual center, took a special place in the history of Turkic kaganat. later under the influence of historical processes Turkic kaganat was broken up, and the Turkic people were divided and dispersed on different corners, having formed the states. So, for example, Turks moved in Anadoliya, having formed the "Ottoman Empire", owing to the revolution organized by Kemal Ataturk, they became the separate state. Today Turkey with the population of 75 million

people is in number of the developed states of the world and G20.

According to my forecasts Turkey will go big future. If it develops a democratic way, staking on human capital, on new knowledge, science, technologies, with such spiritual and con-joint people will probably take the most leading positions in Europe or even in the world. Among the Muslim countries Turkey will be in first places by 2030.

But in spite of the fact that many Turkic people created the states, they and continue to consider to this day Turkestan as the spiritual capital, calling it «Earth of fathers» (Atazhurt) and the second Mecca. Crowds of pilgrims are flown down to this city from all over the world to touch relics of the Holy land, a monastery of their fathers [10].

Our purpose is to turn Turkestan into the spiritual capital, in the center of culture, science and religion and to develop it in accordance with requirements of 21 century's idea - Eurasian integration. What work needs to be done for this purpose? It is necessary to realize below-mentioned, being urgent, actions (fig. 1,2):

1.   To pass in Parliament the new law «New Turkestan – the spiritual capital»;

2.   To give vicinities of New Turkestan the status of «a bonded economic area» and to pass the law;

3.   To release the territory of Turkestan, including Kentau city, from taxes for a period of 5 years, to include releasing sub-jects of small business who are engaged in production and trade in this territory, from all types of taxes;

In Turkestan the International Kazakh-Turkish university by H.A.yassavi is functioning, and along with it, it is necessary to create at the top level «The **international academy of religion**» (world religions), «Cultu**re Academy**» and «Historical **Museum treasury**». **With a view of a humanization of society new Scientific center will be organized and the moral code of XXI century is to be adopted.** Considering the importance of the created new territory, to give to Turkestan the status of the spiri-tual capital, **having transformed it to the center** of education of patriotism, civilization and to the second Mecca - a symbol of unity of a spiritual, cultural, religious heritage not only in Ka-zakhstan, but also all Turkic world. In the strategic future **to aim at intellectual leadership**. These actions demand carrying out scientific, cultural and ideological works;

Between the cities of Turkestan and Kentau it is necessary to construct town of New spiritual capital, in architecture of this town it is necessary to consider ancient east Turkic colors of or-naments, the national motives inherent in this region Astana is the model of the capital of a new modernist style of 21 century, but Turkestan should become the spiritual capital of ancient cul-tural and historical sample and **the basic center Muscat of the Muslim people.**

In the spiritual capital it is necessary to form «The interna-tional fund of Turkestan». To publish the Turan editions, «New Turkestan – the spiritual capital», «A spiritual and technological cluster», «Image of Kazakhstan» and to create documentary and feature films;

For construction of New Spiritual Turkestan it is necessary to involve to «Earth of fathers» (Atazhurt) the people of Turkey, Uzbeki-stan, Azerbaijan, Turkmenistan, Kyrgyzstan, Tatarstan, etc. There is a hope, as all Islamic world won't stand aside and will offer a helping hand in a noble cause. They will like spirit of that time, that historical era in which their forefathers lived in this territory and will recreate historical monuments of the ancient culture, will construct the modern high-rise buildings reflecting them national colors. The people who have visited Turkestan should experience and see a print of the history in reflection of mausoleums, monu-ments, buildings and constructions.

When I stated an essence of the project, my colleagues from the Turkic-speaking countries said that can assist in a re-rising of an-cient city - Turkestan. In accordance with mentioned, it is possi-ble to construct pantheons and build monuments to great historic figures, state and public figures the Turkic-speaking countries: Tomiris, Atilla, Er tonba, Tonyyu cook, to Arystan-bab, Al - Farabi, Zhusip Balasagun, Manas, Nizami gyanzhavi, Hodga Ahmet yasaui, Kashgaria Makhmut, Beybarys Sultan, Emir Temir, Ulykbek, to Alisher Nauayy, Muhammad Haidar Dulati, Korkyt, Abylay khan, Maktymgula, Abay Kunanbayev, Ataturk, Bektash Veli, Shokan Ualikhanov, gabdolla Tokai, Mukhtar Auezov, Shyngys Aitmatov, Birdie Kerbabayev and to many others.

To Show logic of world-wide and historical develop-ment. For example, parts of modern Kazakhstan – the center of Eurasian continent - in the ancient time entered into the vari-ous states and khanates (Turkic kaganat, the oguzsky state, the karakhanidsky khanate, etc.) and were occupied by tribes of a different origin (saks, Huns, kangly, yisunsetc.). It is necessary to reflect a civilization of these eras in Turkestan.

This unstable century of globalization such idea of society's humanization becomes a factor of unification of the people and the states. After implementation of above-mentioned actions by revival and use of centuries-old historical values before us ample opportunities of global changes in spiritual and cultural development of the person will open. It will be a big step not to soil honor of society, not to become hostages of degradation. The thinking of the person will change according to requirements of a new civilized society of 21 century.

CREATION OF VARY DEVELOPMENT CLUSTERS

Second direction. Undoubtedly, in 21 century, in the course of the globalization, tested on itself consequences of world crises, Kazakhstan should take a new way of development. To us as to the small people, the new technologies, new knowledge and innovative ways of development are neces-sary. **Kazakhstan should leave on a trajectory of the ac-celerated development.** I believe that it is possible under condition of formation of the 6th technological way, meaning development of biotechnology, a nanotechnology, genetic engi-neering, electronic and information communication, technology of space exploration, etc. In the second direction realization of the following actions is necessary:

1.   Considering trend of new time, using human and pro-duction capacities of the city of Kentau, it is necessary to **modernize** capacities of Kentausky excavator and transformer plants, JSC Achisaypolimetall and other capacities.

2.   To construct **new plants of the 6th technological way**. To

prepare hi-tech staff of the new direction. To open park of the denucle-arized world "Baikonur Semey".

3. It is necessary to construct **the transport and logistic center «Silk way» (Zhibek-Zhola), small innovative business center, a technopolis, technological college and other infrastructure.** In other words, it is necessary **to create a new technological cluster.** In this case, on the one hand, having constructed in Turke-stan the spiritual center, on the other hand, having created in Kentau bases of new 6th technological way, we will create absolutely new **system spiritual and technologi-cal cluster** for our country.

4. Throughout all great Silk way it is necessary **to create and develop a tourism cluster.** On the one hand, it would give the chance to realize the development program for mono cities.

5. **Cluster creation the Aul of a new sample** is dictated by time. This cluster will give the exact answer what should be the Kazakh aul of 21 century and reflect its characteristics. Developing an aul, we will promote development of all country. Forma-tion «a cluster the Aul» will cause creation of new workplaces, will stop leakage of youth to the cities and will solve a problem of country's demography. It is sure that this project will be an embodiment of centuries-old dream of our great-grandfathers, especially will affect **natural process of fast demographic take-off** and as this problem became priority, it is necessary to give particular attention to it. **Without having in-creased number of our people, we won't become the rich strong state.**

6. As this project is the Euroasian megaproject, it is nec-es-sary to strengthen its geopolitical value by attraction of China, Rus-sia, Turkey and other countries. Attraction of investments of these states in space exploration (Baikonur), in tourism and logistic hold-ing «great Silk way», in construction of plants of new technological way, use of uranium and other resources in the peace purposes really would strengthen positions of Kazakhstan.

ADDITIONAL JUSTIFICATION

At the heart of such large projects for the first time in the world on the basis of two cities - Turkestan and Kentau - will be formed a new spiritual and technological cluster 21 century becomes a century of pioneer introduction of a new model of spiritual, cultural and technological development of society on an example of one region. Here, on the one hand, spiritual and cultural branches, and, on the other hand, components of new 6th technological way, will work for a society humanization. Only spiritual and technological constructivism will give chance to solve consumer possibilities of society optimum. Megapro-ject's implementation of not having analogs in the world, for the first time at the international level, on an example of the presented one region, will solve a problem of development of society in the future that will allow to implant **new model of a humanization of society**. **This is beginning og new stage in forming of culturological way.**

The purpose is to turn Turkestan in the spiritual center (megalopolis) of the international level. At the same time, firstly in history, on an example of one region, having united spiritual and cultural and new technological, innovative development of society, we are to show to the world of possibility of new model of development. In this regard it is necessary to hold the inter-national scientific and practical conference and project presenta-tion at world level. Till today in world practice these problems weren't solved yet in such system form [6].

Round Big Turkestan there are many countries of Central Asia (about about 400 million people can be involved in this idea). Errors of former achievements of technological explosion consisted in a technocratizm, the humanistic purposes and prob-lems of society were not taken into account because of absence of spiritual and technological constructivism.

Difference of this project from USA **"Silicon Valley"** is in directed on the mankind benefit, i.e. on solution of problems of spiritual and cultural development, aul revival according to require-ments of new time together with new innovative tech-nologies. On huge territory position of Turkestan as region in the center of Asian continent transfer it into the center of movement of people, distribu-tions of religions and ideas, cultures and arts, strengthened original unity of this region. The edition of UNESCO included quintessence of long-term researches by archeologists, orientalists, philosophers, culturologists and be-came bright confirmation of capacity of the region, which has carried by in centuries the originality present par-ticipation of its modern civilization.

Within this project for the first time in the center of Eur-asia, on an extent of «great Silk way» the New Turkestani spiritual and technological valley, otherwise, will be formed the new megap-olis of development will be created. If to consider human capacity of this region, in the Turkestan and its vicinities will live about 300 thousand people, and in the city of Kentau about 150 thousand peo-ple will be based. In the future between the cities of Turkestan and Kentau in the new spiritual capi-tal will live more than 100 thou-sand people. In addition to it, it is direct in the southern regions, in the cities - Shymkent, Taraz, Kyzylorda, Almaty lives more than 7,9 million people [11]. It is the most densely populated region in which the most part of the ethnic Kazakh population is concentrated. Influence of such huge human potential (in aggregate with all popula-tion of Kazakhstan) on formation and development of the spiritual and cultural capital will be essential.

As it was already noted above, the region is located at sources of the great Silk way. The founded archaeological opening, such as Otrar listed by UNESCO, Hodzhi Ahmed yasavi's mauso-leum, seldom pictographs, burial of the ancient saks gold person (Esik), Aksu-Dzhabagla's reserve and other archeological excavations, monu-ments, mausoleums - the certificates of the ancient civilization which have become a brand of our coun-try for foreign tourists, draw attention of world community as a cradle of culture of this region [10]. Therefore creation of a **cluster of the International tourism** in the spiritual, cultural capital becomes a measure which is meeting the requirements of our time.

FINANCING SOURCES (LOOK JUSTIFICATION)

1.   The state, republican, local budgets within the law, use of means of the RK National fund.

2.   With a view of revival and transformation of a cradle of the Turkic world of Turkestan into the spiritual capital to create «The international fund».

3.   Attraction of foreign investments into innovative, new technological projects.

4.   Rendering by the Turkic countries of support revived on lands of their fathers (Atazhurt) to the Spiritual capital. There is a hope, as the Islamic countries will participate in it. The new Spiritual capital will gain absolutely new lines, distinct from the former.

5.   Each area should bring the contribution in this project. To create a pantheon of celebrated personalities of the Kazakh his-tory, a fight panorama for national independence and great battles, courage manifestations on historical hills of our distressful earth.

6.   For financing of the project will be obtained funds of physical and legal entities. Asar and other actions will be organ-ized.

Megaproject realization the Spiritual and technological Cluster «the Turkestani Valley» is to be transferred to the jurisdiction of the government and the International fund up to end and to put under Parliament control. For maintenance of the international image this project should be directly **under patronage of the President of RK.**

Special value of the project is that coordination of spiritual and cultural and scientific and technological structures in uniform process and management of its results will allow us to provide effective use of the most valuable potential - human. As such unanimous decision the mega polis project becomes a push for the whole world. **Today in**

the world still there is no such, focused on civilized development, a spiritual and technological center, that is:

1.   Ancient Turkestan becomes the humanized spiritual cent-er of new society. By means of revival of cultural wealth of na-tionalities of many states we will start to develop in a new way, there will be the force, able to unite the people of our country and Central Asia.

2.   The cities centers of a new technological cluster Turkestan and Kentau, a transport and logistic cluster, cluster of spirituality, clusters of an aul and tourism will give an impulse to innovative development of the country.

3.   In the region the city the Spiritual capital in east style will grow. In this new small town each state, each ethnos will see re-flection of the civilization, the culture, development history, cus-toms and traditions. New Turkestan will make changes to spiritual consciousness of people.

4.   Rich power of the territory of Turkestan is defined by two factors: richness of the earth, the capital and a geographical ar-rangement in Eurasia. Thanks to it, ending in 2015 of construction of the road the Western China - Sinking down Europe will revive the great Silk way. Its capacity and efficiency will be much higher at the expense of reduction of time of transportation, than use of ocean, maritime routes. On richness of a subsoil of the earth Ka-zakhstan takes the 9th place in the world, and in uranium – the first one. Their effective development and use is our great task.

Especially actual for today is a statement of the English sci-entist and the politician, the outstanding classic of geopolitics Ch.D.Mak-kinder: «The country supervising Eurasia – supervises also the whole world» [13]. But how to draw domination from the seas on a land? land monitoring much more differs from monitor-ing of waters and it is heavier, because on a land there live million people. One thought if genghis Khan in the XI century subdued the half-world a sword and a spear, our Kazakh people the new project which does not have analogs, new knowledge from here follows, can affect world civilization development and give it a new impulse. This megaproject is presented as a scientific discov-ery (know-how), making contribution to development of mankind and the international security. It is possible to consider that it is an unexpected find of a brilliant idea, so to speak, is a discovery of a new vector in mankind development. In this project spiritual and technological constructivism of society's consumption that wasn't earlier is for the first time reached.

In this project the history and spiritual culture of the Turkic and Islamic worlds, a historical way of development, the concept and state programs of Kazakhstan were considered logic of the world historical development. Also on questions that expect us in the course of globalization, in what direction we should develop that should become a priority and that should take into consideration in 21 century, we tried to give the answers given reason from the scientific point of view.

In the conclusion it would be desirable to note that realiza-tion of the international national megaproject «Transformation of Turkestan into the spiritual capital» will allow not only to increase prestige of the Kazakh people, but also becomes the center of a civilization of all Muslim states, the people and the nationalities, all Islamic world. **Today the project should become a motive power uniting all. It will be a new civilizational call to the whole world, especially rich countries!** The religion together with other religions will call Islam not for dissonance, not to ter-rorism (as infinitely propagandize the western mass media), and to unity, making positive impact on spiritual and safe development of mankind. In other words, it is some kind of fearless step to spir-itual revolution in consciousness of mankind. **This megaproject becomes regional model of new spiritual and technological development of a world order and the international security**.

After implementation of the new project, the district «New Turkestan» it should be legally given the status of administra-tive area. At the international level «new Turkestan» becomes the century spiritual center uniting the West and the East which will promote integration, involving potential possibilities of the great Silk way [14].

New Turkestan, having left a zone of influence of one state, **will turn into the Eurasian integration center – a place of the center of cultural wealth of a set of the countries**. At the ex-pense of it the unity of society and the people as a whole will increase, the scheme of a sustainable development of Kazakhstan will be created. As soon as this regional project will yield the results, its universal use, as the Turkestani spiritual range, becomes the agenda for ideal development of the world. Turkestan as the spiritual capital, probably, will develop under the aegis of the United Nations and with assistance of UNESCO, with creation in its territory of these representations and other international orga-nizations and institutes.

Having potential possibilities to become the strong nuclear power thanks to rich deposits of uranium and Baikonur spaceport ex-istence, Kazakhstan at the same time aspires to nuclear safety and calls other countries for peaceful co-existence. Our denucle-arized state is the largest country in the region of Central Asia and plays an appreciable role in providing both state, and regional security. Thus Kazakhstan makes a certain contribution to world-wide and historical development of a universal civilization.

FINANCIAL AND ECONOMIC CALCULATIONS
OF THE MEGAPROJECT

1.	ProjecT «New TurkesTaN»	Mln. dollars
1.1.	**city of the spiritual capital**	**590**
	1.1.1. Turkish, Uzbek, Kirghiz, Azerbaijani, Turkmen, Tatar projects, project of the Islamic world of the VI-XXI centuries	700,0
	1.1.2. Kazakh project. History and culture reproduction (buildings, pantheons, panoramas) since ancient times and finding of independence	100,0
	1.1.3. International academy of religion, lyceums, madrasah. Religious studies center.	100,0
	1.1.4. Culture academy. Cultural centers: theaters, cinema, hotels, electronic libraries, etc. Cultural and historical museum treasury.	250,0
	1.1.5. Scientific center of a humanization of society. New code of morals.	70,0
	1.1.6. Projects of housing construction. Participation of areas	300,0
1.2.	**kentau's technological cluster**	**1 245,0**
	1.2.1. Plants of the 6th technological way	450,0
	1.2.2. Production modernization. Reproduction	25,0
	1.2.3. Technopolises	120,0
	1.2.4. Scientific, training, production centers. Training of the new direction.	50,0
	1.2.5. Uranium, lead, space, biotechnology, a geninzheneriya, a nanotechnology, etc. innovative and strategic structures (Joint projects with Russia, China, etc.)	200,0
	1.2.6. Youth small town, high technologies	400,0
1.3.	**cluster New aul of 2000 labors**	**850,5**
	1.3.1. Construction project of agro-industrial complex. Construction of 100 new houses	400,0
	1.3.2. Mini-plants: 140 innovative mini-farms, hothouses etc.	180,0
	1.3.3. Social infrastructure: sports, cultural, malls, schools, first-aid posts, kinder gardens	220,0
	1.3.4. Providing with the district food. Research-and- production bases	50,0
	1.3.5. The program of attraction of youth in an aul, training centers	0,5
1.4.	**cluster of Tourism**	**113,0**
	1.4.1. Complexes of cultural and historical heritage: (Ahmet Yassaui, Arystanbab, Otyrar, Taraz, Samarkand, etc.)	3,0
	1.4.2. Investment of Silk way projects	25,0
	1.4.3. Natural and ecological tourism	5,0
	1.4.4. Business tourism. Promotion and advertizing of tourism	10,0
	1.4.5. Tourism infrastructure: hotels, service rest. Services sector workplaces etc.	70,0
1.5.	**Infrastructure**	**4 310,0**
	1.5.1. Transport and logistic center «Silk way»	440,0
	1.5.2. New ways, high-speed trains	850,0
	1.5.3. Airport	1 800,0
	1.5.4. Satellite communication, telecommunications, electronic media, etc.	220,0
	1.5.5. International television center «Turan»	1 000,0
2.	**Project presentation. Carrying out the international scientific and practical conference, business of forums.**	**0,5**
ToTaL		**8 039,0**

REFERENCES

D. Friedman The Next 100 years: A Forecast of events of the XXI century. - M.: Penguin Books, 2010.

Sabden O. Kogamdy izgilendiru men kauipsizdik - Zhana alemdik tartiptin negizi. Almaty: Kazakh University, 2013.

Sabden O. humanization of society and security - the basis of the new world order. Almaty: Kazakh University, 2013.

Vernadsky V.I. Scientific thought as a planetary phenomenon. - Moscow: Nauka, 1991.

Michio Kaku. Physics of the future. - M., 2012.

Sabden O. XXI ғasyrdaғy adamzattyn Omir syru strategiyas-ynyn kontseptsiyasy, Almaty: KR BgM gK IE, 2014.

lama Sharif. Kazakhstan Today. - August 10. In 2011.

T. Mansurov Eurasian project, Nursultan Nazarbayev, em-bodied in life. - M.: Real-Press, 2014.

Sabden O. A new global outlook and a model of the world order. - Almaty Aytumar, 2013.

Baipakov KM, Azimhan A. All roads lead to Turkestan: monuments person - Almaty, 2013.

Regions of Kazakhstan (stat.sbornik). - Astana, 2013.

N. A Nazarbayev Address to the People of Kazakhstan: Ka-zakhstan Today. - 17.01.2014.

Mackinder H.S. Democratic ideals and reality. - New york: Holt, 1919.

Social values, Science and Tehnology (Eng) (pdf). European Commission P / 7-11 / Europa portal (june 2005). Arihivirovano from the original on 21 August 2011.

ABOUT THE AUTHOR

Orazaly Sabden was born on May 20, 1947 in Tastumsyk aul of Tulkubasskiy region of South-Kazakhstani oblast of the Kazakh SSR.

He graduated the Kazakh Institute of Chemical Engineering (1970). Doctor of Economics (1989), Professor (1999), acad-emician of the International News Agency and the Scientific Research Academy of the RK (1992), academician of the Academy of Sciences of HS of the RK and the International Higher Edu-cation Academy of Sciences (1996), academician of the Inter-national Economic Association Eurasia (1998), academician of the Kazakh-stani National Academy of Natural Sciences (2009), President of the Republican public association The Union of Scientists (2006).

In 1970 - 1973 years he worked on Chimkent's lead plant, in Ka-zmontazhautomatica trust.

In 1973 - 1990 years he was a senior economist, junior, sen-ior, chief research worker of the Institute of Economics of the Academy of Sciences of Kazakhstan.

In 1990 - 2001 years he was elected as a deputy of Parliament of the Republic of Kazakhstan four times. He was a chairman of com-mittee of economic reform, on the question of science advance-ment and public education.

In 2001 - 2003 years he was a president of the International Ka-zakh-Turkish University named after Hoja Ahmet yassawi.

In 2004 - 2006 years he was a professor of the Kazakh Acad-emy of Transport and Communications named after M. Tyny-shpaev, president of the Institute of Analysis and Prognosis Ka-zakhstan – USA.

In 2006 - 2012 years he was a director of the Institute of Eco-nomics of the Ministry of Education and Science of the Republic of Kazakhstan.

From 2012 he was a chairman of scientific center, chief research worker of the Institute of Economics of the Ministry of Education and Science of the Republic of Kazakhstan.

He is the author of more than 650 scientific publications including 72 monographies and course books.

In the conditions of international integration of science and education he pays a great attention to the international collabo-ration with the leading foreign scientific and educational centers of USA, CPR, Turkey, EU, CIS, worthily representing abroad the economic science of Kazakhstan. Being one of directors of the constant commission of science and education, culture and means of mass media of the International Assembly of the CIS countries, he significantly contributed to legislative provision of the economic system reforming in the CIS countries.

He is a member of the Scientific Council of the RAS of com-plex problems of Eurasian economic integration, modernization, competitiveness and stable development, created by the order of President of the RAS (No 296 dated from 18.09.2012), a mem-ber of commission of new technologies of the EurAsEC (from 2010), a full member of the International Engineering Academy, the International Supreme Education Academy, the Internation-al Academy of Innovations and the International Academy of global Studies (2015 г.).

Nowadays he worked out five large international projects:

1.   Creation of new spiritually-technological cluster The Turkistan Valley which doesn't have analogues in the world. 2. Method of single universal currency measurement for the whole world in type of Power, i.e. quotient kW/currency.

3.   New global worldview model of the world order.

4.   Humanization of society and safety are the basis of new world order.

5.   Construction of humanity survival strategy in the XXI and the following centuries.

He is a master of sports of the USSR in free-style wrestling, champion of Kazakhstan.

He is the author of idea of the Historical Panoramas of the Turkic Nations album (2003), and also of the historical monu-ment Turkibasy Auliesy (Head of turks saint) (2004), which was built at his expense. The author of ideas and scenarios of the feature films The Broken Feeling (2007), The good Man (2014), «Жер» (2016 г.).

He is a laureate of the leninist Komsomol prize in the sphere of science and techniques (1980), laureate of the State Prize of the Republic of Kazakhstan in the sphere of science, techniques and ed-ucation (2003). For outstanding service in the area of sci-entific co-operation strengthening between Russia and Kazakh-stan in 2007 he was awarded by **the M.V. Lomonosov's Order** by the Security Council of Russia. He has a medal named after the outstanding sci-entist – V.I. Vernadskiy.

THE ARTISTIC PANORAMA OF «THE HISTORY OF TURKIC PEOPLES»

THE ARTISTIC PANORAMA OF
«THE HISTORY OF TURKIC PEOPLES»

SELECTED WORKS
OF ACADEMICIAN O. SABDEN

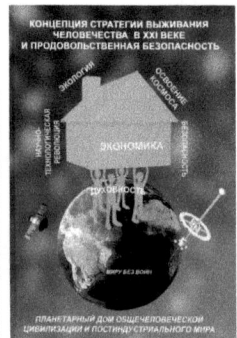

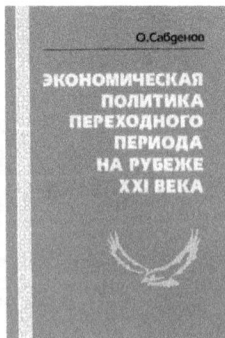

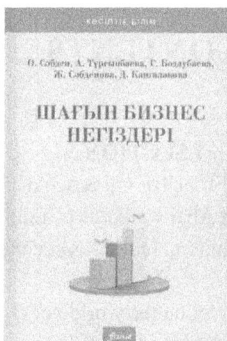

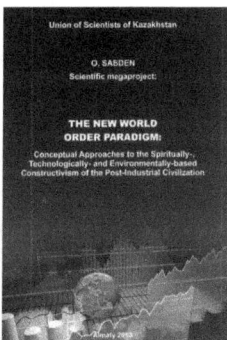

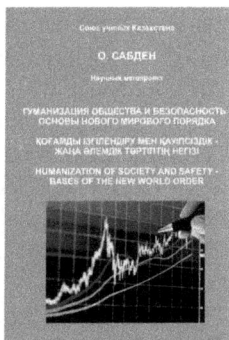

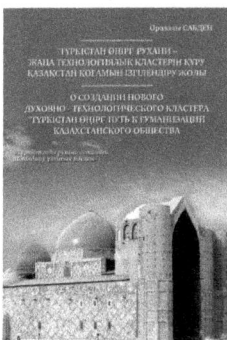

CONTENTS

II SECTION
THE GREAT HISTORICAL PERSONS

III SECTION
SCIENTISTS REVIEWS

IV SECTION
TURKISH WORLD HISTORY MUSEUM

V SECTION
STRATEGY OF SURVIVAL FOR MANKIND
IN XXI AND FURTHER CENTURIES

VI SECTION
ON THE ESTABLISHMENT OF A NEW SPIRITUALAND
TECHNOLOGICAL CLUSTER «TURKESTAN VALLEY»